Cooking
with
Grace

Cooking
with
Grace

A STEP-BY-STEP COURSE
IN AUTHENTIC ITALIAN COOKING

Grace Pilato

St. Martin's Press
New York

To my mother, Rosa Tomaselli,
whose love, courage, independence, and stubbornness
I cherish

To the joys of my life, my grandchildren—
Tyler, Noah, Skye Gina, Guyaton, Carmen,
Jazelle, and Grace Rose.
May we continue the joys of cooking together
in Nonna's kitchen.

To the loving memory of:
my father, Natale Tomaselli
my mother-in-law, Connie Pilato
my sister, Gina Colombo
my nephew, Joseph Tomaselli;
you were with me throughout the writing of this book

www.stmartins.com

Design by Kathryn Parise

Photographs by James Collins

Food stylists: Grace Pilato and Gretl Collins

ISBN 0-312-26138-1

First Edition: June 2001

10 9 8 7 6 5 4 3 2 1

CONTENTS

INTRODUCTION

I welcome this opportunity to share with you how easy and joyful it is to prepare wonderful Italian food to enjoy with your family and friends. It has often been said that the most direct route to a person's heart is through his or her palate and that the character of the Italians and the way that they show their love is most evident in their food and art. Many of the dishes you'll find on these pages are from my family—recipes from my mom, grandma, or other relations. Other recipes come from my own imagination and experimentation, which draw on the old Italian ways but also involve improvisations that have been tested by the lovingly critical palates of my family, friends, and students in my cooking classes. People are an important part of this book because, in a way, they are the most important part of the recipe. Cooking together with children, moms and dads, husbands and wives, grandparents, and friends can foster a strong sense of bonding and mutual satisfaction.

My recipes combine down-to-earth tradition with a bit of today's sophistication. They reflect my Italian heritage and the importance I place on nutrition and healthy eating. As you use the recipes, you will get a feel for working side by side with me as your instructor, just as if you were in one of the many cooking classes I have held in my home. You will be delighted to discover how simple it is to make good food a part of everyday life.

This book puts authentic Italian cooking within the reach of anyone. Both gourmets and beginners will enjoy these recipes. Recipes range from simple (Spinach with Garlic and Olive Oil, prepared in less than 10 minutes) to complex (Graziella's Decadent Cake, a special occasion cake that incorporates five other recipes). No matter which recipe you try, you will find the directions to be clear, helpful, and well tested by a wide variety of people in my cooking classes, including beginners, chefs, and dietitians. Most important, the results are delicious.

As an artist, I consider presentation of food essential. After all, we savor food with our eyes before we taste it. I have been producing pottery and sculpture and selling my work at craft shows and exhibitions for more than twenty-eight years. This profession has brought me into contact with artists from around the country. The photography in this book showcases the work of some of the leaders of the craft movement, with samples of platters, plates, stemware, woven baskets, and elegant flatware and serving pieces. I encourage you to purchase and use handcrafted items in your home—it will truly enhance your lifestyle. My husband and I have collected artwork that adorns our home, works that are used and loved on a daily basis. Choose pieces that will show off your food, your table, your kitchen, and your home, giving you food for the soul, a lasting gift. Think of it as an investment in living.

Traditions and memories make life rich. Sharing wholesome, home-prepared food with family and friends is an important way to bond people in today's hectic society and help families build traditions. Many families no longer eat together around the kitchen or dining room table. They are missing out on precious time to join the people they love most in order to share ideas and the events of their days. Cooking in Italy is an art practiced by and for the family, linking the generations as they participate in this daily sharing of common joy. I encourage you to embrace this philosophy and to make it a part of your life. You will never regret it.

You'll begin your course in authentic Italian cooking with a series of what I call stepping-stone recipes. The "Stepping-Stone Recipes" chapter includes foundation techniques showcased in recipes that build on one another. Start with the simple, fresh marinara sauce and you will discover why it is an all-time favorite among my cooking students. Look at the end of the recipe and you will see how many other dishes you can make using this sauce. The rest of the chapters are arranged in the same order as the courses in a sumptuous Italian meal, moving from antipasti to pasta to soups, progressing to main courses with mouth-watering vegetables, and finishing with elegant desserts.

The quality of your creations depends on using the very best and freshest ingredients to intensify the flavor. Buy the best olive oil affordable to you. It should be 100 percent extra-virgin olive oil, first cold press, with low acidity. Grate a chunk of imported Romano or Parmigiano-Reggiano cheese. Use fresh garlic and herbs. Buy peppercorns and grind pepper as you need it. You won't believe the difference in taste.

Organization is the key to success in the kitchen. Read a recipe all the way through first to be sure you understand the directions and have the necessary ingredients and cooking utensils. Always chop and measure ingredients before you begin to cook. Make sure you keep track of cooking time by using a kitchen timer.

I'll teach you how to cook efficiently, maximizing your time. Plan your menu so that you know what you want to cook and the order in which you want to serve it. Then decide what can be done in advance. For example, chopping enough garlic and onions for several dishes saves on time and clean up. Start cooking what takes the longest first. This way, while one dish is cooking, you can prepare other food; this will be referred to as overlapped cooking time in the chapters ahead.

This book also describes how to stock a pantry with basic ingredients from which a variety of meals can be quickly created. It also provides tips on preparing extra portions to freeze for hectic days so that simple meals of soup, pasta, salad, and homemade bread can be prepared in less than half an hour.

I suggest you use your hands whenever possible in preparing these recipes. They are your best tools. No man-made tool can compare. If you wash them frequently, they are also the cleanest tools in your kitchen. And you can't misplace them!

The recipes in this book list approximate preparation times. *The preparation time given is simply a guideline.* No two people work the same way in the kitchen. Depending on your skill level and style, these times will vary. The first time you make a new recipe, give yourself plenty of lead time so you can enjoy the process. Take notes while you are preparing the recipe so that the next time it will be even easier.

I have dreamed about writing this book for years. I want to encourage you to get in touch with the simple things that make life so rich and full. I have found that it's possible even in the midst of a tumultuous, busy life to summon up the life-enhancing magic of the Italian art of cooking. What it requires is generosity, patience, and the best raw materials. What it returns is worth all you have to give.

ESSENTIAL INGREDIENTS FOR
THE WELL-STOCKED PANTRY

A well-stocked pantry is essential to good cooking, especially if you enjoy creating recipes on the spur of the moment.

The following lists are merely suggestions to help you organize your kitchen. Do not be intimidated by the length of the list; these are items I include in my pantry that I have used to create the recipes in this book. You may need to build your pantry gradually, but if you are enthusiastic about Italian cooking, be prepared to make an investment in time, energy, and money. It will be well worth it.

This pantry list does not include some of the basic items needed in a well-stocked household, such as soaps and cereals, or the full variety of fresh fruits and vegetables, meats, poultry, and fish used as main ingredients in your everyday cooking.

DRY GOODS

Unbleached all-purpose white flour
Cake flour
Wheat flour
Wheat berries
Wheat flakes
Bulgur wheat
Cracked wheat
Oat flakes
Oatmeal
Barley
Steel-ground oats
Cornmeal, yellow and white

Semolina
Crackers
Fine dry bread crumbs
Rice—long grain, Arborio,
   Carnaroli, or Vialone Nano
Yeast

PASTA

Stock fine quality, 100 percent
   durum wheat semolina (preferably
   imported) in a variety of shapes
   and sizes, in 1-pound packages.

Small pasta for soups—orzo, tubettini, pastina, and ditalini

Short tubular pastas—penne, rigatoni, and ziti

Long pasta—fettuccine, linguine, and spaghetti

Pasta for stuffing—large shells and manicotti

Large flat pasta—lasagna

DRIED LEGUMES

Lentils

Assortment of beans, including cannellini

Chickpeas

Green or yellow split peas

DRIED FRUIT

Raisins—golden, sultana

Currants

Sweetened cranberries

Figs

Apricots

Chestnuts

Sun-dried tomatoes

CANNED AND JARRED INGREDIENTS

Cannellini beans

Kidney beans

Chickpeas

Whole plum tomatoes, Italian-style in 28-ounce cans

Tomato puree in 28-ounce cans

Tomato paste in 8-ounce cans

Various broths—vegetable, beef, chicken, and fish in 14½-ounce cans

Clam juice

Fine-quality bouillon cubes (for emergencies only!)

Pumpkin puree in 28-ounce cans

Tuna fish, imported Italian, packed in olive oil

Anchovies, imported Italian, packed in olive oil in 2-ounce tins

Artichoke hearts

Clams, whole, chopped, or minced in 7-ounce cans

Roasted peppers in 8- or 16-ounce jars

Apricot or peach preserves in 10- or 16-ounce jars

Evaporated milk in 12-ounce cans

BAKING SUPPLIES

Salt—kosher, sea, and regular

Sugars—granulated, superfine, confectioners'

Cornstarch

Baking powder

Baking soda

Vegetable shortening

Cocoa powder, unsweetened

Chocolate chips, squares, and bars

Food coloring

Extracts—almond, anise, lemon, orange, vanilla

Sesame seeds—unhulled

Honey

COFFEE AND TEAS

your preference, but include espresso

NUTS

your choice of almonds, walnuts, hazelnuts, pecans, and pine nuts

OILS AND VINEGAR

Extra-virgin olive oil, 32-ounce bottle

*Essential
Ingredients
for the
Well-Stocked
Pantry*

xii

Canola or vegetable oil, 32-ounce
bottle
White distilled vinegar, 8 to 32
ounces
White wine vinegar, 8 to 32 ounces
Red wine vinegar, 8 to 32 ounces
Balsamic vinegar, 8 to 16 ounces

CONDIMENTS

Roasted red sweet bell peppers in 8-
or 16-ounce jars (or from the deli
section of your supermarket)
Olives—cured black (Kalamata,
Gaeta, or Sicilian) and green in 8-
or 16-ounce jars (or from the deli
section of your supermarket)
Olive paste, 4- or 6-ounce jar
Capers, 3-ounce jar
Dijon mustard, 6- or 8-ounce jar

SPICES AND DRY HERBS

Whole peppercorns
Bay leaves
Oregano
Dried pepper flakes
Cayenne pepper
Fennel seeds
Whole nutmeg
Whole cloves
Ground cinnamon
Saffron threads

INGREDIENTS FOR STORING
IN A COOL, DARK PLACE

Potatoes
Onions
Garlic
Shallots
Dried mushrooms, such as porcini
and shiitake

FOR THE REFRIGERATOR

Fresh herbs such as flat leaf Italian
parsley, basil, thyme, rosemary,
and mint
Unsalted butter
Milk, cream, or half-and-half
Eggs, large
Cheeses—imported when possible.
Examples: Parmigiano-Reggiano,
Romano, asiago, fontina,
gorgonzola, fresh mozzarella,
ricotta (whole milk), provolone,
Taleggio, mascarpone, creamed
Havarti, and Gruyère (if fontina is
not available).
Meats, poultry, and fish, buy fresh as
you need it
Celery
Vegetables—buy as needed.
Suggestions: broccoli, spinach,
cauliflower, zucchini, salad
greens, sweet bell peppers.
Fruits—oranges, lemons, apples,
grapes, whatever is in season that
you enjoy eating
Marinated mushrooms, jarred (see
page 13)
Marinated roasted peppers, jarred
(see page 15)
Marinated sun-dried tomatoes,
jarred (see page 18)
Marinated eggplant, jarred (see
page 11)
Olive Paste Sauce, jarred (see page
129)
Fresh mushrooms, your choice—
white button, cremini,
portobello, porcini, oyster,
chanterelle, and shiitake
Salad dressings you have prepared
(see pages 68–72)

Essential
Ingredients
for the
Well-Stocked
Pantry

Deli pressed meats, your choice—
salami, prosciutto, mortadella,
sopressata, coppa

FOR THE FREEZER
Chicken breasts, butterflied and
pounded
Whole roasting chicken
Pork tenderloin, whole or
butterflied and pounded
Pancetta or bacon, sliced in
¼-pound packages
Pesto (see page 25)
Basil cigars (see page 4)
Baby peas
Marinara sauce in 1-cup containers
(see page 5)
Tomato meat sauce, in pint
containers (see page 122)

Homemade soups and broths
(see "Soups" chapter, page 147)
Grated citrus zest and peels
Cookies (see "Desserts and Sweet
Things" chapter, page 253)

WINES, APÉRITIFS, AND LIQUEURS

There are many books on the market
that describe the characteristics
and uses of Italian wines and other
drinks. Refer to these sources as
necessary, or go to your local wine
store and ask for suggestions. Have
several bottles of your favorites
available for your enjoyment and
for cooking.

*Essential
Ingredients
for the
Well-Stocked
Pantry*

x i v

BASIC EQUIPMENT
FOR YOUR KITCHEN

The equipment you will need depends on the number of people in your household, how often you entertain, the size of your kitchen, and the amount of storage space. My advice is to buy what you know you will use and to buy the best equipment and tools you can afford. High-quality pieces of equipment produce the best results and some are lifetime purchases. Do some initial research, ask your family and friends which brands work the best for them, and then visit several kitchenware shops and department stores—become knowledgeable, and then make your purchases.

This list is meant to give you a broad view of what you might need to prepare the recipes in this book; it is only a guide. Pick and choose according to your individual specifications, and every once in a while, treat yourself to a special tool you always wanted.

SAUCEPANS AND STOCKPOTS—
They should be heavy gauge with tight-fitting lids.
1½- to 2-quart size
3- to 4-quart size
8-quart size
12- to 14-quart size
Pasta insert that fits in one of the large pots

SKILLETS
They should be heavy gauge, with good conduction of heat and tight-fitting lids. Their handles should be made of a material that can go in the oven.
6- or 7-inch coated with a nonstick material
12-inch coated with a nonstick material
7-inch with 2-inch-deep sloping sides

9-inch with 2-inch-deep sloping or straight sides

12-inch with 2-inch-deep sloping sides

ROASTING AND BAKING PANS

1 large roasting pan, medium weight, roughly 18 × 12 × 2½ inches deep

1 medium roasting pan, medium weight, roughly 14 × 10 × 2 inches deep

Roasting rack to fit medium-size pan

Tube cake pan

4 cookie sheets / baking sheets 17 × 11 × ½ inches

2 round cake pans, 8- or 9-inch

Cookie rack, large

Pie pan, 9-inch round

KNIVES

4-inch paring knife

6-inch all-purpose knife

10-to-12-inch chef knife

10-inch slicing knife

10-inch serrated bread knife

Steak knives

Kitchen shears

Ordinary scissors

EQUIPMENT

Food processor

Stationary or handheld electric mixer

Blender

Pasta machine

Deep fryer

Food mill

Microwave

Toaster oven

Timer

TOOLS AND ODDS AND ENDS

Measuring spoons

Stackable dry measuring cups

Wet measuring cups, glass or plastic with a pouring spout

Mixing bowls, glass, stainless steel, or clay. Make sure they are stackable and come in a variety of sizes. Have one oversize one to toss salads and pasta.

Mortar and pestle

2 vegetable peelers

Citrus zester

Juicer

Can and bottle opener

Corkscrew

Rolling pin

Wooden spoons with various handle sizes

Whisk

Metal and rubber spatulas

Metal dough scraper

Ladles in several sizes

Large slotted spoon

Large spider mesh skimmer

Long-handled fork for stirring long pasta while it's cooking

Long-handled spoon for stirring short and tubular pasta while it's cooking

Pasta server

Serving spoons and forks

Tongs

Vegetable brush

Salad spinner (avoid models with pull-string attachments)

Colander, one large, one medium, with long metal handle

Strainers, assorted sizes

Serving bowls and platters

Cannoli shell forms (8)

Pasta cutting wheel, straight-edged or fluted
Ravioli press
Pastry bag with a variety of tips
Pastry brush
Round toothpicks
Mallet
Grater, four-sided box type or rotary
Nutmeg grater
Instant-read thermometer
Oven thermometer
Cutting boards, several sizes in wood or polyurethane
Freezer wrap
Aluminum foil
Plastic wrap
Waxed paper
Parchment paper
Heavy-duty plastic freezer bags, various sizes
Kitchen string
Plastic containers with tight-fitting lids, various sizes from 1-cup to 1-gallon
Potholders
Aprons
Kitchen towels
Sponges and cleanup cloths
Expired credit cards—to scrape batter out of bowls, pots and pans, and work surfaces

STEPPING-STONE RECIPES

In this chapter, I present special recipes that showcase techniques that are very important for you to learn early on before progressing to the rest of the book. This chapter also includes helpful hints and suggestions and explains why certain procedures are done in a certain way. I feel that if you understand the whys you will be better able to master the hows.

Stepping-stone recipes will help you assimilate basic techniques and move on to more complex recipes. The recipes build on one another—for example, first you learn how to make marinara, then ricotta and crêpes, and before you know it, you have the skills to turn out beautiful manicotti.

Read the stepping-stone technique section for each recipe thoroughly before using it. Becoming proficient at these techniques will save you time in the kitchen, freeing you to be more creative.

Marinara Sauce
Stepping-Stone Technique

As you proceed to make this very simple but exquisite sauce, you will be amazed at all you will learn. You will use many of these techniques over and over again. They might seem a bit difficult at first, but eventually they will become a part of you and you will not have to think about them again.

Once you make this sauce and taste it, you will be hooked by its delicious fresh flavor. There will be no going back to buying marinara sauce in jars. I suggest you make the whole portion, although initially it might appear to be too much for you. It is not really that much more work; you use the same amount of utensils, and cleanup is the same. You will then have portions to freeze for those days that you just don't have enough time to cook. This is what organization and a well-stocked kitchen are all about.

Get yourself ready by organizing yourself, your equipment, and your ingredients. For this recipe it makes a lot of sense to use a food processor or blender if you have one. It can grind the cheese for you, chop the garlic, and also chop the tomatoes once you have seeded them. Go from processing the dry ingredients first (cheese), to the semidry ingredients (garlic), and lastly to the wet ingredients (tomatoes). No need to clean your processor in between these steps. Save time, energy, and extra cleanup whenever possible.

In this recipe, you'll use the following techniques:

Grating Fresh Romano and Parmesan (Parmigiano-Reggiano) Cheese

Cheese can be finely grated using a box grater or quickly and easily in the food processor. To do it in the food processor, chop the cheese by hand into 1-inch chunks, use the metal S-shaped blade, and with the motor on, drop the pieces through the feed tube. Cheese grated this way can be stored in the refrigerator for your weekly use.

Chopping and Storing Garlic

If you will be using a lot of garlic, I recommend chopping an entire head of garlic at once and storing what you don't use in the refrigerator. It takes about the same amount of time to chop a whole head of garlic as it does to chop a few cloves. Separate the cloves by placing the whole garlic bulb, root end facing up, onto the cutting board. Hit the garlic bulb with a kitchen mallet, or the flat side of a knife; then separate the cloves. Pound the individual cloves, making them easier to peel. Peel away the skins with the tip of a small knife. Trim the woody ends of each clove.

Chopping garlic in the food processor takes no time at all. If you want the garlic to be uniformly minced, turn the motor on, and drop the cloves all at once through the feed tube. If you want it to be chopped in varying sizes, put all the cloves in the bowl of the food processor and pulse until the garlic is chopped to the desired consistency. Of course, you can always chop garlic by hand with a chef's knife.

To store the garlic, place it in a small container and cover with extra-virgin olive oil along with a few drops of fresh lemon juice. (The juice retards bacterial growth.) It will keep for about a week in the refrigerator. Be aware, however, that the flavor intensifies the longer the garlic sits, so depending on your taste, you may wish to use a bit less than a recipe calls for. *One-half teaspoon of chopped garlic is equal to about one clove.*

Selecting and Seeding Canned Tomatoes

The quality of your sauce depends on selecting the best whole plum tomatoes possible. Whole plum Italian tomatoes are what you need; they have a firm, thick pulp with few seeds. There are many brands of canned whole Italian plum tomatoes on the market. You may want to try several brands. After you open them, look for firm meaty tomatoes that contain the fewest seeds possible. Since there are many varieties of canned tomatoes, let's be absolutely clear: *Do not use the round ones, the diced ones, the chopped ones, or the stewed ones.*

It's very important to seed the tomatoes—tomato seeds impart a bitter taste to your sauce. To seed tomatoes, place the tomatoes with their juice in a large bowl. Holding a tomato with one hand, use the fingers of your other hand to open it, revealing the inside of the fruit. Pull out the inside core along with any fibrous pieces and the seeds. Dip the cleaned tomato into the juice; this will remove most of the remaining seeds. It is not necessary to be compulsive about this and get every single seed out, but remove as many as possible. Place the seeded tomatoes in another large bowl. I tell my children, husband, and students that this chore is more fun when shared, as it will go by quickly.

Pour the leftover bits and pieces of tomato, cores, juice, and seeds through a food mill or strainer with small holes so the seeds will remain in the strainer. This juice and pulp also will be used in the sauce. We waste nothing!

Using Nonreactive Pans

Certain vegetables and ingredients react with the metal of the cooking pans to produce a chemical reaction, creating an unpleasant taste and destroying some of the nutritive value. For this recipe you need to choose pans that are nonreactive, such as stainless steel, titanium, enameled porcelain, or nonstick bonded cookware. Do not use aluminum, cast iron, or copper.

This sauce must be made in large skillets rather than saucepots. Shallow skillets with sloping sides allow the juices to evaporate quickly. This helps the sauce to cook faster, giving it a fresher taste. This sauce would taste completely different if you cooked it in a saucepot.

Preserving Fresh Basil to Be Used Throughout the Year

When basil is in season and you have it in abundance, freeze it so you can use it all year round. If freezer space is at a premium, try making these basil "cigars." Remove the basil leaves from the stems. Wash the leaves and dry them completely with paper towels. Using small snack-size recloseable plastic bags, pack the leaves tightly into the bag, as many as will fit, pushing out as much air as possible, and roll the bag into a cigar shape. Close the bag. Make several cigars at once and store them in a larger recloseable plastic freezer bag for extra protection. The portion you need can be sliced as soon as you remove the cigar from the freezer, and the rest can be refrozen.

Marinara Sauce

Salsa Marinara

Preparation Time: 30 minutes • Cooking Time: 1½ hours

5 (28-ounce) cans whole Italian plum tomatoes and their juice
¼ cup plus 2 tablespoons extra-virgin olive oil, divided
6 cloves garlic, minced (about 1 tablespoon)

12 leaves fresh basil, sliced (or 1 tablespoon Pesto, page 25), divided
1 teaspoon freshly ground pepper, or more to taste
1 teaspoon salt (if needed)
1 tablespoon sugar (if needed)

PROCEDURE

1. Seed the tomatoes using the technique on page 3.

2. Coarsely chop the tomatoes using a knife, blender, or food processor, chopping about 2 cups at a time into ¼-inch dice. If using a processor or blender, use the pulse mode. This gives you more control over the size of the pieces. You do not want to overprocess them. Pass the juice and any bits and pieces of tomato through a food mill using the disk with the smallest holes. Combine the chopped tomatoes and their sieved juice in a large bowl.

3. Because of the large quantity of sauce, you will need to use two large skillets. Make sure both skillets are placed on large burners. As you add each ingredient, divide it as evenly as possible between the two skillets.

4. Heat two large, nonreactive skillets on medium heat until warm. Add 2 tablespoons of the olive oil to each skillet and heat until oil is hot and you notice a slight ripple on the surface. Add the garlic and stir until it just turns golden, about 2 minutes. Be careful not to burn the garlic.

5. Next, add the tomatoes and their juice, half the basil, and the pepper. Cook uncovered on medium heat for 1½ hours, stirring every 5 to 10 minutes so the sauce does not scorch on the bottom. If medium heat appears to be too high, turn it down to medium-low. The lower the heat, the longer the sauce will have to cook.

6. Add the remaining 2 tablespoons olive oil, 1 tablespoon to each skillet. Taste the sauce, and season with salt and pepper if desired. (Canned tomatoes

may be packed in enough salt so that you won't need to add any.) If it has a lit-tle acidic flavor, add sugar, 1 teaspoon at a time, wait a few minutes, and taste again. Add more only if needed.

7. You will know the sauce is done when most of the juice has evaporated and the sauce is very thick. Test the sauce by dragging a spoon across the center of the pan. If no liquid seeps back into the center, it is done. Add the rest of the basil leaves at this time, to give the sauce extra-fresh flavor and color.

Yield: 7½ cups
(2 cups will generously sauce
1 pound of pasta)

NOTES

One of the most perfect and simple dishes in the world is pasta with this marinara sauce!

Stored in the refrigerator in covered containers, it will keep for 1 week. It freezes very well and will keep in the freezer for up to 6 months. Store in 1-cup portions. To defrost, place the sauce in the microwave in a microwav-able, nonplastic container. (The plastic and the acid from the tomatoes do not react well together when heated in the microwave.) Cover loosely with plastic wrap and defrost. Alternatively, you can remove the sauce from the freezer the night before and defrost it overnight in the refrigerator. Heat the sauce until hot before combining it with hot, freshly cooked, drained pasta.

Use This Recipe to Make:

- Manicotti Made with Crêpes, page 44
- Breaded Chicken Cutlets, page 52
- Mussels in Spicy Marinara, page 88
- Pasta with Sausage, page 111
- Seafood Lasagna, page 112
- Rice Balls, page 93
- Ricotta Gnocchi, page 137
- Semolina Polenta with Broccoli, page 145

- Tomato-Basil Cream Sauce, page 127
- Soup with Kohlrabi, page 153
- Meatless "Cutlets," page 218
- Fish Stew, page 223
- Fried Green and Red Peppers, page 242
- Eggplant Sicilian Style, page 247
- Pizza, page 188

HOMEMADE FRESH RICOTTA
STEPPING-STONE TECHNIQUE

Ricotta is a soft curd fresh cheese made from pasteurized, homogenized cow, sheep, or goat milk. Ricotta is very light, creamy, and tasty. It has no preservatives and must be refrigerated. It will keep for up to 7 days. It is made throughout most of the regions of Italy and in various parts of the Mediterranean as well as in the U.S. Ricotta has always been very popular throughout Italy and recently is making a wonderful comeback in the United States.

Many people think making your own ricotta is difficult, but once you make it for the first time you will see how truly simple and rewarding it is. Making ricotta involves only a few common ingredients. I suggest that you prepare it with whole milk unless you are on a special restricted diet. The cream in the milk gives it its wonderful flavor. My philosophy is to eat less, but enjoy the best possible taste. I do not use ricotta as a filler but to enhance the flavor of a dish.

There are a few things to be on the alert for when making ricotta. To prevent scorching, you need to stir the milk about every 5 minutes, using a stainless-steel spatula. With this tool, you can scrape the entire bottom of the pan more efficiently. When you measure the vinegar, use a wet measuring cup, one made of glass or clear plastic that has a pouring spout. Place the measuring cup at eye level to make sure you have the exact amount. You will need an instant-read thermometer. I recommend the Taylor instant-read pocket thermometer; it is reliable, inexpensive, and compact. If you happen to make the mistake of overheating the milk, wait until it cools down a bit, checking the temperature. If curds did not form in good numbers or did not separate from the whey, the milk was probably not hot enough or you measured the vinegar improperly. If this happens, check the temperature and add more vinegar, 1 tablespoon at a time. You see, it's not that difficult.

I use ricotta in many different recipes in this book, from savory to sweet, from main courses to desserts.

Homemade Fresh Ricotta

....

Ricotta Fresca

Preparation Time: 5 minutes, plus 2 hours resting and 2 hours draining
Cooking Time: 20–30 minutes

1 gallon whole pasteurized milk
½ teaspoon salt

⅓ cup plus 1 tablespoon distilled
white vinegar

PROCEDURE

1. Use a large, heavy-gauge stainless-steel saucepot. Wash it thoroughly with very hot water, but do not bother to dry it. (Leaving it wet helps prevent the milk from scorching.) Place the milk in the saucepot over medium heat. Add the salt and stir briefly. Allow the milk to heat up slowly, stirring occasionally with a metal spatula. When you notice tiny bubbles and steam forming on the surface of the milk, stir more frequently; don't let it scorch. You want it to reach 190°F, near scalding temperature, just before boiling. Check the temperature with your thermometer periodically.

2. When it reaches the correct temperature, turn the heat off, add the vinegar, and stir gently for 1 minute. You will notice curds forming immediately. Take the pot off the stove. Cover with a dry, clean dish towel and allow the mixture to sit undisturbed for 2 hours. On cold days, you can prepare your ricotta in the morning before going to work and let it sit until you come home.

3. When the ricotta has rested for 2 or more hours, take a piece of cheesecloth, dampen it with water, and lay it out inside a colander. With a slotted spoon or sieve, ladle out the ricotta into the prepared colander. Place the colander with the ricotta inside a larger pan or bowl so it can drain freely. Let it drain for 2 hours or longer.

4. Store the cheese in a covered container in the refrigerator.

Yield: 4 cups (about 2 pounds)

NOTES

Ricotta will keep in the refrigerator for up to 7 days. I do not recommend freezing, because when frozen it loses some of its textural qualities.

Use low-fat or part-skim milk in making ricotta only if you have dietary restrictions. The flavor comes from the cream in the whole milk.

Use This Recipe to Make:
- Manicotti made with Crêpes, page 44
- Cannelloni Stuffed with Spinach and Ricotta, page 114
- Tortelloni with Mushroom Sauce, page 119
- Ricotta Gnocchi, page 137
- Stuffed Bread with Spinach and Olives, page 183
- Lemon Ricotta Drop Cookies, page 260
- Ricotta Puffs, page 270
- Cream Puffs, page 272
- Cannoli, page 274
- Graziella's Decadent Cake, page 284
- Ricotta Cloud Cream, page 271

Marinated Eggplant
Stepping-Stone Technique

Peeling and Debittering Eggplant

If the recipe calls for peeling the eggplant, do so just before using—the flesh discolors quickly! Remove both ends first, then peel with a vegetable peeler or sharp paring knife. Eggplant that are not in season or those that have been stored for a long time may be bitter. To be on the safe side, use the following technique to help remove some of the bitter juices. Sprinkle eggplant generously with salt and place in a large colander or bowl. After ½ to 1 hour, rinse, drain, and pat dry with paper towels. When eggplant are in season and grown locally, it is usually not necessary to debitter them.

Keeping Eggplant Submerged

When boiling vegetables such as eggplant or mushrooms that tend to float on the surface of the water, keep them submerged by placing a colander or strainer directly over the surface of the ingredient. The weight of the colander will help in keeping them submerged.

Squeezing Out Excess Water from Eggplant

The more water that is left in the eggplant, the less marinade it will be able to absorb and the less flavorful it will be. To squeeze excess water from eggplant or other cooked vegetables such as spinach, place the cooked, drained vegetables on a dinner plate. Place another identical plate on top and press the two plates together, holding the plates vertically over the sink to allow any extra water to drain out.

Marinated Eggplant with Garlic and Olive Oil

Melanzane Sott'Olio, Aglio e Aceto

Preparation Time: 10 minutes, plus 30 minutes to 1 hour for debittering, if necessary

Cooking Time: 2 to 3 minutes

Marinated eggplant is excellent to have on hand, stored in the refrigerator for use in many ways. It makes a great gift from your kitchen as well!

2 medium eggplants
2 teaspoons salt (plus more if
    debittering eggplants)
1 quart water
2 cups white distilled vinegar

For the Marinade:
1 cup extra-virgin olive oil
    (more if needed)

3 cloves garlic, chopped or slivered
    (about ½ tablespoon)
20 fresh basil leaves
½ teaspoon red pepper flakes
1 teaspoon freshly ground black
    pepper
2 teaspoons dried oregano, rubbed
    between your hands to release
    its flavor

PROCEDURE

1. Remove the cap and stem ends from eggplants. Peel them with a vegetable peeler and slice into ¼- to ⅓-inch rounds. Lay the eggplant slices on a work surface, sprinkle with salt, place in a large colander, and let drain for ½ to 1 hour. Rinse, drain, and pat dry with paper towels.

2. In a large nonreactive saucepot, bring water, vinegar, and salt to a boil. Add the eggplant. With a wooden spoon, make sure that the eggplant slices are submerged in the liquid. Bring back to a boil and cook for only 2 minutes. (Use a timer to make sure you do not overcook.)

3. Drain the eggplant, run under cold water to stop the cooking process, and drain again. When the slices are cool, gently press out any extra water. Place the eggplant in a large bowl.

4. In a medium bowl, mix the olive oil, garlic, basil, red pepper flakes, black pepper, and oregano. Stir well. Add the eggplant to the marinade and

toss, using your hands to evenly distribute the marinade throughout. Taste for seasonings and adjust accordingly.

5. Wash the canning jars and lids in the dishwasher or sterilize in a large pan of water.

6. Stack the slices in the prepared jars. Pour any leftover marinade over the top. The eggplant should always be completely submerged in olive oil, with at least ½ inch of oil above it. Add extra olive oil if needed. Screw the lids on the jars tightly and refrigerate.

Yield: 1 quart

NOTES

When ready to use, take the eggplant out of the refrigerator 15 to 30 minutes before serving. This will allow the oil that might have congealed in the refrigerator to return to its original liquid state. Also, herbs and spices always taste best at room temperature.

Store eggplant in the refrigerator in tightly sealed containers. Marinated eggplant will keep in the refrigerator for 1 month or longer. I do not recommend freezing.

Use This Recipe to Make:

- An antipasto
- Spreads for bruschetta
- Sandwiches for lunch
- Frittata, page 34

Marinated Mushrooms

Funghi Marinati

Preparation Time: 10 minutes • Cooking Time: 1 minute

Mushrooms preserved in this manner are great to have on hand in the refrigerator. They have a multitude of uses and will liven up many a dish.

2 cups white distilled vinegar
4 cups water
2 teaspoons salt
2 pounds mushrooms, cleaned with
    a damp paper towel and sliced
    ¼ inch thick, quartered, or leave
    whole if they are small

10 fresh basil leaves
1 cup extra-virgin olive oil
    (more if needed)
½ teaspoon salt
¼ teaspoon freshly ground black
    pepper
¼ teaspoon red pepper flakes

For the Marinade:
1½ teaspoons minced garlic
1½ teaspoons dried oregano

PROCEDURE

1. Place a medium nonreactive saucepot on high heat. Add the vinegar and water. Bring to a boil, add the salt and mushrooms, and boil for 1 minute. Drain very well; the less moisture, the better the flavor.

2. Mix all marinade ingredients in a bowl. Add the mushrooms and toss well.

3. Wash a quart-size jar with very hot, sudsy water. Rinse and drain.

4. Fill the jar with mushrooms and marinade. Make sure that the mushrooms are completely submerged in oil, with at least ½ inch of oil above them. Add more extra-virgin olive oil if necessary.

Yield: 1 quart

NOTE

Store these mushrooms in a tightly sealed container in the refrigerator; they will keep for over a month and can be used in sandwiches, for antipasti trays, in green salads, on crusty bread or crostini, or in sauces, soups, and stuffings.

Roasted Peppers
Stepping-Stone Technique

Roasting peppers gives them a unique unbeatable taste that is concentrated in flavor.

Roasting Peppers

Line a baking sheet with aluminum foil to make light work of cleanup. When peppers are broiled, their natural sugars come to the surface, caramelizing them. It's this caramelization that burns the baking sheets.

Wash and dry the peppers. It's important that they are dry so that they will roast properly. I find that 9 medium-size bell peppers, when sliced in half, fit nicely on a baking sheet. Cutting them in half makes the cooking process go faster and allows for more even charring. Both oven setting and oven temperature should be on broil. Cook these peppers under the broiler, placing the cooking rack as close to the heating element as possible. Keep the oven door slightly ajar as you broil them.

As the peppers char, place them in a paper or plastic bag and close tightly. Note that not all of the surface of the pepper will char; don't worry about it. Let the peppers steam inside the bag for 7 to 10 minutes. The steam trapped inside the bag will help to loosen the skins. Don't leave them in the bag too long or the steam will dissipate and the skins will be more difficult to remove. Don't worry if you do not get every last bit of skin removed, but do try to keep the flesh of the peppers intact.

Marinated roasted peppers have a multitude of uses. Use them for garnishes as part of an antipasto platter; put them in green salads to add flavor and color; puree and add them to enrich sauces, marinades, and dressings; use small amounts to flavor stuffings; incorporate them in sandwiches and frittatas; top pizzas with them; or fill unbaked loaves of breads with them.

Marinated Roasted Peppers

Peperoni Arrostiti e Marinati

Preparation Time: 15 minutes • Cooking Time: 30 minutes

Roasted peppers marinated in this way are great to have on hand in the refrigerator. You will reach for them often.

9 medium red, yellow, or orange bell
   peppers
1 cup (or more) extra-virgin olive oil
4 cloves garlic, minced (about
   2 teaspoons)

14 fresh basil leaves, chopped
1 teaspoon dried oregano
¼ teaspoon kosher salt
1 teaspoon freshly ground black
   pepper

PROCEDURE

1. Move the oven rack as close to the top element as possible. Preheat the broiler. Line a baking sheet with aluminum foil.

2. Wash and dry the peppers. Cut them in half and remove the cores and seeds. Place the peppers, cut-side down, on the baking sheet. Push the tops down gently so they lie flatter on the baking sheet.

3. Broil the peppers with the oven door slightly open. First, you will smell the aroma of the peppers; then their skins will blister, start to turn black, and then char. Some pieces will blacken faster than others. Take the peppers out of the oven with tongs when most of the skin of each pepper chars. Place them in a paper or plastic bag, and close the bag tightly. (If there are any more un-cooked peppers, place them on the baking sheet as room permits.) As the remaining peppers char, add them to the bag. Close the top of the bag after each addition. Let the peppers steam inside the bag for 7 to 10 minutes.

4. Remove the peppers from the bag and peel off the blackened skins.

5. Place the peeled peppers in a bowl along with the rest of the ingredients. Toss with your hands, using your fingertips to make sure the ingredients are evenly distributed.

6. Wash a quart jar with very hot, sudsy water. Rinse and drain.

7. Fill the jar with the pepper mixture, making sure the peppers are always submerged in the olive oil by at least ½ inch. Add more oil if necessary. Cover tightly with the lid and refrigerate. Any marinade that is left after you have eaten the peppers can be used as a dressing for salad greens or vegetables. Peppers can also be roasted on a grill. To do so, keep the peppers whole and seed them after removing the charred skins.

Yield: 9 roasted peppers

Use This Technique to Make:
- Roasted Red, Green, and Yellow Peppers with Anchovies, page 79
- Olive, Eggplant, and Red Pepper Salad, page 97
- Chicken Salad, page 215
- Risotto with Seafood, page 132
- Rolled Stuffed Salmon, page 56
- Baked Trout, page 263
- Asparagus with Pancetta and Caramelized Nuts, page 244
- Stuffed Zucchini, page 250
- Pizza, page 188
- Roasted peppers will also enhance such dishes as White Kidney Bean Soup, page 159; Onion, Garlic, and Cheese Focaccia, page 185; and Stuffed Pork Tenderloin, page 201

Marinated Sun-Dried Tomatoes
Stepping-Stone Technique

These marinated sun-dried tomatoes are like having gold in your refrigerator; the flavor is very concentrated and a few go a long way.

Drying fruits and vegetables is a common practice used throughout the world, originating long ago when refrigeration was not available and people had to preserve what they had for harder times ahead. When they needed the dried fruit or vegetables, all they had to do was rehydrate them, making them come to life again. This was accomplished by placing them into boiling water for a short time.

Marinated sun-dried tomatoes have a myriad of uses. You can add them to frittatas, salads, bread dough, and sandwiches. You could use them as part of an antipasto platter, add them to soups, or top pizzas with them. When something you are cooking just doesn't have enough flavor, such as a soup or a sauce, try chopping up a few and adding them at the end of the cooking cycle—they are a great flavor enhancer.

Marinated Sun-Dried Tomatoes

···

Pomodori Secchi Sott'Olio

Preparation Time: 10 minutes • Cooking Time: 1 to 5 minutes

I have vivid memories of watching the ladies in my native village in Sicily slicing whole tomatoes in half, generously salting them, and placing them, on screen-covered racks. Magic would happen when the rays from the sun and the gentle breezes danced over and around them. The smells were glorious. A dried tomato is filled with such concentrated aroma and flavor. Tomatoes are dried at the peak of the growing season when they are in abundance and very sweet. Preserving them in this manner, we were always assured of having a supply that could be used in a variety of dishes throughout the year.

Years ago, before we were able to purchase sun-dried tomatoes in the U.S., my relatives from Sicily would send us care packages. Now sun-dried tomatoes are widely available in Italian specialty shops, natural food stores, vegetarian markets, and even in supermarkets. The recipe that follows is the one my mother learned when she was a young girl in Sicily—simple, flavorful, and elegant.

1½ quarts water
½ pound sun-dried tomatoes
2 tablespoons chopped garlic
½ cup loosely packed fresh
    basil, coarsely chopped
    (about 20 leaves)

½ teaspoon freshly ground black
    pepper
1½ cups extra-virgin olive oil
    (more if needed)

PROCEDURE

1. In a medium nonreactive saucepan, bring the water to a boil. Drop the dried tomatoes in the boiling water for 30 to 60 seconds, rejuvenating them. With a slotted spoon, remove a tomato from the water and check to see how it feels; it should now feel plumper and softer. If tomatoes are still brittle, remove the saucepan from heat and let them stand in the hot water until they soften, about 5 minutes. Drain well and pat dry with paper towels.

2. In a large bowl, mix the garlic, basil, pepper, and olive oil. Add the tomatoes and toss with your fingers, making sure you incorporate the marinade throughout.

3. Place the tomatoes and marinade in prewashed glass quart jars, packing the tomatoes tightly into the jars along with any marinade. The tomatoes should always be submerged in the olive oil by ½ inch. Add extra olive oil if needed.

Yield: 2 cups

NOTES

These tomatoes will keep in the refrigerator for up to a year; take out whatever you need, making sure the tomatoes are always submerged in oil; add more oil if necessary. If you happen to have any extra oil left after you have eaten the tomatoes, use it to flavor soups, vegetables, salad greens, or bread.

Use This Recipe to Make:
- White Kidney Bean Soup, page 159
- Stuffed Turkey Breast, page 216
- Baby Peas with Sun-Dried Tomatoes and Toasted Pine Nuts, page 241

Broiled Eggplant Slices
Stepping-Stone Technique

This technique for creating very flavorful vegetables is quite easy and uses much less oil than would be needed if you were sautéeing or frying. It can be used for zucchini, yellow squash, and an assortment of root vegetables. Broiling brings out the natural sugars in the vegetable, making it sweeter as well as intensifying its flavor.

Our family used to cook these eggplants in the traditional way, first by dredging them in flour, dipping in egg, coating with bread crumbs, and then frying them in oil. The problem with this old approach is that no matter how careful you are, the eggplant acts like a sponge, soaking up unhealthy amounts of oil. The technique presented below is a much leaner and healthier version that does not compromise on flavor. These eggplant slices can be eaten as is, sprinkled with grated cheese and herbs, or used as a foundation for many different recipes.

Broiled Eggplant Slices

Melanzane alla Griglia

Preparation Time: 15 minutes, plus ½ to 1 hour for debittering eggplant if necessary
Cooking Time: 15 minutes

2 medium eggplants
1 teaspoon salt (plus more for debittering eggplant if needed)
¼ cup extra-virgin olive oil
Freshly ground black pepper

¼ cup freshly grated Romano or Parmigiano-Reggiano cheese
6 fresh basil leaves, torn into small pieces (optional)

PROCEDURE

1. To prepare eggplant, trim off cap and stem. I don't peel them, but if you prefer, you may peel them. Cut eggplant into ¼- to ⅓-inch rounds. If the eggplant are small, slice them lengthwise, giving you more surface area. Lay the eggplant slices on a work surface and sprinkle all over with salt. Place the slices in a large colander to drain. After ½ to 1 hour, rinse, drain, and pat dry the eggplant with paper towels.

2. Move the oven rack to the uppermost position, nearest the broiler unit. Preheat oven to broil. Line a baking sheet with aluminum foil.

3. In a small bowl, place ¼ cup extra-virgin olive oil. Have a pastry brush ready. Place eggplant slices in a single layer on baking sheet. Brush both sides of the slices with olive oil; then sprinkle them lightly with salt and pepper.

4. To broil the eggplant slices, place the baking sheet directly under the broiler elements or the flame. As soon as the slices start to turn golden (5 to 7 minutes), turn them and broil the other side. The second side always takes less time to cook. Take individual slices out of the oven as they are done. When you take out one slice, place another in its place until you have broiled all the eggplants.

5. To serve, place a single layer of eggplant slices on a platter and sprinkle with Romano (or Parmigiano) cheese. Add basil as a garnish if desired.

Yield: 4 or more servings depending on its use

NOTES

If you prefer, the eggplant can be grilled on the barbecue; it tastes great.

Store leftover eggplant slices in the refrigerator in a covered container. They will keep up to 1 week. You can freeze them, but they lose some of their texture. They will keep in the freezer for up to 2 months. Defrost and use in whatever manner you like.

Other Possibilities Include:

- Making Eggplant Parmigiana: Simply spoon some marinara sauce over the broiled eggplant slices and sprinkle with Parmesan cheese. Place in a preheated 350°F oven for about 10 minutes. Eggplant Parmigiana slices are wonderful in sandwiches made with homemade bread; try taking them on picnics.

- Placing a spoonful of ricotta and pine nuts on each slice, rolling them up, and serving as an antipasto or a vegetable for lunch or dinner
- Cutting in cubes and combining with Marinara Sauce, page 5, to sauce pasta
- Topping Pizzas, page 188
- Filling a roll-up, combined with sautéed ground lamb and marinated sun-dried tomatoes
- Creating an antipasto, with roasted green and red bell peppers
- Adding to Frittata, page 34

PESTO
STEPPING-STONE TECHNIQUE

In my opinion, one of the greatest gifts the Italians have given to the world is pesto. The word *pesto* comes from the Italian word *pestare* ("to pound"). In the olden days, pesto was always made with a mortar and pestle; the process was slow, meticulous, and carried out with a lot of love. Many villages and restaurants still abide by this tradition.

On our last trip to Italy, we decided to engage in pesto tasting. We sampled a variety of pastas seeped in pesto from four different restaurants. Each dish had its own magnificence with subtle differences in taste and texture. This is the beauty of pesto sauce. One can choose to either toast or not toast the pine nuts, to leave them whole or grind them, to vary the ratio of basil to oil to garlic. Each sauce becomes the unique work of its creator. Some restaurants use a little parsley with their basil, while others thin their pesto with some boiling water from the pasta. Such minute variations do, in fact, make a difference. Still, the most important element is the quality and freshness of the ingredients used.

The basil should always be freshly harvested and aromatic; the olive oil should be 100 percent extra-virgin, first cold press—the best you can afford —and the cheeses imported and freshly grated. To make sure the pine nuts are not rancid, I suggest tasting one before purchasing, if possible. Definitely taste them before starting to make the recipe.

Pasta choices can range from homemade trenetti to commercial dry pasta of 100 percent durum wheat semolina in shapes from linguine to pennete rigati. If you would like to indulge in the old-fashioned mortar-and-pestle method, simply gather your ingredients and pound and grind them together.

Pesto freezes very well and will keep in the freezer for up to 1 year. When I make pesto to freeze, I omit the pine nuts, Romano cheese, salt, and pepper. I prefer to add these to the dish at the last minute. The grated Romano cheese, toasted pine nuts, and freshly ground black pepper lose some of their flavor when frozen.

Depending on the amount you are making and the size of your family, you will need to decide what size container to use. To make small amounts to use in cooking, I use an ice cube tray, wait until the cubes of pesto are completely frozen, and then take them out and freeze them individually in tiny snack-size recloseable plastic bags. If you are doing many batches, line cookie sheets with parchment paper and fill with pesto. When frozen, cut the pesto into 2-inch squares and place the squares in freezer bags. If you have frozen pesto in larger containers, you can always take a small portion out by chiseling away with a knife and then returning the unused portion to the freezer.

Toasting Pine Nuts

Toasting any nuts intensifies their flavor, bringing out their natural oils. To toast pine nuts, heat a small, heavy-gauge or nonstick skillet over medium heat. Add the pine nuts. Stir and toss for 3 to 4 minutes, until nuts just turn a very light golden color. You will smell the aroma, see them turn a golden color, and notice a shiny appearance. It's easy to burn them, so be careful. If you burn them, discard and start over. An alternative method is to toast the nuts in a preheated 350°F oven. This method can also be used for other nuts. Spread the nuts in a single layer on a cookie sheet. Pine nuts take 3 to 4 minutes to toast. Walnuts take 8 to 10 minutes, almonds 5 to 6 minutes, hazelnuts and pecans 8 to 10 minutes. Stir frequently. Remove and cool.

Pesto

Pesto

Preparation Time: 10 minutes

¼ cup pine nuts
4 cloves garlic, peeled
1 cup extra-virgin olive oil (more if the blades on the food processor or blender do not turn because the pesto is too thick)
½ teaspoon salt

½ teaspoon freshly ground black pepper
2 cups fresh basil leaves, stems removed, packed lightly
½ cup freshly grated Parmigiano-Reggiano or Romano cheese, or a combination of the two

PROCEDURE

1. Lightly toast the pine nuts in a small, nonstick skillet using the technique on page 24.

2. In food processor bowl fitted with a metal blade or in a blender, chop the garlic. Add the olive oil, salt, and pepper and pulse several times. Add the basil and pulse until pureed; you may need more oil. Add the cheese and nuts and pulse several times until nuts are coarsely chopped.

Yield: 2 cups (enough to sauce 2 pounds of pasta)

NOTES

The basil in pesto oxidizes quickly when exposed to air, turning the top layer brown. One way to lessen this is to place a piece of plastic wrap on the surface of the pesto before putting the cover on the container. Double protection!

It is best to freeze leftover pesto and use it as needed. It will keep in the freezer for up to 1 year.

You may substitute walnuts or pecans for the pine nuts, but of course, the flavor will be different.

In the winter, when fresh basil is very expensive, Italian flat-leaf parsley may be substituted for a portion of the basil; this will change the flavor but is still very delicious.

To make pasta with pesto: Cook the pasta according to package directions.

Check for doneness a couple of minutes before the package suggests. When the pasta is al dente, remove 1 cup of the pasta liquid and set it aside. Drain the pasta and pour back into the pot. Add 1 cup or more of pesto, and toss lightly. If you feel the pasta is too dry and would prefer it to be moister, add a little of the pasta water and toss again. Pour the pasta onto a platter, sprinkle with extra cheese and freshly ground black pepper, and eat while nice and hot. If you would like to be adventuresome, try boiling green beans and slices of potato and tossing them with your pasta—very unusual, but good.

Use This Recipe to Make:
- Marinara Sauce, page 5
- Pesto Salad Dressing, page 72
- Roasted Red, Green, and Yellow Peppers with Anchovies, page 79
- Sunday Tomato Sauce with Meatballs, page 122
- Spicy Pasta with Capers and Olives, page 107
- Soup with Kohlrabi, page 153
- White Kidney Bean Soup, page 159
- Baked Chicken with Potatoes and Vegetables, page 208
- Green Beans with Balsamic Vinegar and Oregano, page 239

Béchamel Sauce
Stepping-Stone Technique

The Italians and the French are still arguing about the origin of this sauce, both claiming it as their own. Béchamel sauce can be used on vegetables and fish and also to thicken or enrich various dishes. Once you become familiar with the technique, you can incorporate a variety of ingredients to change its flavor, color, and texture. Change the flavor simply by substituting wine for some of the milk or by adding various cheeses. If adding liquid ingredients such as wine or broth, cut back on the milk. If the sauce gets too thick, add more liquid and check for seasonings.

Béchamel is made with milk when accompanying vegetable or pasta dishes. You may substitute some beef broth when serving it with meats, fish broth when serving it with fish, and chicken broth when serving with poultry.

Béchamel Sauce

Salsa Besciamella

Preparation Time: 5 minutes • Cooking Time: 15 minutes

1 quart whole milk
6 tablespoons unsalted butter
6 tablespoons unbleached all-
   purpose flour
1 bay leaf
1 teaspoon salt

Optional:
1 sprig fresh thyme
A pinch of nutmeg
¼ teaspoon freshly ground black
   pepper

PROCEDURE

1. Pour milk into a glass measuring cup and heat in the microwave until almost boiling.

2. Melt the butter in a 2-quart saucepan over medium heat. When the butter has melted and stops foaming, reduce the heat to medium-low. Add the flour and stir continuously with a wooden spoon or a whisk until smooth, about 2 to 3 minutes. Do not let the mixture turn brown.

3. Stir in the hot milk 1 cup at a time, stirring continuously to prevent any lumps from forming. Add the bay leaf and salt, and the optional ingredients if using. Cook gently, stirring continuously, until the sauce has a smooth consistency and coats the end of the spoon nicely. If the sauce is too thick, add a little more milk; if it is too thin, cook it a little longer.

4. Taste for seasoning and adjust accordingly.

5. Place a sheet of plastic wrap directly on the surface of the sauce until you are ready to use it to prevent skin from forming.

Yield: 1 quart

NOTES

Store any leftovers in the refrigerator in a covered container. It will keep for several days. Reheat in the microwave or on top of the stove in a double boiler set over low heat. Béchamel sauce thickens as it sits. When reheating, it will be necessary to add more liquid. Be careful to stir continuously to avoid scorching.

Use This Recipe to Make:
- Seafood Lasagna for Very Special Occasions, page 112
- Rolled Stuffed Salmon, page 56
- Use this as a base to make simple pasta or vegetable sauces

Spinach
Stepping-Stone Technique

I have converted many people into spinach lovers in my classes with the use of this simple cooking technique. You will be amazed at how easy this is. There's no boiling, no frying, no cleanup. You will be hooked.

There are just a couple of things to remember about spinach: It should not be cooked in an aluminum pot or cut with a carbon-steel knife blade. A chemical reaction takes place, which discolors the spinach and produces an unpleasant taste. Baby spinach is becoming readily available in many supermarkets in both the produce section and the salad bar. Many times it is prewashed and, because it is so young and tender, does not need to have the stems removed.

❧

Spinach with Garlic and Olive Oil

....

Spinaci Ripassati con Aglio e Olio

Preparation Time: 10 minutes • Cooking Time: 4 minutes

1 pound fresh spinach, cleaned and
   drained
1 tablespoon extra-virgin olive oil
1 clove garlic, chopped fine (about
   ½ teaspoon)

½ teaspoon salt
¼ teaspoon freshly ground black
   pepper
A pinch of nutmeg (optional)

PROCEDURE

1. Place the spinach in a large reclosable microwavable plastic freezer bag. Drizzle the oil over the spinach, add the garlic, and sprinkle with salt, pepper,

and nutmeg. Zip the bag almost all the way, leaving a 1-inch opening for venting. Shake the bag to evenly distribute seasonings.

2. Place bag in the microwave and cook on High power for 3 or 4 minutes, until the spinach turns bright green and is wilted. (Note: Be careful when opening the bag to prevent steam burns.)

3. Serve as a side dish.

Yield: 1 cup

NOTES

This spinach will keep in the refrigerator for several days. Reheat in the microwave.

This technique also works well for cooking asparagus, Swiss chard, carrots, and frozen peas.

Use This Recipe to Make:
- Frittata, page 34
- Stuffed Mushrooms, page 83
- Seafood Lasagna for Very Special Occasions, page 112
- Cannelloni Stuffed with Spinach and Ricotta, page 114
- Spinach Gnocchi, page 141
- Spinach Sauce, page 144
- Stuffed Turkey Breast, page 216
- Rolled Stuffed Salmon, page 56
- Elegant Shrimp with Spinach, page 229
- Stuffed Bread with Spinach and Olives, page 183
- A topping for Pizza, page 188

Sautéed Swiss Chard
Stepping-Stone Technique

The technique of first boiling vegetables before sautéing them in olive oil and garlic is a classic in Italy. It is very easy to do, takes a short time, and makes the vegetables extremely flavorful. With some strong-flavored vegetables, such as Swiss chard, broccoli, and cauliflower, it is very desirable to dissolve some of their harshness and pungency into the cooking water, making them sweeter, more palatable, and, for some, less gaseous. Boiling enhances the color of many vegetables, but beware not to overcook them. Overcooking turns vibrant colors into dull grays and khaki greens and turns the vegetables into mush. Cook vegetables as quickly as possible to retain the nutritive value. Sautéing vegetables quickly in olive oil and garlic after boiling imparts a wonderful flavor.

Swiss chard is quite pungent in taste when eaten raw and much milder and sweeter when boiled. You may use it in any dish that calls for spinach.

Sautéed Swiss Chard

Bietole Fritte

Preparation Time: 7 minutes • Cooking Time: 15 minutes

1 bunch Swiss chard
    (1½ to 2 pounds)
1 tablespoon salt for boiling water
2 to 4 tablespoons extra-virgin olive
    oil

2 to 4 cloves garlic, chopped
    (1 to 2 teaspoons)
½ teaspoon salt
¼ teaspoon freshly ground black
    pepper

PROCEDURE

1. Remove the Swiss chard leaves from the stem. Wash leaves and stem well under running water and then soak in a large bowl of cold water. Swish leaves around to release any extra sand and soil from crevices. Remove leaves and stalks from the water and place in a colander to drain. Chop the stalks and the leaves separately, placing them in individual bowls.

2. Bring a large pot of water to a boil. Once it is boiling, add 1 tablespoon salt and the chopped stalks. When stalks are fork-tender, about 4 to 5 minutes, add the chopped leaves, stir, and cook until the leaves are just wilted, about 1 to 2 minutes. Drain well.

3. Place a large skillet over medium-high heat. When skillet is warm, add the oil. When the oil is hot, add garlic, and stir and sauté for 2 minutes or until garlic turns golden. Add the Swiss chard, salt, and pepper, and stir and sauté for several minutes, blending all the flavors together. Taste for seasoning and adjust accordingly. Serve hot, warm, or at room temperature.

Yield: 4 to 6 servings

NOTE:

Store leftovers in the refrigerator in a covered container; they will keep for several days.

Use This Recipe to Make:
- Frittata, page 34
- Stuffed Mushrooms, page 83
- Pizza toppings, page 188
- Fillings for Ravioli, page 116; Lasagna, page 112; Tortelloni, page 119
- And to compose the ultimate sandwich, page 242

FRITTATA
STEPPING-STONE TECHNIQUE

A frittata is a simple, unassuming open-faced omelet that is both inexpensive and easy to prepare. The same technique can be used with a wide variety of ingredients. I usually make frittata when I have a lot of leftovers in the refrigerator that I need to use up.

Here Are Some of the Ingredients You May Want to Use in Your Frittata:
- oil or butter
- fresh herbs such as basil, thyme, mint, sage, parsley, and chives
- aromatics such as onions, shallots, scallions, garlic
- salt and freshly ground black pepper for seasoning
- raw vegetables such as shredded zucchini, carrots, onions
- sautéed vegetables such as spinach, bell pepper, Swiss chard, eggplant, mushrooms, broccoli, and peas
- marinated vegetables from your refrigerator such as sun-dried tomatoes, eggplant, and mushrooms
- cooked meat, poultry, or fish
- ricotta or leftover pasta or rice
- cheeses such as Romano, Asiago, or Parmigiano-Reggiano, mozzarella, and fontina
- black and green olives

Frittata

....

Frittata

Preparation Time: 5 to 10 minutes • Cooking Time: 10 to 15 minutes

Follow this simple recipe, get the technique down, have fun creating your own.

6 large eggs
2 tablespoons milk or water
1 teaspoon chopped fresh herbs of
   your choice
¼ cup chopped ham or 4 slices of
   cooked crumbled pancetta
   (optional)
2 to 3 tablespoons of freshly grated
   Romano, Asiago, or Parmigiano-
   Reggiano cheese or 1 cup
   shredded fontina cheese

3 to 4 tablespoons extra-virgin olive
   oil or a combination of butter
   and oil, divided
1 medium or small yellow cooking
   onion, chopped
½ cup or more raw or sautéed
   vegetables of your choice
1½ teaspoons salt, divided
¼ teaspoon freshly ground black
   pepper

PROCEDURE

1. In a medium bowl, beat the eggs lightly with the milk or water. Add herbs, ham, or pancetta (if using), and cheese.

2. Place a large nonstick skillet over medium heat. When skillet is warm, add 1½ tablespoons of the oil. When the oil is hot, add the onion. Stir and cook for 3 to 4 minutes.

3. Add the raw or partially cooked vegetables and season with salt and pepper. Stir and sauté 3 to 5 minutes, or until tender. Allow to cool slightly.

4. With a slotted spoon, remove the vegetables from the pan and place in the bowl with the egg-and-milk mixture. Return the pan to medium heat, add remaining oil, and when it is hot, pour the stirred egg and vegetable mixture into the skillet and cook for 5 to 7 minutes on the first side, or until the frittata is puffed and golden and the top begins to solidify.

5. To turn the frittata, place a large plate upside down over the skillet and, holding it firmly with pot holders, turn the pan with the frittata over onto the dish. (If this seems a bit intimidating, do a couple of trial runs with an empty pan, plate, and oven mitts; you will get the hang of it.) Be brave. Remember, you learn from your mistakes. Slide the frittata back into the hot pan and continue cooking the second side until golden, about 3 to 4 minutes more. Alternatively, if you have an ovenproof pan, you could put the skillet under the broiler to cook the top of the frittata, circumventing the need to flip it over.

6. Remove the pan from the heat and slide the frittata onto a platter. Cut into wedges and serve hot, warm, or at room temperature.

Yield: 4 servings

NOTE

Store leftovers in the refrigerator in a covered container; they will keep for several days. I do not recommend freezing.

VEGETABLE FRITTERS
STEPPING-STONE TECHNIQUE

This stepping-stone technique works very well with a variety of vegetables. For success with fritters, there are some important points to remember. Parboil the vegetables only until they are fork-tender. Drain them well, or the liquid clinging to them will dilute the batter. Make the batter thick, not runny. You want it to adhere to the vegetables, forming a coating around them. Use a good heavy, large nonstick skillet to sauté them. Wait for the oil to get nice and hot before beginning the sautéing process. The oil should sizzle when the fritters are added to it.

The fritters taste best when eaten right after they are cooked, but they can be held in a warming oven for an hour or so. They can also be prepared in the morning and reheated just before you are ready to serve them—put them in a 350°F oven for 7 to 10 minutes, until they are warm.

You will want to experiment with other vegetables. You can even use the batter as a base for veggie burgers. These are some of the vegetables I use:

- broccoli
- mushrooms
- julienned carrots
- red, green, and yellow bell peppers
- cardoons
- Swiss chard stalks

St. Joseph's Cauliflower Fritters

Cavolfiore di San Giuseppe

Preparation Time: 20 minutes • Cooking Time: 15 minutes

Every year, throughout Italy and the U.S., families join together on March 19 to keep alive the tradition of the St. Joseph table, sharing special foods with others. My family has been involved with the reenactment of this feast day in many aspects, from my Dad's portrayal of St. Joseph to my role as the Virgin Mary to the actual preparation of the feast and to hosting the table by my brother and his wife in honor of their son Joseph.

Our family prepares several traditional dishes for St. Joseph's Day, including this recipe, St. Joseph's Bread (page 172), and Ricotta Puffs (page 270).

These fritters are prepared very early in the morning and kept at room temperature until they are presented at the St. Joseph table. This is probably our children's all-time favorite vegetable dish to eat.

4 quarts water
1 tablespoon salt
1 large head cauliflower broken into
    small florets (about 4 cups);
    reserve stalks and stems for
    vegetable broth or discard

For the Batter (Pastetta):
WET INGREDIENTS
4 large eggs, beaten
¼ cup cold water
⅓ cup freshly grated Romano cheese
¼ teaspoon minced garlic
1 tablespoon finely chopped fresh
    mint

DRY INGREDIENTS
2 tablespoons cornstarch
1 cup unbleached all-purpose flour
1 teaspoon baking powder
½ teaspoon salt
⅛ teaspoon freshly ground black
    pepper

For Frying:
3 tablespoons extra-virgin olive oil,
    divided (more if necessary)
3 tablespoons canola oil, divided
    (more if necessary)

PROCEDURE

1. Bring the water to boil in a large pot. Add salt and the cauliflower to the boiling water. Bring back to a boil and cook for 7 to 10 minutes, or until the

florets are fork-tender but not mushy. Drain in a colander and rinse under cold water to stop the cooking. Drain again very well and set aside to cool.

2. Mix the eggs, water, Romano cheese, garlic, and mint in a medium bowl. In another medium bowl, mix together the cornstarch, flour, baking powder, salt, and pepper. Add the dry ingredients to the egg mixture several tablespoons at a time, and beat with a fork or mixer until no lumps remain, about 1 minute. The consistency should be like a *thick* pancake batter. If the batter is too thin, sprinkle in more flour and stir. If too thick, add a teaspoon or so of cold water. If you have the time, place batter in the refrigerator for ½ hour to set before using.

3. Add the cauliflower to the batter and gently mix with your fingers to coat each floret.

4. Place a large skillet over medium-high heat. When skillet is warm, add 1½ tablespoons of the olive oil and 1½ tablespoons of the canola oil. When the oil is hot (indicated by ripples on the surface of the oil), spoon the batter-dipped florets into the oil 1 tablespoon at a time. Do not crowd the pan. You should hear the oil sizzle as you add the florets to the pan. If not, allow the oil to get hotter before proceeding.

5. Cook until one side is golden brown; then turn and cook the other side. Place the cooked fritters on paper towels to drain. Cook the rest of the fritters in the same way. Add additional oil as necessary to cook the remaining fritters. Serve warm or at room temperature.

Yield: 8 servings

NOTES

Store leftovers in the refrigerator in a covered container; they will keep for up to 3 days. They make unusual, tasty sandwiches. To reheat, place in microwave for 45 seconds or in a 350°F oven for 7 to 10 minutes. Freezing is not recommended.

Homemade Pasta
Stepping-Stone Technique

I am giving you three different techniques for making homemade pasta dough: first, making it from scratch by hand; second, using the food processor; and third, using a stand-up mixer with a dough hook.

Although it takes a little time, making pasta at home is a relatively easy process that requires few ingredients. Making pasta, like making bread, has an elemental sense of taking simple ingredients and creating your own product. If time is a concern, I suggest leaving the project for another day and going to your local Italian market, where you are likely to find good fresh pasta for sale. However, if you are free from time constraints, the following recipe will allow you to fall into the rhythmic joy of this simple process.

The first time you make homemade pasta it will probably take you longer than the suggested preparation time. As you continue to make it, however, you will become more proficient, taking less time. Make pasta with children! They really enjoy rolling the pasta through the machine and seeing it come through the disks in different shapes and sizes.

I suggest making more than you need. I always make a double batch, either saving it for another meal during the week or placing it on a paper plate and into a reclosable plastic freezer bag and freezing it. Fresh pasta will keep in the freezer for up to 6 weeks. Place frozen pasta directly into salted, boiling water, stir, and cook it for about 1 minute.

The proportions given are an approximation and will probably vary with the size of the eggs used, how you measure the flour, the brand of flour you use, and how humid the weather is on the day you are making the pasta. Pay attention, and you will find it is easy. If the dough is too sticky, add a bit more flour; if it is getting too dry, don't use all the flour called for, or add a small sprinkling of water. In the end, allow your eyes and hands to see and feel. *You have to be able to knead the dough—it should not be too sticky or too dry.*

Use homemade pasta with many of the sauces in this book. Also try using it in some of the soup recipes, making them into main-course dishes.

Basic Egg Pasta Dough

....

Preparation Time: 25 minutes, plus 30 minutes for allowing the dough to rest

2½ cups unbleached all-purpose
    flour
5 large eggs, beaten
½ teaspoon salt (optional)

1 tablespoon extra-virgin olive oil
    (optional)
Water (if necessary; add 1 teaspoon
    at a time)

PROCEDURE

To Make the Pasta Dough by Hand:

1. Heap the flour in a mound on your work surface. Make a deep well in the center of the flour and add the beaten eggs and the olive oil and salt (if using). Working from the center outward, using a fork or your fingers, gradually incorporate the eggs into the flour to make a dough; only use as much of the flour as is necessary to make a pliable dough that is not sticky. If the dough is too crumbly, add water, 1 teaspoon at a time.

2. When the dough starts to get firm, begin kneading it while incorporating more flour if necessary. Use the palm and heel of your hand and knead as you would bread dough, pushing it against the work surface and turning it constantly for about 5 minutes. It should feel smooth and elastic and not too sticky. It should be fairly firm, not too soft or too hard, moist without being damp, and have a uniform texture and color.

3. Cover the dough completely in plastic wrap, and place in the refrigerator for at least 30 minutes. This allows the gluten in the flour to rest, making it easier to roll out and stretch.

To Make the Pasta Dough in a Food Processor:

1. Fit the processor with the metal blade, add flour and salt to the work bowl. Pulse four times. With motor on, add eggs and oil. Process until the ingredients are uniformly blended and start to form a ball (30 to 60 seconds). Add water if necessary.

2. Remove the dough from the machine and place on your work surface. Knead for 1 minute. It should feel smooth and elastic and not too sticky. It should be fairly firm, not too soft or too hard, moist without being damp, and have a uniform texture and color.

3. Cover the dough completely in plastic wrap, and place in the refrigerator for at least 30 minutes.

To Make the Pasta Dough in an Electric Mixer:

1. Fit the mixer with the dough hook and place all the ingredients into the bowl. Run the mixer at medium speed until the dough forms a ball and pulls away from the sides of the bowl.

2. Remove the dough from the bowl and place on your work surface. Knead for 1 minute. It should feel smooth and elastic and not too sticky. It should be fairly firm, not too soft or too hard, moist without being damp, and have a uniform texture and color.

3. Cover the dough completely in plastic wrap, and let rest in the refrigerator for at least 30 minutes.

To Roll Out the Pasta by Hand:

1. After the dough has rested, prepare the work surface with a dusting of flour. Flatten the rested dough into a disk shape with the palm and heel of your hand. Dust your rolling pin with flour and roll out dough to the desired thinness. Usually $\frac{1}{32}$ inch is the right thinness for linguine or fettuccine, and a little thinner for filled pastas that have one layer over the other.

2. If the dough tries to shrink back as you roll it, allow it to rest for a few minutes in between the rolling and stretching process.

3. Allow the pasta to dry for about 10 minutes before cutting into strands. Roll sheets of pasta into a cylinder and, with a sharp knife, cut crosswise strips of the desired width.

4. Spread the strips on clean dish towels and allow to dry for 10 minutes, turning them from time to time.

To Roll Out the Pasta with a Basic Pasta Machine:

1. After the dough has rested, prepare the work surface with a dusting of flour. Cut the dough into six equal pieces (the size of a medium egg).

2. Secure the pasta machine to your work surface with the clamp provided. Set the rollers of the machine at the widest opening.

3. Working with one piece of dough at a time, dust lightly with flour and flatten with the palm of your hand. Pass the dough through the flat rollers with the regulating knob at position 1 or the widest setting.

4. Fold the piece into thirds and pass through rollers again.

5. Continue rolling, folding, and lightly flouring the pasta sheets each time they are passed through the machine at the widest setting. Do this about three times. This works the dough, making it smooth and uniform. Repeat this procedure with the remaining pieces.

6. Reset the rollers one width narrower. Working with one piece of dough (do not fold into thirds), dust lightly with flour and pass through rollers again. Roll all the pieces once through this setting. Dust with flour as necessary. Repeat the rolling procedure, decreasing the width by one notch each time until you reach the desired thinness (which is usually the second to the last). The strips become longer as the pasta gets thinner.

7. If you are going to cut the pasta into shapes, do not dry the pasta for too long; it must be pliable enough not to crack and split as it goes through the cutting disks. Nor can you cut it if it is too soft and moist; the pieces will stick to each other. Choose the cutting disk you prefer—linguine, fettuccine, and so on. As the ribbons of pasta come through the cutting disk, separate and spread them on your dish towel, sprinkling them with additional flour if necessary.

Yield: about 1¼ pounds (about 4 to 6 servings)

NOTES

If you would like to add flavorings and color to pasta, such as spinach and herbs, do so when adding the liquid ingredients. *To make a firmer homemade pasta,* use 2 cups unbleached all-purpose flour and 1 cup semolina flour for the flour in this recipe. You will also need to add 2 or more additional tablespoons of water to help form the dough into a pliable ball. This firmer dough is a little more difficult to work with, but it has more tooth. Semolina can be purchased at natural foods stores, Italian markets, and in some supermarkets.

To cook fresh pasta, place it in a large pot of salted water, stir, and boil for 1 to 2 minutes depending on its thinness.

Use This Recipe to Make:
- Cannelloni Stuffed with Spinach and Ricotta, page 114
- Shrimp-Stuffed Ravioli, page 116
- Tortelloni with Mushroom Sauce, page 119
- Seafood Lasagna for Very Special Occasions, page 112

CRÊPES (CRESPELLE)
STEPPING-STONE TECHNIQUE

Crêpes are very thin pancakes made with flour and milk. They are perfect wrappers for a variety of fillings and create a myriad of dishes from sweet to savory.

The manicotti recipe that follows showcases crêpe-making as the basis for this savory pasta dish. It builds on techniques you've already learned. You know how to make the marinara sauce, ricotta has been added to your repertoire, and now you will learn to make crêpes—all the ingredients necessary to create delicious authentic Italian manicotti.

You can also make other savory dishes using crêpes. Fill them with cooked vegetables, meats, poultry, or seafood. Or spread with Pesto (page 25), roll up or fold, and pour Béchamel Sauce (page 27) over them, and bake at 350°F until heated through, about 15 minutes. Use your imagination to create a multitude of stuffed baked pasta dishes.

The batter can also be used as a base for dessert crêpes—just add a tablespoon or two of sugar to taste and be sure to cook the crêpes on both sides. The second side of the crêpe cooks almost instantly. You can fill dessert crêpes with Mama Rosa's Lemon Custard Cream (page 74), Ricotta Cloud Cream (page 271), Chocolate Custard Cream (page 278), or Fresh Fruit Salad (page 255). To embellish them, top with whipped cream or toasted nuts or both. Drizzle with melted chocolate or liqueurs.

Manicotti Made with Crêpes

Manicotti

Preparation Time: about 1 hour (not including the time needed to prepare homemade ricotta)
Baking Time: 25 to 30 minutes

I was introduced to manicotti made with crêpes rather than pasta shortly after our marriage, when my husband, Guy, and I moved to New York City. I had never been away from home before, and I was very homesick. Guy was in the navy and stationed in Bayonne, New Jersey, where he worked with a charming Italian-American named Lou Iazetti. They quickly became friends, and I met the entire Iazetti family when we were invited to their home for dinner. Their closeness, love for each other, joy, and generosity were infectious and just what the doctor ordered. We went home that evening revitalized and filled with the spirit of the Iazetti family and their delicious food. This recipe was inspired by Lucille Iazetti. I cannot make this recipe without recalling the wonderful times we shared together and all the delicious Italian food she made for us.

For the Crêpes:
6 large eggs
1 cup milk (whole or 2%)
⅛ teaspoon salt
1 cup unbleached all-purpose flour
1 teaspoon oil to season skillet

For the Filling:
1 recipe Homemade Fresh Ricotta
    (page 8), or 4 cups commercial
    ricotta
2 large eggs (if ricotta is very dry, use
    1 additional egg)

½ cup freshly grated Romano cheese
1 cup shredded fresh mozzarella
    cheese
2 tablespoons chopped Italian flat-
    leaf parsley

For the Assembly:
4 cups Marinara Sauce (page 5)
    or Tomato-Basil Cream Sauce
    (page 127)
½ cup shredded mozzarella, fontina
    cheese, or freshly grated Romano
    cheese to sprinkle on top

PROCEDURE

For the Crêpes:

1. In a medium bowl, using an electric mixer on low speed, combine the eggs, milk, and salt. Add the flour a little at a time, mixing until it has all been incorporated. Continue beating until the batter is smooth and there are no lumps. Place the mixture in the refrigerator for 30 minutes. This allows the flour to absorb the liquid, yielding a crêpe with superior texture.

2. You cook these crêpes on one side only. The other side cooks when it is baked in the oven.

3. Place 2 large sheets of parchment or wax paper on your work surface.

4. Soak a small piece of paper towel with the oil. Lightly grease a 6-inch nonstick frying pan or crêpe pan. Place the pan over medium heat. When the pan is hot, use a small ladle to spoon about 2½ tablespoons of batter into the center of the pan. Quickly tilt and rotate pan with a twisting motion of the wrist, distributing the batter evenly to cover the bottom of the pan. The evenness of the crêpe is determined by how quickly you do this. If there are little holes in the crêpe, just fill them in with a little more batter. You know the bottom is cooked when the top of the crêpe loses its wet look and the edges of the crêpe start to look lacy, about 30 to 45 seconds.

5. When the bottom of the crêpe is done (just *barely* golden), remove the pan from the burner and turn it upside down over the parchment or wax paper. Tap the pan lightly on the table to dislodge the crêpe. It should fall right onto the paper. If you have difficulty, try releasing the edge with a blunt knife first; then turn the pan over.

6. Return the pan to the stove. Repeat the process until all the batter has been used. Grease the pan occasionally if necessary. You should have 16 to 18 crêpes. As your skill improves, so will the yield. They tend to be thicker when you are just starting out.

7. The first crêpe is usually a test crêpe and a throwaway. So don't get discouraged. Also keep in mind that the crêpes are going to be filled and covered with sauce, so any imperfections won't be noticeable. Don't be too critical. You will get a feel for this crêpe-making technique easily if you allow yourself to make a few mistakes. It will get easier and you will wonder why you didn't try this method of making manicotti sooner.

8. These crêpes can be made a day in advance or on the morning of the day you plan to use them. To store, stack in between layers of wax paper, place in a reclosable plastic bag, and refrigerate.

For the Filling:

1. Place all the ingredients—ricotta, eggs, cheeses, and parsley—in a medium bowl and mix with your hands or a fork until well blended.

2. This too can be prepared a day in advance. Cover the bowl tightly with plastic wrap and store in the refrigerator until ready to use.

For the Assembly:

1. Preheat the oven to 325°F.

2. Spread a thin layer of the marinara sauce in the bottom of a nonreactive baking pan about 17 × 12 × 2 inches.

3. Lay a crêpe, cooked-side up, on the parchment paper. Place 2 heaping tablespoons of filling in the center horizontally. Roll the crêpe into a tubular shape with the top edges overlapping. The uncooked surface will hold the flap together. Continue filling the rest of the crêpes.

4. After the crêpes are filled and rolled, place them in the sauce side by side but not touching each other, using a small amount of sauce in between each one. The sauce will separate them, prevent them from sticking together, and make them easier to serve. Spoon some marinara sauce over the top of the crêpes and sprinkle with the remaining cheese.

5. Bake uncovered for 30 to 40 minutes, until the sauce is bubbly and the manicotti are cooked throughout. Remove from oven and serve immediately.

Yield: 8 servings (16–18 filled manicotti)

NOTES

Although the filling and the crêpes may be made in advance, separately, once the crêpes are filled, they should be baked within an hour or two, or some of the liquid from the ricotta may seep out and make the sauce watery.

Leftovers will keep fresh in the refrigerator for up to 4 days and can be reheated in the microwave or oven. Freezing the filled, cooked manicotti is not recommended.

The individual crêpes may be frozen for up to 6 weeks. Be sure to wait until they are cool before wrapping them up. Stack the crêpes between pieces of wax paper or parchment paper; then wrap with plastic wrap and place in freezer bags.

Risotto
Stepping-Stone Technique

Risotto, when made properly, is one of the great joys of Northern Italian cuisine. I offer you this simple version so you can begin to get a feel for the technique of making risotto without becoming too intimidated. Risotto can be made with one or a multitude of different ingredients. Depending on the ingredients used, you will produce a rice with various flavors, textures, and colors, a dish that will excite all your senses. It can be prepared to be rustic or elegant. Once you learn how to make risotto, you will be spoiled for life.

A variety of ingredients can be used in preparing risotto. Try substituting different spices, herbs, nuts, truffles, vegetables, meats, poultry, seafood, and cheeses. The variations are endless. Some ingredients are placed in the broth at the very onset to impart flavor to the base, and some, such as shellfish, are added at the end.

Use heavy-bottomed skillets or saucepans. They conduct heat more evenly and are less likely to scorch the rice. Always cook risotto uncovered on medium heat, stirring continuously. You need to baby-sit this rice and not let it out of your sight. After you become comfortable with this technique, go on to trying the other risotto recipes, and then to improvising by creating your own signature risotto with ingredients that you are particularly fond of.

Simple Risotto

....

Risotto Semplice

Preparation Time: 5 minutes • Cooking Time: 30 minutes

3 cups Vegetable Broth (page 62),
    Chicken Broth (page 60), or Beef
    Broth (page 61)
1½ tablespoons extra-virgin olive
    oil or butter or a combination
    of the two
1 small yellow cooking onion,
    chopped
1 cup Arborio, Carnaroli, or Vialone
    Nano rice

4 sprigs fresh thyme
1 bay leaf
2 tablespoons butter
2 tablespoons freshly grated
    Parmigiano or Romano cheese
Salt, only if the broth has not been
    seasoned

PROCEDURE

1. In a small saucepan, heat the broth to simmering; keep hot throughout the duration of the cooking process, ready to be added in stages.

2. Place a heavy-gauge medium skillet over medium-high heat. When the skillet is warm, add the oil. When the oil is hot, add the chopped onion and sauté for 3 minutes, until the onion becomes transparent and lightly colored. Add the rice and stir. Continue to sauté the rice and onion for a few minutes. The rice will change from white to opaque and shiny.

3. Stir in ½ cup of the simmering broth and the herbs. Make sure to stir the entire surface of the bottom of the skillet to prevent scorching. Cook uncovered over medium heat, stirring continuously, until the broth has been absorbed by the rice. Add another ½ cup simmering broth to the rice and continue to stir and cook. As the broth is absorbed, keep adding more broth, repeating the process.

4. Test for doneness about 20 minutes into the cooking cycle. Toward the end, if you happen to run out of broth, substitute hot water. When the rice is tender and cooked throughout and the liquid is absorbed, remove from the stove. Add the butter and cheese, stirring vigorously until they are incorporated. The risotto should be creamy, not sticky. Serve immediately.

Yield: about 4 cups

NOTES

Use homemade broths whenever possible; they add a richness of flavor that is incomparable.

I recommend making a double batch of this risotto. It will come in handy in your cooking the rest of the week. You can add it to soups, salads, or stuffing. Try pureeing it to thicken soups and salad dressings.

It will keep in the refrigerator for up to 1 week.

Use This Recipe to Make:
- Risotto alla Bolognese, page 134
- Risotto alla Milanese, page 130
- Risotto with Seafood, page 132
- This risotto can also be used to enrich many of the soups in this book, making them main-course meals. It can also also be used as an ingredient in the stuffing of vegetables, meats, fish, and poultry.

Breaded Cutlet Stepping-Stone Technique

This process of making cutlets features chicken, but it can also be used to prepare beef, veal, pork, fish, and even vegetables. The technique will, for the most part, remain the same. Becoming comfortable with this technique will help you create many new dishes, expanding your repertoire.

When the cutlets have been sautéed and are fully cooked, they may be served as is or with fresh lemon wedges as in Chicken Milanese. Or they can be topped with Marinara Sauce (page 5) and cheese to make Chicken Parmesan.

Butterflying Chicken Breasts

Place a boneless breast of chicken on your cutting board and look at it. You will notice that one end is much plumper than the other, and if you were to cook it in this way, the result would be a piece of chicken that was properly cooked on one side and overcooked on the other. In order to make these pieces even in thickness so they will cook uniformly, butterfly the plumper portion only.

First trim off any fat and cartilage. To butterfly, slice the plumper part, holding the knife parallel to the cutting board with one hand, and place the other hand on top of the breast. Slice the portion almost in half, stopping ¼ inch from the end. Take this flap and open it up like a book.

You now need to flatten the chicken. Place a large sheet of parchment or wax paper on a cutting board. Place the breast shiny-side down on the paper, covering with another sheet of paper. Pound it with a kitchen mallet, using a pound-slide motion. You want the chicken to be between ¼ and ⅛ inch thick. Pounding not only helps tenderize the chicken, but it also makes the pieces larger. Cut the chicken breasts in half if they are too large for a single portion.

Breading the Cutlets

Think of breading as an assembly-line process. First, dredge all the pieces of chicken in flour, then dip each one in the egg mixture, then press them into the bread crumbs. This will save time and also steps to the sink to wash breading off your fingertips. The more organized you are with this technique, the faster the process will go.

Sautéing the Cutlets

When sautéing the cutlets, here are some pointers to remember. For the best flavor, use a combination of olive oil and butter. Make sure the oil and butter are nice and hot before adding the cutlets; they should sizzle when they hit the pan. Do not overcrowd the pan. Turn the cutlets when the first side has turned golden. The second side takes less time to cook. After you remove the cutlets, place them on paper towels to drain.

Breaded Chicken Cutlets

··

Cotolette di Pollo

Preparation Time: 30 minutes • *Cooking Time: 4 to 5 minutes per cutlet*

Baking Time: 10 minutes for entire dish once assembled
(if making optional Chicken Parmesan)

This is a dish that everyone loves—it is so dependable, inexpensive, and deliciously appetizing, and the presentation works beautifully. You can either serve the cutlets plain, or add Marinara Sauce and cheese to make Chicken Parmesan. Paying attention to butterflying the breasts so they are fairly even in thickness, pounding them gently and firmly to tenderize and thin them, using the best, freshest cheese, and, of course, using the wonderful homemade Marinara Sauce make this dish *fantastico*. The cutlets are so tender, they positively melt in your mouth. You definitely don't need a knife to cut them. My son Michael, who lives about five blocks away, has a special sensory detector. Every time I make this, he just happens to be in the neighborhood. It's his and his daughter Skye's favorite.

8 boneless skinless chicken breast
    halves
Salt and freshly ground black
    pepper

For the Breading:
6 large eggs
2 tablespoons milk or water
½ cup freshly grated Parmigiano-
    Reggiano or Romano cheese
¾ cup unbleached all-purpose flour
3 cups plain dried bread crumbs
    (more if necessary)

For Sautéing Cutlets:
3 tablespoons extra-virgin olive oil,
    divided (more if necessary)
3 tablespoons butter, divided (more
    if necessary)

*For Assembling Optional
Chicken Parmesan:*
1½ cups Marinara Sauce (page 5)
¼ cup freshly grated Parmigiano-
    Reggiano or Romano cheese for
    sprinkling on the top or 1½ cups
    shredded fresh mozzarella cheese

PROCEDURE

1. Rinse the chicken pieces under cold running water, drain, and pat dry with paper towels.

2. Trim any excess fat, cartilage, or connective tissue from the chicken

breasts. Butterfly the plump portion at the top of the breast so you will have a large piece of uniform thickness which will cook more evenly (see page 50).

3. Flatten the breasts with a kitchen mallet between sheets of parchment or wax paper (see page 50). Season both sides with a light sprinkling of salt and pepper.

4. In a medium bowl, beat the eggs, water, and cheese together until blended. Tear off four 12-inch pieces of parchment or wax paper. On the first piece, place the flour and on the second, place the bread crumbs. Save the third and fourth to put the cutlets on after they have been breaded.

5. Dredge the seasoned chicken breasts one at a time in the flour. Then dip each floured piece of chicken into the egg-and-cheese mixture, shake off the excess liquid, and place them into another bowl. After all have been dipped in egg, place each breast on the bread crumbs and press with your fingers to coat both sides well. The bread-crumb coating should not feel wet. Place the breaded cutlets on a clean piece of wax paper.

6. Refrigerate the breaded cutlets for 30 minutes if possible. This allows the breading mixture to set and gives you time to clean up before proceeding.

7. Line a baking sheet with a layer of paper towels to absorb any excess grease. If you're making the Chicken Parmesan, preheat oven to 350°F.

8. Place a large skillet over medium-high heat. When the skillet is warm, add 1½ tablespoons each of butter and olive oil. When the butter and oil are hot, add the cutlets, one at a time. They should sizzle as they go in. If not, let the oil heat up a little longer. Do not crowd the skillet. Cook the cutlets until the bottom side is light golden-brown and crusty. Turn and cook the other side until golden. Remove the cooked cutlets from the skillet onto the baking sheet.

9. You may either serve the cutlets as is, or add sauce and cheese to make Chicken Parmesan.

10. To make Chicken Parmesan, layer a thin amount of the Marinara Sauce on the bottom of a large ovenproof serving platter. Place the cutlets on top of the sauce, and spoon another thin layer of sauce on top of the cutlets. Top with cheese and heat in the oven for 10 minutes until the sauce has mingled with the chicken and the cheese has melted.

Yield: 8 generous main-course servings

NOTES

When properly stored, the chicken cutlets or the Chicken Parmesan will keep in the refrigerator for up to 4 days. To reheat, simply warm in the microwave or place in a toaster oven that has been preheated to 350°F and bake for 7 to 10 minutes until hot. This dish also freezes well and will keep in the freezer for up to 2 months.

If you want to handle some of the preparation in advance, you can prepare and pound the chicken and refrigerate it for up to 1 day before continuing.

The uncooked breaded cutlets can be refrigerated for up to 1 day before sautéeing. Use pieces of wax paper in between the cutlets to prevent them from sticking. The cutlets can also be frozen for up to 2 months (if the chicken has not been previously frozen). To use the cutlets, simply defrost in the refrigerator and proceed according to the recipe.

Rolled Stuffed Salmon
Stepping-Stone Technique

This rolled stuffed salmon is the festive centerpiece of an elegant meal. It is not only tasty, healthy, and inexpensive, but light, attractive, and impressive.

I have done a variation of this technique throughout this book. I'm particularly drawn to the layering and rolling process. This technique is simple and basic and allows for a variety of presentations and improvisations depending on what raw ingredients are used and how much you trust your instincts.

The idea is always the same. You choose a wrapper, fill it, roll it, cook it, and serve with a quick sauce that complements it. The wrapper can be a circular or rectangular piece of chicken, turkey, beef, veal, pork, fish, pasta, vegetable, or even bread. The choice of fillings is endless—your imagination is the only limit. Ingredients are placed on top of the wrapper or base layer, incorporating a variety of colors, textures, and flavors that blend well together. The piece is then rolled up and sometimes tied with kitchen string or held in place with toothpicks or skewers. It is then cooked in one manner or another, in a specially created sauce or in the pan drippings to which some wine is added to create a simple sauce. After it is taken from the oven, it is allowed to settle for a few minutes and is then cut into beautiful slices and plated. Give yourself plenty of time the first time you do this technique; that way you won't get frustrated. Remember, this technique gets easier and easier as you use it.

Since much of this dish can be prepared in advance (the day before or the morning of) and there is a lot of overlap in cooking time, it is hard to give specific times for preparing and cooking. Take it one step at a time and do as much in advance as possible. For example:

- The rice can be prepared the day before.
- The mushrooms and scallions can be sautéed the morning of.
- The spinach can be prepared the day before.
- The roasted peppers can be prepared the day before or purchased in jars or from the deli.
- The Béchamel Sauce can be prepared the morning of.
- The salmon can be sliced, pounded, and refrigerated earlier in the day.

Rolled Stuffed Salmon

....

Preparation Time: 30 minutes, plus 25 minutes for preparing the rice, 4 minutes for the spinach, 20 minutes for the Béchamel, and 10 minutes for the peppers (times will overlap)

Cooking Time: 20 minutes

The many colors and textures revealed in this dish are a visual treat. The flavors are equally impressive.

1 2-pound salmon fillet, center cut, skin and any bones removed, sliced lengthwise into 2 or 3 long thin fillets

Butter, for greasing the baking pan

For the Stuffing:
1 tablespoon butter
1 tablespoon extra-virgin olive oil
8 ounces mushrooms, wiped clean and sliced thin
4 to 5 scallions, white part only, sliced thin
1 recipe Spinach with Garlic and Olive Oil (page 29)

1½ cups prepared Quick, Delicious, and Simply Elegant Rice (page 136)
¼ pound fontina cheese, shredded
1 roasted red or yellow bell pepper (see page 14), sliced lengthwise into ⅛-inch strips
Juice and zest of 1 lemon

For the Sauce:
½ recipe Béchamel Sauce (page 27)
½ roasted red bell pepper (see page 14)
Any stuffing left after the salmon has been rolled
Milk, if needed

PROCEDURE

To Prepare the Salmon for Stuffing:

1. Place a large piece of wax or parchment paper on the work surface. Butterfly each piece of salmon by cutting lengthwise, starting at one edge of the fish and cutting up to, but not completely through, the opposite edge. Open each piece like a book, and flatten. Arrange the fillets on the paper side by side lengthwise so they overlap each other by ¼ inch, making a rectangle.

2. Place another piece of wax or parchment paper over the fillet and *gently* pound the pieces together with a mallet so you have a rectangular sheet of salmon a little less than ¼ inch thick. If you make a small hole, place a small piece of salmon from the edge into the hole and pound the area lightly. Refrigerate the salmon on the paper until ready to assemble.

To Assemble and Cook:

1. Preheat the oven to 400°F. Butter a baking pan.

2. Place a medium skillet over medium-high heat. When the skillet is warm, add the butter and oil. When the butter has melted and the oil is hot, add the mushrooms and scallions. Stir, sprinkle with salt and pepper, and sauté for 4 minutes, or until the mushrooms are tender. Place in a small bowl and set aside.

3. Remove salmon from refrigerator. Leave a ⅓-inch border around the edge of the salmon as you layer. Start with the spinach, layering it all over the salmon; then dot with the mushroom and scallion mixture. Spread the rice on as the next layer. Sprinkle the shredded cheese all over. Lay strips of roasted pepper lengthwise over the rice and cheese. Proceed to roll the salmon horizontally, starting with the edge nearest you and rolling away from you to form a long, fat, sausage-shaped roll.

4. Lift the salmon by lifting the paper underneath it and roll it carefully into the baking pan. Sprinkle the top with the lemon juice.

5. Bake for 20 minutes, until fish is cooked, turning a nice salmon color and opaque. Do not overcook or it will become dry.

6. While the salmon is baking, make the sauce. Heat the Béchamel Sauce in a saucepan. Place the roasted pepper along with any leftover stuffing mixture into the blender or food processor. Puree and add to the Béchamel. Cook over medium heat together for 1 minute to blend flavors. The sauce should be thin; add more milk if necessary.

To Serve:

1. Remove the salmon from the oven and allow it to rest for a few minutes. Slice into ½- to 1-inch rounds. Place a thin layer of Béchamel Sauce on the individual serving plates, then place the salmon rounds on top of the sauce. Spoon several tablespoons of sauce around the salmon rounds; then sprinkle with lemon zest. If there is extra sauce, serve it in a gravy boat.

Yield: 6 to 8 servings

NOTES

Store any leftovers in the refrigerator in a covered container; they taste best when eaten the following day. I do not recommend freezing this dish.

Broth
Stepping-Stone Technique

Broths form the base of many soups, stews, and sauces and are very useful when making risotti. If you are looking for a low-calorie lunch, broth with the addition of rice or small pasta certainly fits the bill. Broth can be used as is for a quick picker-upper. An excellent broth is prepared by adding bones, bits and pieces of meat, chicken, vegetables, or fish frames and shells. These ingredients are placed in a large stockpot and covered with cold water. The water is brought to a boil, and any scum is skimmed off with a slotted spoon. The broth continues to cook at a simmer for anywhere from 1 to 3 hours, depending on the ingredients. This long, slow cooking gently extracts the flavor from the ingredients. For a richer, more intense flavor, add more vegetables, meat, chicken, or fish.

Save any extra trimmings, bones, and shells in a heavy-duty freezer bag and freeze. Add these to the broth at the beginning of cooking.

Defatting Homemade Broth

I suggest that whenever possible you make your broth a day in advance and re-frigerate it. This allows any fat to rise to the surface and solidify. The next day the fat is very easy to remove and discard, leaving you with a fat-free, guilt-free broth.

If you are in a hurry and have to use the broth the same day, take a paper towel and place it on top of the surface of the broth. Wait a few seconds for the toweling to absorb the fat; then remove and discard. Repeat this process until you have removed all the fat. When all the fat has been removed, the paper towel will then absorb the broth, which is of a different consistency, liquidy, and is not yellow and greasy. This is a very important step and should not be overlooked. Save those calories!

Using Canned Broth

For those times that you want to make a recipe that calls for broth and you have none in your freezer, keep a couple of cans of broth in your cupboard. When using canned broth that is not fat-free, defat it by removing the fat that is on the surface of the broth with a spoon. Often canned broths are very salty—look for low-sodium broths or adjust the amount of salt you use in the recipe accordingly.

Fish Broth

Brodo di Pesce

Preparation Time: 10 minutes • Cooking Time: 1 hour

3 pounds fish frames (heads, bones, shells, etc.)
1 pound perch fillets
3 quarts cold water
2 cups dry white wine
1 large onion, coarsely chopped
2 ribs celery, coarsely chopped
3 carrots, coarsely chopped
1 tablespoon black peppercorns
6 sprigs Italian flat-leaf parsley
1 bay leaf

PROCEDURE

1. Rinse the fish frames and fillets under cold running water. Drain.

2. Combine all the ingredients in a large stockpot. There should be 2 to 3 inches of water above the fish. Bring to a boil over medium heat. Using a skimmer or slotted spoon, remove and discard any scum that has come to the surface.

3. Reduce the heat to low and gently simmer uncovered for about 1 hour.

4. Strain the broth through a sieve using two layers of cheesecloth. Discard the solids. Cool the broth to room temperature and refrigerate until ready to use. Defat before using.

Yield: about 3 quarts

NOTE

Store broth in the refrigerator in a covered container; it will keep for up to 3 days, or freeze for up to 2 months.

Chicken Broth

Brodo di Gallina

Preparation Time: 10 minutes • Cooking Time: 2½ hours

1 whole chicken (about 3 pounds)
3 pounds chicken bones (backs,
    necks, ribs, wings, etc.)
1 medium yellow cooking onion,
    coarsely chopped
2 ribs celery, coarsely chopped
2 carrots, coarsely chopped

3 Italian plum tomatoes, seeded
    (see page 3) and chopped
5 sprigs Italian flat-leaf parsley
2 sprigs fresh thyme
1 bay leaf
1 tablespoon salt (or more to taste)

PROCEDURE

1. Place the chicken and chicken bones in a stockpot and cover with water. There should be 2 to 3 inches of water above the chicken.

2. Bring to a gentle boil uncovered over medium heat; then reduce the heat to low. Skim off and discard any scum that comes to the surface with a skimmer or slotted spoon.

3. Add the remaining ingredients except the salt. Simmer uncovered for about 1½ to 2 hours. Season with salt. Taste for seasonings and adjust accordingly.

4. Remove the chicken and reserve for another use. Strain the broth into a large bowl and discard the bones and vegetables.

5. If you need the broth right away, remove the fat with paper towels, as described on page 58, before using. Otherwise, allow it to cool, and refrigerate. The next day, remove the fat from the surface.

Yield: about 4½ quarts

NOTE

When properly stored, this broth will keep in the refrigerator for up to 4 days or can be frozen for up to 2 months.

Beef Broth

Brodo di Manzo

Preparation Time: 10 minutes • Cooking Time: 2 to 3 hours

3 pounds beef chuck, cut into 2-inch
    cubes, seasoned with a
    sprinkling of salt and pepper
3 pounds beef bones, seasoned with
    a sprinkling of salt and pepper
1 medium yellow cooking onion,
    coarsely chopped
2 ribs celery, coarsely chopped

2 carrots, coarsely chopped
3 Italian plum tomatoes, seeded
    (see page 3) and chopped
5 sprigs Italian flat-leaf parsley
2 sprigs fresh thyme
1 bay leaf
1 tablespoon salt (or more to taste)

PROCEDURE

1. Place the meat and bones in a stockpot and cover with water. There should be 2 to 3 inches of water above the meat.

2. Bring to a gentle boil over medium heat; then reduce the heat to low. Skim off and discard any scum that comes to the surface with a skimmer or slotted spoon.

3. Add the remaining ingredients except the salt. Simmer uncovered for about 3 hours. Season with salt. Taste for seasonings and adjust accordingly.

4. If desired, remove the meat and reserve for another use. Strain the broth into a large bowl and discard the bones and vegetables.

5. If you need the broth right away, remove the fat with paper towels, as described on page 58, before using. Otherwise, allow it to cool and then refrigerate it. The next day take it out of the refrigerator and remove all the fat from the surface.

Yield: about 4½ quarts

NOTE

Store the broth in the refrigerator in a covered container; it will keep for up to 4 days or can be frozen for up to 2 months.

Vegetable Broth

···

Brodo di Verdura

Preparation Time: 30 minutes • Cooking Time: 1 hour 45 minutes

Do not let the number of ingredients in this broth intimidate you. If an ingredient is not readily available, feel free to substitute another. You can store leftovers in the freezer for making quick soups, sauces, and gravies.

¼ cup extra-virgin olive oil
2 leeks, white portion only, cut into
    quarters and cleaned very well
2 yellow cooking onions, peeled and
    quartered
1 garlic clove, peeled and crushed
4 carrots, cut into 2-inch pieces
2 celery stalks, cut into 2-inch pieces
3 kohlrabies, chopped coarsely

3 turnips, chopped coarsely
3 parsnips, chopped coarsely
1 bulb fennel, chopped coarsely
1 red bell pepper, chopped coarsely
2 bay leaves
6 sprigs fresh thyme
½ bunch Italian flat-leaf parsley
1 teaspoon peppercorns
1 tablespoon salt (or more to taste)

PROCEDURE

1. Place a large skillet over medium-high heat. When skillet is warm, add the oil. When the oil is hot (indicated by ripples on the surface of the oil), add the leeks, onions, and garlic. Sauté for 4 minutes.

2. Add the carrots, celery, kohlrabies, turnips, parsnips, fennel, and red pepper and sauté for another 5 minutes.

3. Place this mixture of vegetables into a large stockpot, and add enough water to cover the vegetables by 1 inch. Bring to a boil over medium-high heat, reduce heat to simmering, and cook uncovered for 1 hour.

4. Add the bay leaves, thyme, parsley, peppercorns, and salt and cook for an additional ½ hour. Taste for seasonings and adjust accordingly.

5. Strain the broth through a sieve that is lined with a double thickness of cheesecloth. Discard the solids.

6. If not using the broth right away, place in the refrigerator after it has cooled.

Yield: about 3 quarts

NOTES

Store broth in the refrigerator in covered containers for up to 4 days, or freeze it for up to 4 months. It is a good idea to freeze broth in 1-cup containers.

BASIC ITALIAN BREAD
STEPPING-STONE TECHNIQUE

I am a tough taskmaster and I'm asking you to start out making bread using 5 pounds of flour. "Five pounds?" you say, with a little quiver. Put your trust in me. With a bit of patience, perseverance, and a positive attitude, you will be able to do it. Making 5 pounds of bread is just as easy as, if not easier than, making 1 pound. One pound is not enough to get a feel for what the process is all about. Another advantage is that flour comes in 5-pound packages, so you won't have to measure the flour, which can be time consuming. Bread freezes very well and is a delight to share with family, friends, and neighbors; they are always so appreciative.

The common belief among most people is that bread-making is too difficult. I will prove to you that this is not so. Making bread is very inexpensive, as it requires only a few ingredients, but it does require a commitment of time and energy and an understanding of how the bread-making process works. In the introduction to the "Breads, Pizza, and Focaccia" chapter, (page 163), I describe the chemistry of bread-making. Please be sure to read it. Once you understand how the process works, you will go on to make a good loaf of bread. Those loaves will get better and better in texture, taste, and appearance as you become more skilled. For inspiration, take a look at the photos showing you the many possibilities.

Basic Italian Bread

Pane Semplice

Preparation Time: 30 minutes • Rising Time: first, 2 hours; second, 1 hour
Baking Time: 30 minutes per baking sheet

Whenever I bake a batch of bread that uses 5 pounds of flour, the first loaf to come out of the oven has to be baptized. This is a tradition in my family. As the loaf comes out of the oven, it is allowed to rest for 2 minutes and then is sliced in half horizontally to expose the inside. With the steam escaping, it is dressed with sprinklings of coarse salt, several grinds from the pepper mill, and then anointed with a generous drizzle of extra-virgin olive oil. If we have extra grated Romano cheese, we sprinkle that on too. The two pieces of bread are then put back together to form a loaf and we wait another minute before slicing (or tearing) it into individual serving-size pieces, giving the bread time to absorb the ingredients into the crumb. Memories of my dad holding and slicing the bread, close to his body, pulling the knife close to his chest and then stopping just at the right time, are precious to me. With every bread-making class I teach we do this with the very first loaf and I tell the story of my dad. That helps keep his memory alive in my heart as this tradition is shared and passed on to others.

Proofing Mixture:
1 cup warm water (105°–115°F;
    see Notes)
2 tablespoons active dry yeast
1 teaspoon sugar

For the Dough:
5 pounds unbleached all-purpose
    flour
2 tablespoons salt

5½ cups warm water
¼ cup extra-virgin olive oil

**For the Work Surface and
Baking Sheets:**
Extra flour for kneading
    (if necessary)
½ cup yellow or white cornmeal
1 tablespoon extra-virgin olive oil

PROCEDURE

1. To proof the yeast, pour the warm water into a small bowl. Sprinkle the yeast and sugar over the surface, and stir with a fork for about 30 seconds.

Let stand for 5 minutes, until the mixture is frothy. (Note: If yeast does not froth, it is no longer active and should be discarded. Check the expiration date on the yeast packets or buy bulk yeast from a reputable source such as a natural foods store or bakery supply house.)

2. While the yeast is proofing, place the flour and salt in a large bowl, mixing the flour and salt together. Make a deep well in the center of the flour by pushing flour up the sides of the bowl. Pour the proofed yeast mixture, along with the water and ¼ cup olive oil, into the well in the flour.

3. Holding the edge of the large bowl with one hand, use the other hand to mix the liquid with the flour. Starting from the center, slowly work your way around the bowl, incorporating a little of the flour at a time. Keep going around until all the flour and liquid is combined to form a soft dough. Rub the extra dough clinging to your hand into the mixture. If the dough is too sticky, add a little more flour, a tablespoon at a time, until the stickiness is gone. If there is flour left in the bowl, add a little more water to the flour, a tablespoon at a time, until all the ingredients are combined into a nonsticky mound of dough.

4. For kneading, you will work with half the dough at a time. Divide the dough in half. Turn the dough out onto a lightly floured surface. Lightly oil your hands to prevent the dough from sticking.

5. To knead, fold the dough toward you with your fingers; then push down and away from you with the heels of your hands. You are pressing and pushing the dough, rotating it a quarter turn each time. Use the weight of your whole body to put pressure on the mass of dough. Allow yourself to enjoy the rhythmic motion of your body and hands and how it affects the dough. Continue to knead for about 10 or 15 minutes, alternating between the two halves of dough. The dough will become smooth, elastic, and satiny, feeling sensuous when it has been properly worked.

6. Place 1 tablespoon extra-virgin olive oil in the palm of your hand and rub the oil over the entire surface of the dough. Place the dough in a large, unscented plastic bag. Push all the air out of the bag and close it at the top with a twist tie, leaving room for the dough to rise and double in bulk inside the bag. Place in a draft-free, warm place (about 80°F). It takes bread longer to rise in a cold environment. A good spot is inside the oven with the light on; the oven light provides just enough heat to make a cozy, warm atmosphere for the dough.

7. In about 1½ to 2 hours, the dough should be ready. To check on its progress, press two fingertips about ½ inch into the dough. If the indentations remain when your fingertips are removed, the dough is ready. Remove it from the plastic bag, punch it down, and knead briefly to distribute the air bubbles, about 30 seconds.

8. For the second rising, place the unbaked loaves on 2 to 3 baking sheets. This accomplishes two very important things: The crusts will be unsurpassed in texture and you will be able to bake more loaves at the same time. Sprinkle the cornmeal on the 17 × 11–inch baking sheets. Divide the dough into six equal parts and shape into loaves. There are many shapes you can make, but the simplest are long thin baguettes and flat round loaves. Use these while you are mastering the bread-making process. Take a look at the photos for other ideas. Place the loaves on the baking sheets in a warm place, allowing enough room for them to double in size. This second rising will take about 1 hour.

9. While the loaves are rising, prepare the oven by arranging one oven rack on the bottom shelf and the other on the second from the top shelf. Preheat the oven to 400°F.

10. Place one baking sheet on the bottom rack and bake for 15 minutes, then transfer it to the upper rack. Place another baking sheet on the bottom rack; this is a staggering technique—you now have two sheets baking at the same time, making good use of oven space and heat. When the first sheet is done, move the second sheet up to the top rack to finish baking. The loaves take a total of 30 minutes to bake. You will know the bread is done if the loaves make a hollow sound when you tap on them; you can also tell by their golden brown color. Resist peeking into the oven during the first 10 minutes of baking; sudden drafts may deflate the loaves.

11. When done, remove the bread from the baking sheets *immediately* and place on wire racks or kitchen towels to cool. This allows the moisture from the bottom of the loaves to evaporate, keeping the crust crispy.

Yield: 6 loaves, 1¼ pounds each

NOTES

Use an instant-read thermometer to help you determine the temperature of the proofing water. As you get more experienced you will be able to tell by touch. If you are going to use the bread the same day or the following day, store the baked loaves at room temperature in a brown paper bag. This will help retain a good crust. The bread will keep fresh this way for up to 2 days.

This bread freezes very well and will keep in the freezer for up to 3 months. Wrap the individual loaves in heavy-duty aluminum foil and place in reclosable plastic freezer bags. To reheat frozen bread, allow it to defrost at room temperature. Remove bread from the plastic bags and place in a preheated 350°F oven, directly on the oven rack, for 7 to 10 minutes.

Salads and Salad Dressings
Stepping-Stone Technique

The best salads are a study in art composition, balancing textures, flavors, and colors—crunchy to soft, tangy to sweet, bright colors to more subdued neutrals. The result is a feast for the senses!

Always dress salad greens just before serving so they won't become soggy. Use only enough salad dressing to coat the greens lightly, usually 1 tablespoon of dressing per person. Too much salad dressing will weigh down the ingredients and mask their flavors. Stir the salad dressing well, drizzle it over your salad, and with clean hands or salad utensils, toss salad well, making sure the leaves have been lightly coated, producing a nice sheen.

Think about different ingredients that will add interesting flavors, colors, and textures, and present your salads in bowls or plates that will complement them.

Preparing Salad Greens

Some of the choices to consider when building your salad are green- and red-leaf lettuce, Romaine, Boston head, Bibb, spinach, arugula, radicchio, dandelion greens, escarole, and mesclun (a wonderful mixture of baby salad greens). When buying lettuce or other greens, look for those that have a good color, feel crisp, are free of blemishes, and smell fresh.

Your greens will last longer if you wash them right when you get home. To wash salad greens effectively, fill a clean sink or a very large bowl with cold water and add salad greens, removing tough stalks and wilted leaves. Allow the greens to sit in the water for several minutes. Agitate and toss the greens with your hands gently. Lift the greens up and place them in a colander. Drain the water. If you notice any sand or residue in the bottom, repeat the process until the water is clean. The mistake many people make is putting the leaves and vegetables into a large container and then pouring the water along with the greens into a strainer or colander. When the water runs over the greens, so does any dirt and soil, making the greens gritty again.

All greens should be thoroughly dry before using or storing. If you have a salad spinner, spin the salad dry. (If you have a lot of greens, dry them in batches.) If not, use a clean dish towel. Layer the leaves on top of the towel, roll the towel up in jelly-roll fashion, and gently tap it on the table. After you dry the greens, and if you are not going to use them within the next half hour, place them in the refrigerator in a reclosable plastic bag with tiny holes that has been designed for storing salad greens so they stay fresh and crisp.

Building the Salad

Building your salad can be as simple as using one or two salad greens to a more complex version with a multitude of ingredients. Some choices for your consideration are:

Cheeses—Gorgonzola, goat cheese, Parmigiano-Reggiano, and Romano: grated, slivered, or crumbled

Nuts—Pine nuts, walnuts, pecans, almonds, and hazelnuts; toast them briefly in a skillet for added flavor

Fresh fruit—Tomatoes, apples, pears, oranges, and seedless grapes

Dried fruit—Golden raisins, cherries, and cranberries

Olives—Green, black, and oil-cured

Beans—Cannellini, kidney, black beans, and chickpeas

Try combining two or more of the above ingredients with your salad greens. Remember, simplicity is often the key to a great salad.

About Salad Dressings

Throughout most of Italy dressing for salad greens is very simple. The ingredients to choose from are a fine wine vinegar, lemon juice, or balsamic vinegar, extra-virgin olive oil, coarse salt, and freshly ground black pepper, using a ratio of 2-to-1, 3-to-1, or 4-to-1 oil-to-vinegar depending on your personal taste. Many an Italian household and restaurant simply has cruets of oil and vinegar on the table for people to dress their own salads according to their personal tastes. When serving large numbers of people, it is much easier to have the salad already tossed and plated before bringing it to the table.

Being organized and having a variety of salad dressings prepared in advance in the refrigerator will make your life easier. It takes only 5 minutes to make most dressings, and you can use the same bowls and mixers to make cleanup easier. Salad, soup, and homemade bread make a wonderful supper. When you're tired or you've come home from work late and just don't have the energy for another thing, there you are with soup and bread from the freezer and the salad dressing made. Wash the salad greens, heat up the soup, set the table, and you are ready to eat in 10 minutes. You can't beat that!

I offer these simple salad dressing recipes for variety and convenience. If you feel adventuresome, adapt some of these to make your own or buy a couple of cruets to place on your table.

Easy Salad Dressing

Condimento Facile per Insalata

Preparation Time: 10 minutes

¼ cup wine vinegar
1 teaspoon salt
¼ teaspoon sugar
½ teaspoon freshly ground black
    pepper
2 tablespoons freshly grated Romano
    cheese

2 cloves garlic, finely minced
    (about 1 teaspoon)
1 teaspoon finely chopped Italian
    flat-leaf parsley
¾ cup extra-virgin olive oil

PROCEDURE

Place all the ingredients except the oil in a glass jar. Cover and shake vigorously to dissolve the salt and sugar. Add all the oil to the jar, cover, and shake vigorously again.

Yield: 1 cup

NOTE

To store this salad dressing, label the jar with the date. Often when olive oil is stored in the refrigerator, it congeals. Take the dressing out of the refrigerator 5 to 10 minutes before you are ready to toss the salad and allow the oil to come back to room temperature. Shake and pour the appropriate amount on the salad. Refrigerate any unused portion—it will keep for more than 2 weeks this way.

Pesto Salad Dressing

Condimento al Pesto

Preparation Time: 5 minutes

2 tablespoons Pesto from your freezer—1 ice-cube-size chunk (page 25) or use commercial pesto if homemade is not available
2 cloves garlic, peeled
2 tablespoons freshly squeezed lemon juice

2 tablespoons balsamic vinegar
2 tablespoons freshly grated Romano cheese
¼ cup water
1 teaspoon salt
½ teaspoon freshly ground black pepper
1 cup extra-virgin olive oil

PROCEDURE

Place all the ingredients except the olive oil into a blender or food processor and process for 1 minute. With the motor on, add the oil slowly in a steady stream until emulsified.

Yield: 1¾ cups

NOTE

Pour dressing into a jar and label with the date. Often when olive oil is stored in the refrigerator, it congeals. Take the dressing out of the refrigerator 5 to 10 minutes before you are ready to toss the salad to allow the oil to come back to its original state. Shake, and pour the appropriate amount on the salad. Refrigerate any unused portion. When properly stored, it will keep for more than 2 weeks.

Mama Rosa's Lemon Custard Cream
Stepping-Stone Technique

This recipe is the ultimate comfort food for me and holds many a tender memory of my growing-up years. My mother would make this often for us. Learning to make creams will give you a quick dessert to have in your repertoire that is extremely pleasing in taste, velvety smooth in texture, simple and inexpensive to make, and nutritious.

Cornstarch and egg yolks are the thickening agents used in making this cream. When adding cornstarch, always add it to cold liquid and stir immediately. (You don't want it to settle to the bottom of the bowl, where it hardens very quickly.) Add the egg or other ingredients after the cornstarch has dissolved. If you happen to let it settle for a while, it will harden; get a fork, break up the clumps, and stir to reconstitute.

Mama Rosa's Lemon Custard Cream stands on its own without any extra adornment. It is soothing, not too sweet, with a delightful subtle flavor. Omitting the lemon peel and adding other ingredients such as chocolate, vanilla or almond extract, or various liqueurs into the base cream transforms the flavor, creating other recipes.

Serve it as a quick and light dessert to end any meal, or use it to fill cream puffs, crêpes, cookies, cakes, pies, and cannoli. Add it to whipping cream or homemade ricotta in various proportions to create a richer, lighter, fancier dessert. Garnish it with citrus zest, toasted nuts, or chocolate curls. The possibilities are endless. Take a look at the photo of the cream; you will want to make it right now. I suggest you get to know the base recipe by heart and use it often.

Mama Rosa's
Lemon Custard Cream

....

Crema di Limone alla Mamma Rosa

Preparation Time: 5 minutes • Cooking Time: 10 minutes

4 cups milk (whole or 2%), divided
¾ cup sugar
Peel of 1 medium lemon

½ cup cornstarch
5 large egg yolks, lightly beaten

PROCEDURE

1. Combine 3 cups of the milk, the sugar, and the lemon peel in a heavy, medium-size saucepot. Place over medium heat and stir to dissolve the sugar.

2. In a separate bowl, place the remaining 1 cup milk. Add the cornstarch and stir vigorously with a fork until the cornstarch is dissolved. (This prevents lumps.) Add the beaten egg yolks, stir, and add to the warm milk mixture in the saucepot in a steady stream.

3. Continue to cook the custard over medium-high heat, stirring continuously with a wooden spoon. Be alert; the sauce will start to thicken as the milk heats. Continue to stir, starting from the center of the pot, going to the outside and coming back to the center. Stirring in one direction will help the custard to cook more quickly. Make sure you stir the whole bottom surface of the pot to prevent scorching.

4. The top surface of the custard will start to get steamy, and then you will notice, just before the boiling point, it will start to get lumpy. *Don't panic.* Stir very quickly until the mixture comes to a boil; then turn off the heat, keeping the pot on the burner. Stir briskly for 1 minute longer. This will make the cream velvety. Remove the cream from the burner.

5. Discard the lemon peel. Pour the custard into small individual bowls or goblets or into one large bowl. It can be eaten right away, hot or warm, or placed into the refrigerator to cool and eaten cold. If you don't eat it immediately, place a sheet of plastic wrap directly on the surface of the custard to prevent a skin from forming, making sure the entire surface is covered.

Yield: 4½ cups (serves 6 to 8 as a cream;
or fills 24 small to medium cream puffs or 1 layered cake)

NOTES

If using as a filling for a dessert, place it in the refrigerator to cool for about 3 hours. It will keep fresh for 3 to 4 days in the refrigerator. If stored for several days, before using, beat it with an electric mixer or in the food processor for 30 to 60 seconds on low. This will bring back its creaminess. Freezing is not recommended.

Use This Recipe to Make:
- Sicilian Creams, page 268
- Cream Puffs, page 272
- Cannoli, page 274
- Graziella's Decadent Cake, page 284

ANTIPASTI

The antipasto course is served before the pasta or main course and consists of a harmonious combination of ingredients that are big in taste but small in portions. Antipasti are meant to tease the appetite, not satisfy it. They are light and flavorful and, more often than not, simple to prepare. Many can be prepared one or two days in advance, and served either at room temperature or warm or hot.

In the everyday meals of most Italians, antipasti do not play a significant role. They are usually served when we entertain, celebrate special family events or holidays, or dine out. Antipasti are among the most creative dishes I prepare in the kitchen, the assortment being mouthwatering nuggets of flavors and eye-catching textures and colors.

A bit of planning and my simple step-by-step instructions with each recipe will help you remain calm, cool, and collected. Do as much in advance as possible so you can have fun in the preparation and enjoy time with your guests. Remember, no guest feels comfortable when the host or hostess is in the kitchen most of the evening preparing the food.

Antipasti are versatile. They can be eaten as a light lunch or in conjunction with soups or salad or as a hearty dinner. They can serve as a snack or as the vegetable course, sometimes as the salad course, and always as the appetizer that precedes courses. You can choose to serve only one in a larger quantity or serve many in individual plates or platters. Do what feels comfortable for you, keeping in mind what the rest of the meal will comprise.

For me it is exciting and fun anticipating the presentation of the antipasto, whether it is on individual plates or large platters. It is like a painting with your fingers, moving colors and textures around to make a pleasing image. The visual elements are very important; the appetite is first stimulated by the image, then by the aroma, and finally by the flavors.

When anticipating your antipasto presentation, consider using some of the following: cheeses; fresh-cut vegetables; olives; anchovies; capers; roasted peppers; beans and chickpeas (rinsed, drained, and marinated); fried polenta, bread, focaccia, crostini, or bruschetta; and a drizzle of your best olive oil or vinegar or both. But most of all, have fun in the preparation, the presentation, and the eating!

Roasted Red, Green, and Yellow Peppers with Anchovies

Peperoni Arrostiti con Acciughe

Preparation Time: 30 minutes

Cooking Time: 15 minutes (to roast the peppers)

I would say that about 80 percent of the family and friends for whom I prepare this recipe comment on its unique and delicious flavor, but cannot place it. They just know they love it. If you are convinced you don't like and couldn't possibly eat anchovies, you must try this dish. The anchovy blends into the marinade, enhancing the wonderful flavor of the roasted peppers. This is one of my favorite recipes to teach my cooking students—especially those who don't eat anchovies. I have caught many of them using bread or their fingers to sop up the very last drops of the marinade from their plates. A wonderful crusty bread is a must to accompany this treat.

3 large green bell peppers
3 large red or yellow bell peppers

For the Marinade:
1 tablespoon Pesto from your freezer
   (page 25)
1 (2-ounce) can flat anchovies in
   olive oil

¼ teaspoon dried oregano
1 clove garlic, chopped
   (about ½ teaspoon)
¼ cup extra-virgin olive oil
¼ teaspoon salt
¼ teaspoon freshly ground black
   pepper
2 tablespoons balsamic vinegar

PROCEDURE

1. Roast the peppers according to the instructions on page 14 and cut them into strips about ½ inch wide.

2. Place the marinade ingredients, including the olive oil from the anchovies, in a food processor or blender. Process for about 1 minute, or until the anchovies and garlic are pureed.

3. Place the pepper strips and the marinade in a medium-size bowl and toss gently with your fingers or a fork so that each piece of pepper is completely coated.

Antipasti

4. Make bundles of marinated pepper strips: Take three strips of one color, wrap them with one strip of another color, and place the bundle on a serving tray. Continue making bundles, alternating colors, and arrange the bundles in a decorative pattern. When all the peppers are bundled, drizzle the remaining marinade over the top. Serve at room temperature.

Yield: 8 or more servings as an
appetizer or part of an antipasto tray

NOTES

Feel free to substitute all red bell peppers when they are in season and reasonably priced.

To help you get organized, the peppers can be roasted several days in advance and refrigerated until ready to be marinated and assembled. Make the marinade and marinate the peppers the day you are going to serve them. The dish can be assembled several hours in advance and stored in the refrigerator. Remove from the refrigerator 30 minutes before serving to bring to room temperature.

Place leftovers in the refrigerator; they will keep for up to 5 days. Remember, the flavor of the anchovies will become stronger over time. Any extra marinade can be used over salad greens. I do not recommend freezing.

Eggplant Appetizer

Caponata

Preparation Time: 30 minutes, plus ½ to 1 hour for debittering if necessary
Cooking Time: 20 minutes

This story was told to me by my mother, and I tell it in my cooking classes. I really think it is a tale that gets better with the telling. The way to judge eggplant "gender" is to look at the blossom end of the eggplant. If the end is round and smooth, it is a male, and if the end is indented and concave, it is a female. The male eggplant is said to have fewer seeds than the female eggplant, and since too many seeds tend to make the eggplant bitter, you want to choose an eggplant with the least amount of seeds, a male. Of course, females reproduce so they have many more seeds. What happens to all those poor female eggplants that are left on the grocery store shelves? Someone is buying them . . . is it you? I always go through all the eggplants and choose only the ones with the smoothest bottoms, feeling somewhat guilty, I must admit.

This is one of my favorite antipasto dishes. It incorporates readily available and inexpensive produce. It is hearty, nutritious, and—of course—very flavorful.

2 pounds eggplant, ends removed, peeled, diced into ¾-inch cubes, sprinkled with 2 teaspoons salt and placed in a colander for ½ to 1 hour to remove bitterness (see page 10)
½ cup extra-virgin olive oil, divided (more if necessary)
2 medium cooking onions, chopped
2 cloves garlic, chopped (about 1 teaspoon)
3 ribs celery, cut into ½-inch slices
6 canned Italian plum tomatoes, seeded (see page 3) and chopped

1 tablespoon tomato paste
10 ripe Kalamata or Gaeta olives, pitted and coarsely chopped
2 tablespoons capers, drained
6 fresh basil leaves, chopped
½ teaspoon salt
⅛ teaspoon freshly ground black pepper
3 tablespoons wine vinegar
2 teaspoons sugar
2 tablespoons toasted pine nuts (see page 24), optional

PROCEDURE

1. Rinse the salted eggplants and pat them dry with paper towels.

2. Heat a large skillet over medium-high heat until warm. Add 3 to 4 tablespoons of the olive oil and heat until the oil is hot. (Ripples will start to form on the bottom of the pan.) Add the eggplant cubes and sauté for 5 to 7 minutes, until the eggplant is soft and starts to turn golden. If the eggplant absorbs all the oil and starts to burn, add a little more oil. Remove the eggplant with a slotted spoon, place it in a large bowl, and set it aside.

3. In the same skillet (do not wash it), heat 2 tablespoons of the remaining oil. When it is hot, add the onion and sauté for 4 to 5 minutes. Add the garlic, stir, and continue to cook for 2 minutes. Using a slotted spoon, remove the onion and garlic and place them in the same bowl with the eggplant. Do not wash the skillet yet.

4. Place the same skillet over medium-high heat. When the skillet is warm, add 2 tablespoons of the remaining oil. When the oil is hot, add the celery and cook for 4 minutes, stirring occasionally.

5. Add the tomatoes, tomato paste, olives, capers, basil, salt, and pepper. Cook for another 4 minutes. Add the cooked eggplant, onion, and garlic to the skillet along with vinegar and sugar. Turn the heat up to high and cook for another 2 to 4 minutes, until the vinegar has been absorbed. Taste for seasonings and adjust accordingly. Add the toasted pine nuts if you are including them. Serve warm or at room temperature.

Yield: 10 servings as part of an antipasto platter

NOTES

Store leftovers in the refrigerator in a covered container; they will keep for up to 1 week. Caponata freezes well and will keep in the freezer for up to 2 months.

This dish can be given as a gift to friends for special occasions and holidays. Although the recipe is in the antipasto chapter, feel free to serve it for lunch or a light dinner with a couple of slices of crusty bread.

Stuffed Mushrooms

Funghi Ripieni

Preparation Time: 30 minutes • Baking Time: 25 minutes

1½ pounds white button
   mushrooms, wiped clean with a
   damp paper towel, caps intact,
   stems removed and diced

For the Stuffing:
1 pound fresh spinach or Swiss
   chard, washed and drained
4 tablespoons extra-virgin olive oil,
   divided
½ cup finely diced celery
½ pound ground pork or beef
   (optional—see Notes)

2 cloves garlic, chopped fine
   (about 1 teaspoon)
1 cup cracker crumbs (preferably
   Ritz or Townhouse)
1 large egg, lightly beaten
4 tablespoons minced Italian flat-leaf
   parsley
½ cup shredded fontina cheese
1 tablespoon butter
½ cup sherry or dry white wine
Freshly grated Romano cheese, for
   sprinkling

PROCEDURE

1. Preheat the oven to 350°F.

2. Cook the spinach or Swiss chard in the microwave to directions on page 00. Chop it fine.

3. Place a large skillet over medium-high heat. When the skillet is warm, add 2 tablespoons of the olive oil. When the oil is hot, sauté the celery for 2 minutes. Add the ground meat if using, and sauté until just cooked. Add the diced mushroom stems and garlic and sauté for 2 additional minutes. Place these ingredients in a medium bowl and set aside.

4. Add the cracker crumbs, egg, parsley, spinach, and fontina cheese and toss lightly. Set it aside.

5. Butter a medium baking dish. Sprinkle the mushroom caps with 2 table-spoons olive oil, place them in the baking dish, and bake in 350°F oven for 8 minutes. Drain off any liquid, remove the mushrooms from the baking dish, and stuff by placing the stuffing in a mound into each cap.

6. Pour the sherry into the bottom of the baking dish. Place the stuffed mushrooms back in the baking dish and bake for another 15 minutes. Sprinkle

with Romano cheese, place under the broiler, and broil for 1 to 2 minutes, or until the tops are golden.

7. Transfer mushrooms to a serving platter and serve hot, warm, or at room temperature.

Yield: 20 to 25 mushrooms (depending on size of mushrooms used)—6 to 8 servings

NOTES

If you are a vegetarian or just prefer not to add the ground meat, add a bit more spinach or Swiss chard to the stuffing.

If you are not going to eat the mushrooms right away, save the broiling step until just before you plan to serve them. They taste best when eaten the same day or the following day. The mushrooms oxidize, darkening in color as the days go by. Store any leftovers in the refrigerator in a covered container. I do not recommend freezing them.

Sweet-and-Sour Olives

Olive Fritti in Agrodolce

Preparation Time: 5 minutes • Cooking Time: 10 minutes

Get that fresh bread ready and make enough of this olive antipasto treat to go around. Everyone loves it. Be forewarned: it is absolutely impossible to eat it without bread. A truly unique dish—and definitely a crowd pleaser—it is nice to have extra for snacks or quick lunches.

¼ cup extra-virgin olive oil
2 large sweet onions, chopped
4 cloves garlic, chopped
    (about 2 teaspoons)
1 pound Kalamata or Gaeta olives,
    pitted

¼ cup wine vinegar
3 tablespoons sugar
½ teaspoon freshly ground black
    pepper
4 fresh basil leaves, torn

PROCEDURE

1. Place a large skillet over medium-high heat. When the skillet is warm, add the oil. When the oil is hot (indicated by ripples on the surface of the oil), add the onions. Cook 3 to 4 minutes, until the onions are tender and just start to turn golden.

2. Add the garlic and cook for 2 minutes more. Add the olives, stir, and cook for 1 more minute. You will notice the olives start to puff up.

3. Turn the heat on high, add the vinegar, sugar, and pepper. Stir and cook until most of the vinegar has been absorbed, about 4 minutes. Add the basil and toss. Serve warm or at room temperature.

Yield: 8 to 10 servings

NOTES

These olives can be prepared several days in advance. Place any leftovers in the refrigerator in a covered container; they will keep for several weeks. Remove from the refrigerator 15 minutes before serving to allow the oil to return to its natural state. The olives taste best at room temperature.

Antipasti

Marinated Olives

....

Olive Marinata

Preparation Time: 5 minutes • Cooking Time: 1 minute

My 93-year-old mother provides me with an abundance of wonderful memories. She visits my sister Pina and her husband, Tony, in California often, sometimes staying for only a week and other times staying for several months. Her last visit had my sister calling me on the phone in stitches. Mom apparently told my sister that she was going to sit in the garden. When Pina went to check on her, Mom was nowhere in sight. Pina started to become worried and she went out looking for her. She found Mom several streets away with a long stick in one hand and a plastic grocery bag in the other. Mom was harvesting olives from someone's olive tree, using the stick to tap the olives down. She already had the bag half full and was so surprised to see my sister. Of course, she then engaged Pina in gathering and filling the rest of the bag, which they carried together. Mom said she rang the bell and got permission, but my sister was not absolutely convinced. There didn't seem to be anyone around.

My mother cures olives in the hot sun and uses them in a variety of recipes, but best of all, she brings them to me when she comes to Pennsylvania for a visit. She packs one whole suitcase of olives, nuts, figs, dates, frozen cardoons, and wild fennel that she wraps in newspapers very carefully so that they will still be frozen when we pick her up at the airport. These are the memories that enrich my life and spice up my cooking.

1 pound sun-dried oil-cured olives
½ cup extra-virgin olive oil
4 cloves garlic, finely minced
   (about 2 teaspoons)
½ teaspoon freshly ground black
   pepper

½ teaspoon red pepper flakes
   (more or less to taste)
1 teaspoon dried oregano, crushed

PROCEDURE

1. Wash a quart jar in very hot, sudsy water and rinse well.
2. Fill a 2-quart saucepan about two-thirds full of cold water. Bring to a

boil over high heat. Add the olives and boil for 1 minute. Drain the olives immediately and place them in the quart jar.

3. Add the rest of the ingredients to the jar. Cover and shake well to distribute the ingredients throughout. Place in the refrigerator until ready to use. Remove from the refrigerator 15 minutes before you are ready to serve, and bring to room temperature. Toss to distribute ingredients, and plate.

Yield: 1 pound

Antipasti

Mussels in Spicy Marinara

Cozze Fra Diavolo

*Preparation Time: 30 minutes, plus 1 extra hour for soaking if desired,
and 30 minutes to prepare a small portion of Marinara if you have none available*

Cooking Time: 20 minutes

I especially enjoy serving this delectable dish for the holidays—either Christmas Eve or New Year's Eve. It makes a wonderful presentation with the pinkish color of the mussels, the striking black shells, and the lovely red color of the marinara sauce.

Mussels must always be bought alive and absolutely fresh. Make sure you have plenty of crusty bread available to sop up all the wonderful sauce.

2 pounds mussels

1 gallon cold water

2 tablespoons salt

⅓ cup oatmeal, flour, or semolina

3 tablespoons extra-virgin olive oil

4 medium yellow cooking onions,
    peeled, cut in half lengthwise,
    and sliced

4 cloves garlic, chopped
    (about 2 teaspoons)

2 cups Marinara Sauce (page 5)

2 cups dry white wine

½ teaspoon freshly ground black
    pepper

½ teaspoon red pepper flakes
    (or more, depending upon
    your taste)

2 tablespoons chopped Italian flat-
    leaf parsley

PROCEDURE

1. Soak the mussels in a large bowl of cold water to which you have added 2 tablespoons salt. Throw away any mussels with broken shells and any that don't close when tapped. Add ⅓ cup oatmeal, flour, or semolina to the soaking water and let them soak for 1 hour. The live mussels will feed on the oatmeal and excrete any dirt and sand. Scrub the shells with a stiff brush. Using a knife, scrape away any loose seaweed-like strands (beards) which protrude from the shells. Rinse the mussels in several changes of cold water until the water runs clear.

2. Place a large skillet over medium-high heat. When the skillet is warm,

add the oil. When the oil is hot, add the onions. Stir and sauté for 4 to 5 minutes, until the onions are tender; then add the garlic. Stir and sauté for 2 to 3 additional minutes. Add the marinara, white wine, black pepper, and red pepper flakes. Stir and cook 4 to 6 minutes, until the wine has been reduced by about half. Taste for seasoning and adjust accordingly.

3. Drain the mussels well, add to the marinara mixture, and toss gently. Place a cover over the skillet. (If you don't have a cover big enough, improvise with aluminum foil.) After 3 minutes, remove the cover, add the parsley, and toss again. Cook for 1 to 2 minutes longer, until all the shells are open. (Discard any that don't open.)

4. Place the piping-hot mussels along with sauce in large individual bowls. Eat while hot, and don't forget to use that crusty bread to soak up all those wonderful juices. I don't know which I like better—the mussels or dunking the bread in the juice!

Yield: 8 servings

NOTES

You may choose to serve this as a main course accompanied by a salad. As a main course it will serve 4.

Any leftover mussels should be taken off the shells and put along with the sauce in a covered container and placed in the refrigerator. They should be eaten the next day. If you have a lot of sauce left, you can boil some long pasta and pour the heated sauce and mussels over it. I do not recommend freezing leftovers.

Magnificent Stuffed Artichokes

Carciofi Imbottiti con Formaggio

Preparation Time: 45 minutes

Cooking Time: 45 minutes to 1 hour (depending on the size of the artichokes)

This recipe is one of my children's all-time favorites: a meal in itself—delicious, magnificent in presentation, and featuring many wonderful combinations of subtle tastes. It is both a crowd pleaser and a conversation piece. Please don't be intimidated by the multiple steps—the scrumptious taste is definitely worth the extra effort. Make a few extra so you will have leftovers.

8 medium artichokes
1 lemon, cut in half
Salt and freshly ground black
    pepper
2½ cups water (more if necessary)
1 teaspoon salt
Combination of any of the following
    herbs to flavor the water: Italian
    flat-leaf parsley, thyme, bay leaf,
    mint
Kitchen string

For the Stuffing:
2½ cups dried bread crumbs
1¼ cups freshly grated Romano
    cheese
1 medium or large onion, chopped

Stems from the artichokes, peeled
    and chopped (make sure you
    strip off the hard fibrous outer
    layer)
4 cloves garlic (about 2 teaspoons
    chopped)
4 tablespoons chopped Italian flat-
    leaf parsley
2 tablespoons chopped fresh mint
    (a very important ingredient;
    do not omit or substitute)
½ teaspoon salt
½ teaspoon freshly ground black
    pepper

For Basting:
1 cup extra-virgin olive oil

PROCEDURE

1. Prepare the artichokes using stainless-steel knives and scissors; carbon blades will darken and discolor the flesh. Also, use nonreactive saucepans to cook them in (either one large saucepan or two medium saucepans).

2. To prepare the artichokes for cooking, slice off the stems to form a flat base. Retain the stems for use in the stuffing. Snap off the tough outer leaves

closest to the stems. With a knife, cut off ½ to ¾ inch of the top of the artichoke and discard. Use scissors to snip off the prickly tips of each of the remaining leaves. Rinse under cold running water and drain. Rub all cut edges with the lemon halves to help retard discoloration. Sprinkle artichokes with salt and pepper.

3. In a large pot, place the water, salt and herbs. Add the artichokes, stem-end down. Bring to a boil over high heat, reduce the heat to medium-low; then cover and boil for 7 minutes. Remove the artichokes with tongs. Place on a working surface and allow to cool briefly so you can handle them. You will be using the pan and the cooking liquid again, so set it aside.

4. While the artichokes are cooling, in a large bowl, mix the stuffing ingredients and set it aside.

5. When the artichokes are cool enough to handle, place the artichokes on the work surface stem down, and open each artichoke by spreading the leaves in the center. Scoop and scrape out the prickly inner leaves, including the fuzzy portion called the "choke," using a melon baller or teaspoon. Leave the artichoke bottom intact.

6. Portion out eight equal amounts of stuffing and proceed to stuff each artichoke. Beginning at the outer leaves, start stuffing each leaf, working toward the center, remembering that the center gets stuffed also. Tie each artichoke with string and place it back into the pot with the seasoned water. If they don't all fit in one pot, cook them in two, making sure you have at least 1 inch of the seasoned water solution on the bottom of each pot.

7. Place the pot on the burner over high heat and cover. When it comes to a boil, turn the heat to medium-low. After 10 minutes of cooking time, uncover and drizzle 1 tablespoon olive oil on top of each artichoke. Cover and continue to cook, making sure there is at least 1 inch of water on the bottom of the pan. Add more water if necessary. After another 10 minutes have gone by, add 1 additional tablespoon of oil on top of each artichoke. Continue to cook and test for doneness. The artichoke is done when the leaves pull off easily and the base can be easily pierced with the tip of a knife, about 35 minutes. If you have any oil left, drizzle it over the tops. Remove the artichokes with tongs, place on individual plates or a large serving platter, and remove the strings. Allow to cool for a few minutes before serving. They can be served hot, warm, or at room temperature.

Yield: 8 stuffed artichokes (8 servings)

NOTES

Eating artichokes for the first time need not be intimidating. Go with the flow and have fun with it. First you need to remember that the edible portion of the artichoke is at the base of each leaf, and the closer you get to the center, the more edible leaf there is. Sometimes as you get to the center you can eat the whole leaf. Begin by pulling the leaves off the lower portion one at a time with your fingers, making sure not to lose any of the stuffing. Place the leaf in your mouth and scrape the edible portion and the stuffing off with your teeth. Discard the rest of the leaf. It is nice to have a discard plate. Pull off another and start again. The artichoke bottom is reputed to be the most succulent part. Enjoy!

If baby artichokes are available, the cooking time is much less. Reduce the stuffing by half or double the number of artichokes. I prefer buying these smaller artichokes because they are more tender, take less time to cook, and don't require removing the choke.

This dish can be prepared in advance (for example, in the morning on the day you are going to serve it) and refrigerated. To serve, heat in the microwave or oven to just warm.

Any leftovers taste even better the next few days. Store any leftovers in a covered container in the refrigerator; they will keep up to 5 days. I do not recommend freezing.

Rice Balls

Arancini di Sarena

Preparation Time: 25 minutes (not including preparation time for the Marinara Sauce)
Cooking Time: 20 minutes for the risotto; 15 minutes for frying

These rice balls are popular throughout Italy, served as an appetizer, as a first course light lunch or as a snack. To make *arancini,* you start with a simple risotto. This recipe may seem a bit time consuming, but if you love risotto, give it a try. The *arancini* look very elegant and artistic when served on an antipasto tray. Sometimes I slice a few in half to show how beautiful they look inside.

For the Risotto:
6 cups Chicken Broth (page 60)
   or Vegetable Broth (page 62)
6 tablespoons butter, divided, or part
   butter and part extra-virgin
   olive oil
½ cup chopped onion
2 cups Arborio rice
3 ounces freshly grated Parmigiano-
   Reggiano
3 large eggs
A pinch of salt and pepper
1 to 2 tablespoons dried bread
   crumbs (if necessary)

For the Filling:
1 cup Marinara Sauce (page 5)
3 ounces frozen baby peas (petite or
   early June), microwaved on High
   for 1 minute or until defrosted
½ pound fresh mozzarella cheese,
   cut into ¼- to ⅓-inch cubes

For the Coating:
1 large egg
A pinch of salt and pepper
2 cups dried bread crumbs

For the Frying:
1 quart vegetable or canola oil

PROCEDURE

1. In a medium saucepan, heat the broth to a simmer and continue to keep hot while cooking the rice.

2. Place a heavy-gauge medium skillet over medium-high heat. When the skillet is warm, add 3 tablespoons of the butter. When the butter has melted and starts to foam, add onion. Stir and sauté for 3 minutes. Then add the rice. Continue to sauté for 3 minutes until it turns opaque. Do not burn.

3. Slowly add 1 cup simmering broth, stirring frequently until most of the liquid has been absorbed. Add another ½ cup broth. Keep adding broth

½ cup at a time as the broth is absorbed. After 15 minutes of cooking, start to test the rice for doneness. Rice should be tender but al dente when done. Total cooking time varies from about 25 to 30 minutes. Taste for seasoning and adjust accordingly. Add the remaining butter and the grated cheese. Stir.

4. Allow the rice to cool completely. Mix the marinara and peas together in a bowl and set aside.

5. Beat 3 eggs with a pinch of salt and pepper. Mix the eggs with the cold rice. If the mixture is too moist, add a tablespoon or so of dried bread crumbs.

6. Place a piece of parchment paper on a baking sheet. Take a heaping tablespoon of the rice mixture (about the size of a small egg) and, using the palms of your hands, roll it into a ball. (If you have a cookie dough scoop, this also works well for forming the balls.) Place the balls onto the parchment paper. After you have rolled all the balls, take one ball at a time, poke a hole in the center, and fill it with just a thimbleful of the mozzarella cheese; then add about the same amount of the marinara-and-pea mixture. Close the hole over with the rice, rolling it into a ball again. Continue the process until all balls are filled. If you have enough time, place the baking sheet in the refrigerator for 30 minutes to 1 hour to allow the rice mixture to set.

7. Heat the oil to 360°F in either a deep-fryer or a medium-size heavy-gauge saucepan.

8. While the oil is heating, beat the remaining egg in a shallow bowl. Sprinkle with salt and pepper and stir. Place the bread crumbs in another shallow bowl.

9. Roll the balls in the egg mixture and then in the bread crumbs, making sure all areas are coated. Place the balls of rice on the same parchment-lined baking sheet.

10. Test the oil by placing a small piece of rice into the oil. If it sizzles, it is ready. Fry the rice balls in the hot oil several at a time until golden and crispy. Do not overcrowd. Drain on paper towels and place in a warm oven while you continue to cook the remaining balls. Serve hot.

Yield: 8 to 10 servings

NOTES

You may make the balls several hours in advance and keep them in the refrigerator until you are ready to fry them. Store any leftovers in a covered container in the refrigerator; they will keep for several days. They can be frozen for up to 2 months.

Marinated Mushroom Salad

Insalata di Funghi Marinati

Preparation Time: 15 minutes, plus 2 hours for marinating

1½ pounds white button mushrooms

For the Marinade:
Juice of 1 medium lemon
(about 3 tablespoons)
2 tablespoons wine vinegar
½ cup extra-virgin olive oil
(more if needed)
1 to 2 cloves garlic, chopped very
fine
¼ cup chopped Italian flat-leaf
parsley

1 teaspoon dried oregano
¼ teaspoon freshly ground black
pepper
½ teaspoon salt
½ teaspoon red pepper flakes

For the Garnish:
1 head Boston lettuce
2 tablespoons toasted pine nuts (see
page 24), chopped or ground
(optional)

PROCEDURE

1. Combine all the marinade ingredients in a large bowl and stir.

2. Clean the mushrooms by using a damp piece of paper towel to gently remove any soil particles. Cut the mushrooms in ⅛-inch slices and add to the marinade. Toss lightly to coat the mushrooms. Taste for seasoning and adjust accordingly. You might need to add more oil—there should always be a very tiny bit of oil in the bottom of the bowl. Place plastic wrap directly onto the surface of the mushrooms and refrigerate for 1 to 2 hours.

3. To serve, arrange a tender inside leaf of lettuce on a plate, and place marinated mushrooms on top. Sprinkle with toasted pine nuts if desired.

Yield: 8 servings

NOTES

Any leftover marinated mushrooms will keep in the refrigerator in a covered container for several days.

Orange Salad

Insalata di Arance

Preparation Time: 10 minutes, plus 30 minutes for marinating

Fruit trees grow abundantly throughout Italy. When fruit is in season, it is beautiful to behold. The colors of oranges, lemons, plums, apricots, and pears dot the countryside. In Italy we had our own trees and would eat fruit freshly picked as well as add them to salads and desserts. My mother taught us to can and make preserves, taking advantage of their abundance. When fruit was out of season, she would go to the cellar to get some for us.

As is true of many of the foods I grew up with, orange salad is very inexpensive, wonderfully unique in flavor, and colorful in its presentation. In looking at the ingredient list, you might think that this combination of ingredients could not be complementary. Not so. Try it!

Orange salad can be served for lunch, before a main course, or to cleanse the palate after a main course. The juices are so flavorful, it's hard to eat this salad without bread.

4 large navel oranges
½ small purple onion, sliced into thin rings
¾ cup fresh orange juice

¼ cup extra-virgin olive oil
1 to 2 tablespoons sugar
⅛ teaspoon freshly ground black pepper

PROCEDURE

1. Peel the oranges, making sure to remove the white part of the rind (pith). Cut them into irregular bite-size chunks and place in a medium bowl.

2. Add the remaining ingredients and toss gently. Refrigerate for at least ½ hour before serving to allow the flavors to blend together.

Yield: 4 servings

NOTES

Make sure to save the orange zest for future use.

Store leftovers in the refrigerator in a covered container; they will keep for 3 days.

Olive, Eggplant, and Red Pepper Salad

Muffaletta

Preparation and Cooking Time: 30 minutes, plus ½ to 1 hour for debittering

This is one of my favorite dishes to give as a gift to family and friends. Purchase small, attractive 1-cup canning jars, tie pretty ribbons around the lids, and give them along with loaves of homemade crusty Italian bread. This recipe begs to be shared.

1 medium eggplant, ends removed, peeled, diced into ½-inch cubes, sprinkled with 1 teaspoon salt and placed in a colander for ½ to 1 hour to remove bitterness (see page 10), rinsed, and patted dry with paper towels

¼ cup plus 3 tablespoons extra-virgin olive oil, divided

1 large clove garlic, minced (about 1 teaspoon)

¼ teaspoon salt

¼ teaspoon freshly ground black pepper

2½ tablespoons wine vinegar

1 tablespoon sugar

2 to 3 tablespoons tomato paste

6 fresh basil leaves, washed, dried thoroughly, and torn into pieces

1 teaspoon dried oregano

1 teaspoon fresh thyme

¼ pound sun-dried, oil-cured olives, pitted and chopped

½ pound Kalamata or Gaeta olives, pitted and chopped

½ pound green olives, pitted and chopped

2 red bell peppers, roasted (see page 14), skins removed, chopped

PROCEDURE

1. Rinse the eggplant and pat dry with paper towels.

2. Place a large skillet over medium-high heat. When the skillet is warm, add 3 tablespoons of the olive oil. When the oil is hot, add the eggplant and sauté for 5 minutes. It should be slightly soft.

3. Add the garlic, salt, and pepper and sauté for another 3 minutes, turning and stirring frequently. Add more if necessary.

4. Add the vinegar, sugar, and tomato paste and sauté for another 3 to

5 minutes. Add all the herbs and stir. Taste for seasoning and adjust accordingly.

5. In a large bowl, mix the olives and roasted peppers. Add the eggplant mixture. Toss lightly but thoroughly, add the remaining ¼ cup extra-virgin olive oil, toss again, and refrigerate in a covered container until ready to use. The ¼ cup extra-virgin olive oil can be omitted if you are on a restricted diet.

Yield: 3½ cups

NOTES

This dish can be served as part of an antipasto platter with freshly baked crusty Italian bread for lunch, or as a snack with toast (bruschetta). It is also delicious when made into a paste using the blender or food processor. The paste has a multitude of uses, including as a sauce for pasta.

Store any leftovers in a covered container and refrigerate; leftovers will keep for about 1 week. To use, allow to come to room temperature.

Mozzarella, Tomato, and Basil Salad

Insalata Caprese

Preparation Time: 5 minutes

This very popular and easy salad is considered a classic in Italian homes and restaurants. Look closely: the three ingredients in the recipe—tomatoes, basil, and mozzarella—are the colors of the Italian flag. Make this salad only when tomatoes are in season, using *fresh* mozzarella and your best extra-virgin olive oil. Fresh mozzarella can be purchased at the Italian markets, cheese shops, and even in the dairy sections of some grocery stores. This salad should be served freshly prepared.

4 large ripe tomatoes, washed, dried, cores removed
1 pound fresh mozzarella cheese
4 tablespoons extra-virgin olive oil

10 fresh basil leaves
Salt and freshly ground black pepper

PROCEDURE

1. On a clean work surface, slice the tomatoes and mozzarella into ¼-inch rounds. Arrange the tomatoes, mozzarella, and basil in overlapping slices on a serving dish. Just before serving, drizzle generously with the extra-virgin olive oil and sprinkle with salt and freshly ground black pepper.

2. Serve slightly chilled or at room temperature.

Yield: 4 to 6 servings

NOTES

Store leftovers in the refrigerator in a covered container; they will keep for a couple of days.

Antipasti

PASTA, RICE, GNOCCHI, AND POLENTA

Pasta followed by a green salad and fresh fruit that is in season is my idea of a perfect meal. If I didn't have pasta a couple of times a week, it would affect my mood and disposition and discolor my view on life. I simply love pasta, with its many shapes and sizes: tiny, large, short, long, thick, thin, flat, tubular, plain, ridged. It can be paired with simple sauces that take minutes to whip up or with more complicated long-cooking sauces that are robust or delicate, chunky or smooth. It can be twice-baked and layered or filled.

Dry Pasta

When buying dried pasta, always read the labels and buy brands made only with 100 percent durum wheat semolina. Semolina is a very hard wheat that absorbs less water when cooked, giving you a pasta that has a nice bite—not mushy. Dried pasta made with semolina will last almost indefinitely when stored in a cool, dry, dark place in the original unopened carton or in airtight glass or plastic containers in a cool, dry, dark place.

Depending on the shape of the pasta, 1 pound usually yields about 7 to 9 cups of cooked pasta. Long-strand, spaghetti-like pasta yields less. If you plan on serving pasta as a side dish, 2 ounces of dry pasta per person will suffice. If the pasta is to be the main course, use 4 ounces per person.

The secret to cooking a wonderful dish of pasta: Have a large pot of water (4 to 5 quarts of water per pound) at a rolling boil, then add 1 tablespoon of salt, then add the pasta. Stir until the water comes back to a boil and the pasta is moving around on its own; once this happens, it is not necessary to keep stirring the pasta constantly—just every so often. Most commercial dried pasta needs less time to cook than the manufacturer suggests. Start to check for doneness a couple of minutes before the stated time. Bite into a piece—it should not be hard and crunchy; if the center is too hard, it is not done yet. Another way is to cut a piece of pasta in half and look closely at the center; if you notice a line running through the thickest part, it is not done yet.

To save on cleanup, I usually sauce my pasta either in the same pot in which I have boiled it or in the skillet in which I prepared the sauce. Take the cooked pasta to the sink and drain in a colander. Shake the colander to remove any excess water. (Excess water will cling to the pasta and prevent the sauce from adhering to it, diluting the sauce and making it runny.) While the pasta is draining, place half the sauce into the pasta pot. Pour your thoroughly drained pasta on top of the sauce, toss lightly and see how much more sauce you want to add, and then toss and stir until the pasta is sauced to your satisfaction. Place onto a beautiful serving platter or bowl and serve at once. "Pasta waits for no one."

TIP: A special pasta boiling pan with a removable perforated inner basket makes light work of draining pasta—especially when you are using large fresh pasta sheets, lasagna noodles, or pasta squares for cannelloni.

TIP: The trick to eating long strands of pasta without getting too much on your fork, making it difficult to fit into your mouth, is to take a few strands from the edge of your plate, and with the tines of the fork down on the plate, begin twisting your fork around making a small tight bundle.

Fresh Pasta

Fresh pasta is made simply of flour and eggs, sometimes with the addition of oil, water, salt, or other ingredients. In Italy, semolina flour is usually not used for fresh pasta; softer flour comparable to our unbleached all-purpose flour is used to achieve the proper texture. The dough is not extruded by machines, but rolled out into sheets and cut into various shapes. Most people in Italy serve fresh pasta the day they make it, while it is still somewhat soft and pliable.

Many people think that fresh pasta is better than factory-made dried pasta. Such a comparison is, however, meaningless; they are simply two different products. Italians use fresh and dried pasta in different ways for different dishes. I suggest you try both and discover which one you like better with various sauces.

A recipe for Basic Egg Pasta Dough is given on page 40. You may choose to add flavoring and coloring ingredients to it. If these additions have a high moisture content, such as spinach, adjustments have to be made to the basic recipe by increasing the flour. If adding a dry flavoring ingredient such as ground mushroom powder, you will have to increase the liquid slightly. Use common sense.

If you are going to add flavoring ingredients that have moisture content, try to squeeze out as much moisture as possible. Add all flavoring ingredients to the flour and eggs at the beginning of the mixing period. The following are ingredients you may choose to flavor and color your pastas (remember, do not get carried away!): herbs, chilies, hot oils, flavored oils, cracked pepper, spinach, Swiss chard, beets, lemon or orange zest, saffron, mushrooms, black squid ink, tomato paste, garlic and onion, and even fresh flowers.

If you make double the amount of fresh pasta that you need, the leftover portion can be wrapped in an airtight reclosable plastic freezer bag and refrigerated for up to 3 days or frozen for up to 4 months. Frozen fresh pasta should go directly from the freezer into the pot of boiling salted water. In some larger cities, fresh pasta is available at the Italian markets and grocery stores; also in some smaller towns with sizable Italian populations.

The yield for fresh pasta per pound is about 6 to 7 cups, slightly less than for dry pasta. This is because the fresh pasta has a higher water content. You can count on 3 ounces for a side dish serving and at least 5 to 6 ounces for a main dish serving.

The secret to cooking a wonderful dish of fresh pasta is not to overcook it. Sometimes 30 seconds to 1 minute is all it takes. Have your colander ready in the sink so you can drain it immediately. The pasta will continue to cook if allowed to sit in the pot of hot water too long, leaving you with mushy pasta. After you place the fresh pasta into the boiling water, stay with the pasta for the minute or two that it takes to cook, stirring and tasting every 30 seconds.

Saucing Pasta

A general rule for saucing different shapes and sizes of pasta is that thin smooth pasta noodles require a light smooth sauce that won't overpower or weigh down the pasta, while sturdier shapes like ziti or rigatoni can handle chunkier sauces.

Pasta with Olive Oil and Garlic

Spaghetti Aglio e Olio

Preparation Time: 5 minutes • Cooking Time: 10 minutes

This pasta finds its place at our dinner table often. My mother-in-law, who lived with us and passed away recently just short of her hundredth birthday, boasted of its healing powers, humble beginnings, and peasant roots. It is a wonderfully simple dish to prepare, with a fantastic aroma, beautiful appearance, and mouthwatering flavor. I recommend that everyone learn to make this dish and have it as a part of his or her repertoire. This is a dish that my husband has mastered and makes often when he cooks.

4 to 5 quarts cold water
1 tablespoon salt
1 pound pasta
½ cup extra-virgin olive oil
6 to 8 cloves garlic, sliced very thin
   (slivered)
1 cup freshly grated Romano cheese,
   divided

½ teaspoon freshly ground black
   pepper (more or less to taste)
Chopped fresh Italian flat-leaf
   parsley or basil, for garnish
   (optional)

PROCEDURE

1. Bring the water to a boil in a large pot over high heat

2. While the water is heating, place a small skillet over medium heat. When skillet is warm, add the oil. When the oil is hot (indicated by ripples on the surface of the oil), add the garlic, turn the heat down to medium-low, and allow the garlic to carmelize slowly. The garlic is done when it turns a golden color (5 to 7 minutes).

3. When the water begins to boil, add the salt and pasta. Cook the pasta until al dente, stirring frequently. Reserve 1 cup of the pasta water; then drain the pasta.

4. Return the drained pasta to the pot and add the garlic–and–olive oil mixture, ½ cup of the cheese, and freshly ground black pepper to taste. Toss well to incorporate the pasta with the sauce, cheese, and pepper. Add as much of the

pasta water as is needed to moisten the pasta. Start with ¼ cup; sometimes that's all you will need. It's a matter of taste; some people like their pasta drier than others.

5. Serve immediately, garnished with chopped parsley or basil if desired. Pass the remaining cheese for sprinkling and a pepper mill for those who want to grind more pepper over their pasta.

Yield: 4 to 6 servings

NOTES

As a variation, add ¼ cup or more heated light cream instead of the pasta water.

Store any leftover pasta in a covered container in the refrigerator; it will keep for up to 5 days. To reheat, add 2 tablespoons water or milk and microwave until hot, or place in a skillet, add water or milk, and reheat. I do not recommend freezing.

Spicy Pasta with Capers and Olives

Pasta Puttanesca

Preparation Time: 20 minutes

Cooking Time: 40 minutes (plus overlapped cooking time for pasta)

According to various legends, this recipe may have originated with groups of Gypsies traveling in caravans by day and setting up camps by night, needing to make a meal that was inexpensive, quick, and delicious. This dish matches in appearance their colorful, multilayered costumes. Another version of the story is that the dish originated in one of the red-light districts of Naples. The prostitutes, after working late hours, needed to replenish their energy with a dish that was easy to prepare, nutritious, delicious, and spicy; I offer you my version of this celebrated recipe.

2 tablespoons extra-virgin olive oil
½ (3-ounce) can anchovy fillets
1 small yellow onion, chopped
4 cloves garlic, finely chopped
2 (28-ounce) cans whole Italian plum
    tomatoes, seeded and chopped
    (see page 3; reserve juice for
    another use)
4 tablespoons tomato paste
1 cup dry white wine
4 tablespoons capers, drained
    (whole or coarsely chopped,
    as desired)
10 to 15 Kalamata or Gaeta olives,
    pitted and coarsely chopped

6 fresh basil leaves, chopped, or
    1 tablespoon Pesto from your
    freezer (page 25)
½ teaspoon red pepper flakes (or
    more as desired)
¼ teaspoon salt
¼ teaspoon freshly ground black
    pepper
5 quarts water
1 tablespoon salt
1 pound pasta (spaghetti, linguine,
    vermicelli, penne rigate, or
    fusilli)
Freshly grated Parmigiano-Reggiano
    or Romano cheese

PROCEDURE

1. Place a large skillet over medium-high heat. When the skillet is warm, add the oil. When the oil is hot, add the anchovies. With tines of a fork, mash the anchovies in the olive oil and sauté for 45 seconds. Add the onion and sauté for 2 minutes, until tender. Add the garlic and sauté for another 2 minutes.

2. Add the seeded, chopped tomatoes. Dilute the tomato paste with the wine and add it to the sauce. Bring the contents of the skillet to a boil and boil for 2 minutes. Turn the heat down to medium and add the capers, olives, basil (or pesto), red pepper flakes, salt, and pepper.

3. Simmer uncovered for 25 to 30 minutes, stirring occasionally, until thickened. Taste for seasoning and adjust spices accordingly.

4. To serve, cook the pasta *al dente* according to the package directions. Set a timer so you can check the doneness 2 minutes before the package says it should be done.

5. Before draining the pasta, remove 1 cup of the pasta cooking water and set it aside. Drain the pasta and return it to the cooking pot. Pour half the sauce over the pasta, toss, and stir. Add more sauce as desired. If necessary, add about ¼ cup or more pasta water to loosen up the sauce. Place the pasta on a large platter and sprinkle with grated cheese.

Yield: 4½ cups sauce; 6 to 8 servings

NOTES

Store any leftover sauce in the refrigerator in a covered container; this sauce will keep in the refrigerator for up to 3 days. The sauce also freezes well and will keep for up to 3 months. To reheat, place in the microwave or in a skillet until just hot; you don't want it to get mushy. I do not recommend freezing leftover pasta.

Pasta with Bacon

Spaghetti con Pancetta

Preparation Time: 10 minutes • Cooking Time: 10 minutes

This pasta dish is uncomplicated, tasty, very satisfying, and can be served up in minutes. The pasta can be cooking while you are preparing the sauce. Both will be done at about the same time. With a little help, your family will be enjoying supper together at the table in no time. I teach this recipe in both my adult and children's classes. It is very simple and very flavorful.

This recipe calls for pancetta, a salt-cured Italian bacon. Pancetta comes from the center cut of pork belly. It can be purchased in Italian markets and grocery stores specializing in Italian foods. If you can't find pancetta, you can substitute bacon or lean salt pork, but bear in mind that pancetta is much leaner and has its own special flavor.

5 quarts cold water
1 tablespoon salt
5 large eggs
½ cup freshly grated Parmesan or
   Romano cheese, divided
4 tablespoons butter
1 medium yellow cooking onion,
   chopped
2 cloves garlic, chopped
   (about 1 teaspoon)

1½ pounds spaghetti, linguine, or
   fettuccine
½ pound pancetta, sliced into
   ½-inch strips
¼ cup milk
Freshly ground black pepper to taste
3 to 6 fresh basil leaves, chopped, for
   garnish

PROCEDURE

1. Bring the water to a boil in a large pot over high heat.

2. While the water is coming to a boil, beat the eggs and ¼ cup of the cheese in a medium bowl. Set aside.

3. Place a medium skillet over medium-high heat. When skillet is warm, add the butter. When the butter has melted and stops foaming, add the onion. Cook for 2 minutes, stirring occasionally. Add the garlic and cook for 1 to 2 minutes, until golden; remove the onion and garlic with a slotted spoon into a small bowl and set aside. Leave the drippings in the skillet.

4. Using the same skillet, set it over medium-high heat. Add the pancetta. Sauté for 1 minute without stirring; then stir and sauté for about 4 minutes more, until it just starts to get crispy. Spoon off all but 1 tablespoon of fat. Sometimes when you use very lean pancetta or bacon, there is no extra fat.

5. Return the skillet with the pancetta to medium heat. Add the cooked garlic-and-onion mixture and cook for 1 to 2 minutes, allowing the flavors to blend. Do not allow the mixture to burn. You are looking for the pancetta to become crispy.

6. When the water comes to a boil, add the salt and pasta. Cook the pasta al dente according to package directions. Set a timer so you can check for doneness 2 minutes before the package says it should be done.

7. Microwave the milk so it is very hot.

8. Check the pasta for doneness; drain and place back into the cooking pot.

9. Working quickly while the pasta is still hot, pour the beaten egg-and-cheese mixture over the pasta. Stir and toss. The egg will cook instantly as it comes in contact with the hot pasta. Pour in the hot milk and the pancetta mixture. Stir and toss again.

10. This pasta waits for no one, so call your family and guests to the table as you prepare the pasta for serving. Place it on a large serving platter, sprinkle with the remaining cheese and the chopped basil and pepper. Serve immediately.

Yield: 6 servings for main course

NOTES

Store any leftovers in a covered container in the refrigerator; leftovers will keep for up to 4 days. To reheat leftovers, place in the microwave with 1 tablespoon water and heat, or place in a skillet over medium heat, add 1 tablespoon water, and heat.

Pasta with Sausage

Rigatoni con Salsiccia

*Preparation Time: 5 minutes (not including preparation time
for making Marinara Sauce and sausage)*

Cooking Time: 17 minutes (plan your pasta cooking to overlap with making the sauce)

This dish is substantial and filling—perfect for all seasons. The marinara, fresh sausage, and peas make it colorful, tempting, and very appetizing.

2 tablespoons extra-virgin olive oil	**5 quarts cold water**
1 pound fresh sweet Italian sausage	**1 tablespoon salt**
1 cup dry white wine	**1 pound pasta, tubular**
2 cups Marinara Sauce (page 5)	**Freshly grated Parmesan or Romano**
3 tablespoons heavy cream	**cheese for the table**
¾ cup frozen baby peas	

PROCEDURE

1. Place a large skillet over medium-high heat. When skillet is warm, add the oil. When the oil is hot, add the sausage. Brown on all sides, about 5 to 6 minutes. Add the wine and place a cover on the skillet slightly askew. Cook for another 5 minutes. If the wine evaporates too quickly, add a little more.

2. Remove the sausage to a cutting board and cut into ½-inch-thick slices.

3. Using the same skillet, combine the marinara sauce, cream, peas, and sliced sausage. Stir and cook for another 5 minutes or so. Adjust seasoning.

4. While the sauce is cooking, bring the water to boil in a large pot. Cook the pasta al dente according to package directions. Drain, and place the pasta back into pot. Toss with the sauce and place on a platter or in a serving bowl. Serve hot, and pass freshly grated Parmesan or Romano cheese.

Yield: 6 to 8 servings

NOTE

Store leftovers in the refrigerator in a covered container for up to 4 days.

*Pasta, Rice,
Gnocchi,
and Polenta*

Seafood Lasagna for Very Special Occasions

Lasagne al Forno con Gamberetti e Capesante

Preparation Time: 45 minutes (not including preparation of Béchamel Sauce, Marinara Sauce, and Spinach)

Baking Time: 30 to 40 minutes

Rich and creamy, this flavorful, unusual lasagna makes an exquisite dinner party dish. Although this recipe requires more time and expense than traditional lasagnas, it is well worth it. The presentation is spectacular, using the colors of the Italian flag. The blending of flavors from the sauces, seafood, and vegetables make this a small masterpiece to delight the eye and the palate.

4 cups Béchamel Sauce (page 27)

4 cups Marinara Sauce (page 5)

1 recipe Spinach with Garlic and Olive Oil (page 29), drained well but not squeezed dry

5 quarts cold water

1 tablespoon salt

1 pound fresh pasta sheets or 1 pound packaged 100% durum wheat semolina lasagna noodles

2 tablespoons extra-virgin olive oil, divided

2 tablespoons butter, divided, plus additional butter for greasing baking dish

1 pound jumbo shrimp, shelled and deveined (see page 224), rinsed, and patted dry

1 pound scallops, rinsed and patted dry—remove tiny white muscle tab from the side of each scallop (it is tough and fibrous)

½ cup freshly grated Romano cheese

1 cup shredded fontina cheese—or other soft cheese of your choice

Salt and freshly ground black pepper to taste

PROCEDURE

1. Have ready the béchamel sauce, marinara sauce, and spinach. Place a large bowl of cold water near the stove. Spread out 2 sheets of parchment paper on your work surface.

2. Place water in a large pot; cover, bring to a boil, and add salt and pasta. If using fresh pasta sheets purchased from the Italian market, cut each sheet in half and cook four halves at a time for 45 seconds. Remove the pasta with a one-handled colander or large sieve and place in the bowl of cold water. Repeat process until all sheets are used. If using packaged lasagna, cook al dente according to package directions. Set a timer so you can check for doneness 2 minutes before the package says it should be done. Drain the pasta and place on parchment paper. Pat dry with paper towels. If making your own pasta, follow directions on page 40.

3. Place a large skillet over medium-high heat. When the skillet is warm, add 1 tablespoon olive oil and 1 tablespoon butter. When the butter is melted and the oil is hot, add the shrimp, season with salt and pepper, and sear quickly, stirring, for 2 minutes or until the shrimp turns pink. Remove shrimp and juices from pan, and place in a bowl. When cool enough to handle, chop into big chunks. Set aside.

4. In the same skillet, heat 1 tablespoon butter and 1 tablespoon olive oil until hot over high heat. Add the scallops, season with salt and pepper, and sear for 2 minutes on each side, or until golden brown. Remove from the pan, place in a separate bowl, cool and cut in ¼-inch slices. Set aside.

5. Preheat the oven to 350°F. Generously butter a 17 × 12 × 2½–inch baking dish.

6. To assemble the lasagna: Place one layer of noodles on baking pan. Spread a layer of béchamel sauce, and dot with shrimp. Cover that layer with another layer of noodles, followed by some béchamel sauce, spinach, and Romano cheese. Add another layer of lasagna noodles, followed by marinara sauce, fontina or Romano cheese, and scallops. Continue layering in this manner until all the ingredients have been used, ending with either the béchamel sauce or the marinara. Top with a sprinkling of Romano or fontina.

8. Bake uncovered at 350°F for 35 to 40 minutes, until bubbly and golden. Cut into serving pieces and serve hot.

Yield: 10 servings

NOTES

Store any leftovers in a covered container in the refrigerator; leftovers should be eaten within a couple of days. I do not recommend freezing.

Cannelloni Stuffed with Spinach and Ricotta

....

Cannelloni Ripieni con Spinaci e Ricotta

*Preparation Time: 30 minutes (not including preparation time
for spinach and ricotta, or if you are going to make your own pasta)*

Baking Time: 30 minutes

Children love to help make and eat this pasta dish. The pasta is tender and delicate. The fontina cheese has a mild nutty flavor, blends well with the other ingredients, and melts perfectly. This is one of the easiest stuffed pasta dishes to prepare and can be made almost completely in advance. Make the pasta and assemble the dish the morning you plan to serve it. The only thing left to do before dinner is to pour the cream over the top, sprinkle with fontina, place in the oven, and bake.

Make your own pasta according to the recipe on page 40. If you don't have the time or the inclination to make your own, pasta sheets may be purchased from many pasta shops and some Italian delis throughout the U.S. Hopefully, you have become proficient at making your own ricotta, but if you have to purchase store-bought, purchase it fresh from a cheese shop or an Italian deli. If the ricotta seems liquidy, place a coffee filter in a strainer and strain for several hours. This recipe remains one of my students' favorites. Try it and see for yourself.

For the Pasta:
5 quarts cold water
1 tablespoon salt
½ recipe of Basic Egg Pasta Dough,
    firm version (page 40), or
    ½ pound fresh pasta sheets
1 tablespoon butter
    (for greasing)

For the Filling:
1 recipe Spinach with Garlic and
    Olive Oil (page 29), drained well
    and chopped

3 cups Homemade Fresh Ricotta
    (page 8)
2 large eggs
1 cup shredded fontina cheese
1 cup freshly grated Romano or
    Parmigiano-Reggiano cheese
2 tablespoons finely chopped Italian
    flat-leaf parsley
A pinch of nutmeg

For the Sauce:
2 cups heavy cream
1 cup shredded fontina cheese

PROCEDURE

1. Grease the bottom and sides of an 8 × 12–inch baking dish generously with the butter.

2. In a medium bowl, combine the filling ingredients and blend lightly with a fork or your fingers.

3. Put the water on to boil in a large pot set over high heat. Preheat the oven to 350°F. Place a large bowl of cold water near the stove.

4. While the water is heating, cut the pasta sheets into 4-inch squares. When the water boils, add the salt.

5. Drop half the pasta squares into the boiling water one at a time, stir gently, and boil for 30 to 60 seconds. Remove with a one-handled colander or sieve and place in the cold water. Repeat the process with the rest of the squares. Drain all the pasta squares well and place on parchment or wax paper. Dry with paper towels.

6. Spread 2 heaping tablespoons of stuffing mixture horizontally in the center of each square. Beginning with the edge nearest you, roll up the square to form a cylinder. Arrange the cannelloni, seam-side down and side by side, in a single layer in the buttered baking dish.

7. Pour the cream evenly over the top and sprinkle with the fontina cheese. Move each cannelloni a little so the cream goes in between the pieces; this will prevent them from sticking to each other.

8. Bake for 30 minutes, or until the tops turn golden. If you would like the tops crispier, place under the broiler for 2 minutes. Serve immediately.

Yield: 18 cannelloni; 8 servings

NOTES

Store any leftovers in the refrigerator in a covered container. Leftovers will keep for several days and may be reheated in the microwave or oven. Add 1 or 2 tablespoons of milk before heating.

Shrimp-Stuffed Ravioli

....

Ravioli Ripieni con Gamberi

Preparation Time: 45 minutes to 1 hour if using purchased pasta sheets;
add another 30 minutes if making your own sheets.

Cooking Time: 4 to 8 minutes

Making homemade ravioli can be a project that the whole family enjoys together. My children and grandchildren savor the ravioli-making process almost as much as the final product. I am an avid believer that dishes requiring more energy and patience become, in essence, a bonding time with those helping.

You will need a pasta machine and a ravioli form that makes 2-inch square ravioli to make this recipe.

For the Stuffing:
1 pound large shrimp, shelled and
    deveined (see page 224), rinsed,
    and patted dry
4 tablespoons unsalted butter,
    divided
Salt and freshly ground black
    pepper
3 scallions, white and light-green
    portions only, chopped
½ clove garlic, minced
½ pound white button, oyster,
    shiitake, or porcini mushrooms,
    cleaned and sliced
2 tablespoons dry white wine
1 cup loosely packed grated fontina
    cheese
Fine dry bread crumbs (to use if
    filling is too wet)

For the Pasta:
1 recipe Basic Egg Pasta Dough
    (page 40)
1 egg beaten with 1 tablespoon water
5 quarts cold water
1 tablespoon salt

For the Sauce:
1 stick (8 tablespoons) butter
2 tablespoons chopped Italian flat-
    leaf parsley
1 teaspoon fresh thyme leaves

For Garnish:
Chopped Italian flat-leaf parsley

PROCEDURE

To Make the Stuffing:

1. Place a large skillet over medium-high heat. When the skillet is hot, add 2 tablespoons of the butter. When the butter has melted and is foaming, add

the shrimp, season with salt and pepper. Sear quickly, stirring and tossing until they just start to turn pink (2 to 3 minutes at the most). Remove them from the skillet with a slotted spoon and place in a medium bowl.

2. Add the remaining 2 tablespoons butter to the same skillet. When the butter foams, add the scallions, garlic, and sliced mushrooms. Sauté on medium-high for 3 to 4 minutes, until the mushrooms are tender. Remove with a slotted spoon to the bowl with the shrimp.

3. With the heat on high, deglaze the pan: Pour the wine into the pan drippings and stir with a wooden spoon for about 1 minute. Pour into the bowl. Add the fontina.

4. Place the stuffing ingredients into the food processor or blender and pulse a few times, until all the ingredients are finely minced. If stuffing is too wet, add a small amount of dry bread crumbs starting with one teaspoon. Taste for seasoning and adjust accordingly. Set aside.

To Make the Ravioli:

1. Divide the dough into eight equal pieces. Using a pasta machine, roll out pasta sheets to 12 inches long, starting with the rollers at the widest setting and stopping at the next-to-last setting. (On my Allas Pasta machine it is number 6.) The finished pieces should be rolled out to 13 inches long and 5½ inches wide. See Basic Egg Pasta Dough, page 40, for detailed instructions.

2. Place a pasta sheet over the ravioli form maker. Place the top plate over the dough and press uniformly to form cavities that will house the filling.

3. Brush the pasta sheet lightly with the egg wash and load cavities with about 1 teaspoon of filling. Place a second sheet of dough on top as a cover. Using a rolling pin, roll the entire top to seal and cut the individual ravioli. Turn form upside down to release ravioli. Dust the ravioli with flour as you move along.

4. Line two baking sheets with parchment or wax paper and sprinkle generously with flour. Set the individual ravioli on the sheets. Do not allow them to touch. Cover with a clean kitchen towel.

5. Repeat the process until all the pasta sheets have been used. You may choose to rework the scraps of dough to make more ravioli.

To Cook the Sauce and the Ravioli:

1. Put the water on to boil in a large pot. While waiting for the water to boil, heat the butter and herbs together in a medium skillet. Remove from heat after the butter is melted; do not allow it to darken.

2. When the water comes to a rolling boil, add the salt. Drop the ravioli into the boiling water, being careful not to crowd them. Cook for about 4 minutes, depending on the thickness of the pasta sheets. The ravioli should be tender but not mushy. Taste for doneness.

3. Remove ravioli and return it to the empty cooking pot. Add the hot sauce, toss very lightly, and plate in individual plates or a large platter. Garnish with parsley and serve.

Yield: 40 to 50 medium ravioli; 8 servings

NOTES

Store any leftovers in a covered container in the refrigerator; they will keep for 3 days. To reheat, place in a skillet with 2 tablespoons of milk and heat until warm, or microwave until hot. Do not overheat or the pasta will become mushy and the shrimp will turn rubbery. I do not recommend freezing cooked ravioli.

To simplify the preparation of this dish, the sauce can be made a day or two in advance and kept in the refrigerator. Prepare the ravioli the morning of the day you are going to serve it, and refrigerate.

To freeze uncooked ravioli, arrange in a single layer on a flour-dusted cookie sheet and place in freezer. When the ravioli are thoroughly frozen (about 4 hours), place them in reclosable plastic freezer bags, seal tightly, and label with the date. They will keep in the freezer for up to 6 weeks. Don't thaw them before cooking; add the frozen ravioli directly to salted boiling water and allow 2 to 3 minutes additional cooking time. Taste one to check doneness.

For variations on stuffing raviolis, open your refrigerator and see what kind of leftovers you have. Combine with any cheeses and herbs and you have come up with your own signature ravioli recipe.

Tortelloni with Mushroom Sauce

Tortelloni con Salsa di Funghi

Preparation Time: 1½ hours (not including making your own ricotta)
Cooking Time: 4 minutes

These tortelloni are definitely worth the extra time it takes to make them. Like ravioli and cannelloni, tortelloni can be stuffed and sauced with a variety of savory concoctions. The filling combinations for this recipe makes for an unusual, delicate, and delicious flavor. Make the pasta dough following the Basic Egg Pasta Dough recipe on page 40, adding 1 tablespoon of extra-virgin olive oil to the base recipe. The olive oil helps soften the dough, making it easier to seal. If you do not have time or don't want to make your own dough, buy the pasta sheets from your local pasta store or Italian market. If using these sheets, cut them in half lengthwise and pass through the pasta machine rollers once at the thinnest setting. You can also decide to use this mushroom sauce with store-bought tortelloni or linguine. So many options!

For the Mushroom Sauce:
3 tablespoons butter
2 tablespoons extra-virgin olive oil
2 tablespoons finely chopped
    shallots
2 cloves garlic, chopped
    (about 1 teaspoon)
1 pound mushrooms, sliced, cleaned
    with a damp paper towel
½ teaspoon salt
⅛ teaspoon freshly ground black
    pepper
2 cups whipping cream
1 cup half-and-half
½ cup freshly grated Romano or
    Parmigiano-Reggiano cheese

For the Filling:
½ boneless, skinless chicken breast
1 tablespoon butter
Salt and pepper to taste
2 ounces mortadella, minced (can be
    purchased at an Italian deli or
    grocery store)
⅓ cup Homemade Fresh Ricotta,
    page 8
1 large egg
¼ cup freshly grated Romano or
    Parmigiano-Reggiano cheese
Pinch of nutmeg
1 tablespoon chopped Italian flat-
    leaf parsley

(cont'd)

For the Pasta:
Make 1 pound of fresh pasta, rolled into sheets (use Basic Egg Pasta Dough recipe, page 40)
or
1 pound fresh pasta sheets (purchased from an Italian market or pasta store)

Egg wash (1 egg and 2 tablespoons water beaten)

For the Table:
Freshly grated Parmigiano-Reggiano or Romano cheese

PROCEDURE

For the Mushroom Sauce:

1. Place a large heavy-gauge saucepan over medium heat. When saucepan is warm, add the butter and the oil. When the butter has melted, add the shallots. Stir and sauté for 2 minutes. Add the garlic and sauté for another 2 minutes. Add the mushrooms and sauté for about 4 minutes, making sure that any extra liquid added by the mushrooms during cooking has been reabsorbed. Season with salt and pepper.

2. Stir in the cream and half-and-half and heat to boiling. Reduce the heat to low. Taste for seasoning and adjust accordingly.

3. Simmer uncovered for 5 minutes.

4. Add the cheese, stir, and simmer for a few minutes longer. Remove from the heat and set aside. Place plastic wrap directly over the sauce.

For the Filling:

1. Brown the chicken breast in the butter for about 4 minutes, until cooked. Season with salt and pepper. Cut breast in small chunks and grind with the mortadella in a food processor or blender.

2. Add the remaining filling ingredients and combine.

For the Tortelloni:

1. Place 1 sheet of parchment or wax paper on baking sheet.

2. Place 1 sheet of parchment or wax paper on work surface.

3. Cut pasta sheets into 3-inch squares. Place six of the squares on the parchment paper at an angle in a diamond shape. Brush with egg wash.

4. Place a small amount of filling (½ teaspoon or so) in the center of each square.

5. Dip your fingers into a bowl of hot water and wet two sides of the

square. Fold the dough over onto the moistened edges to seal the dough. With the point facing away from you, place both thumbs under tortelloni and both index fingers over tortelloni, turn edges of tortelloni under and around thumbs, joining and sealing the two ends together, sealing with a dab of water. The shape resembles a wonton. As you complete each series of five, dust with flour and place them individually and not touching on the baking sheet in a single layer and cover with wax paper. Continue this procedure until all tortelloni are finished.

6. Tortelloni may be kept in the refrigerator for 2 to 3 hours before cooking or frozen in a single layer on a baking sheet (see Notes for details).

7. If the tortelloni are to be cooked at once, bring a large pot of water to a boil. Once the water is at a rolling boil, add 1 tablespoon salt to the water. Drop the tortelloni gently, a few at a time, into the boiling water. They will be cooked in 3 to 5 minutes. Check for doneness.

For the Assembly:

1. When the tortelloni are cooked, scoop them out of the water with a slotted spoon or strainer.

2. Place about half the sauce onto the serving platter. Place tortelloni over the sauce and top with the remaining sauce and sprinkle with additional cheese. Serve immediately. Place extra grated cheese along with a pepper mill on the table.

Yield: 8 servings

NOTES

Place any extra, uncooked tortelloni in a single layer on a parchment-lined cookie sheet and store in the freezer. When tortelloni are thoroughly frozen (about 4 hours), place them in reclosable plastic freezer bags and label the bags. The tortelloni will keep in the freezer for up to 6 weeks. Don't thaw them before cooking; instead add the frozen tortelloni directly to boiling water and allow 2 to 3 minutes of additional cooking time.

Having a pasta strainer insert for your pot makes the removal of the tortelloni much easier. Store cooked and sauced tortelloni in a covered container in the refrigerator; they will keep for several days. To reheat, microwave until warm or heat in skillet. I do not recommend freezing cooked and sauced tortelloni.

Pasta, Rice, Gnocchi, and Polenta

Sunday Tomato Sauce with Meatballs

Sugo per la Domenica con Carne e Polpette

Preparation Time: 2 hours   •   Cooking Time: 4 to 4½ hours

This was a special sauce my mom served on Sundays and special occasions. From the early morning when it would awaken us until the early afternoon when it was ready, the smell of this sauce would filter throughout the house. After breakfast and church, the aroma beckoned us into the kitchen, where it was understood that everyone stirred the pot whenever they were near the stove. When we children stirred the sauce—and Mom was not looking—we would break off little pieces from the meatballs to eat. The meatballs definitely became smaller but never fewer; we were absolutely sure that Mom counted every single one as they went into the pot and as they were dished into the pasta plates. (I still wonder if she caught on. Somehow, I suspect she did.)

Children can have fun making the meatballs or seeding the tomatoes. Once everything is in the pot, all you really need to do is keep an eye on it, stirring once in a while. The juices from the meat and the flavor from the bones and the tomatoes give this sauce its traditional authentic flavor and texture. You can't buy this sauce in jars!

For the Sauce:
2 (28-ounce) cans Italian plum tomatoes, including their juice
2 tablespoons extra-virgin olive oil
3 cloves garlic, chopped (about 1½ teaspoons)
2 (28-ounce) cans tomato puree
6 cups warm water
2 (6-ounce) cans tomato paste
1 teaspoon salt
½ tablespoon freshly ground black pepper

10 basil leaves, chopped, or 1 tablespoon Pesto from your freezer (page 25)
2 bay leaves
2 tablespoons extra-virgin olive oil
½ pound beef chuck, cut into 1-inch cubes
½ pound pork butt or pork roast, cut into 1-inch cubes
½ pound pork spareribs or country-style ribs, cut into pieces

1 pound combination of beef and
    pork bones (neck bones are best;
    ask your butcher to cut the
    bones into manageable pieces)
A light sprinkling of salt and freshly
    ground black pepper to season
    the meat and the bones

For the Meatballs:
1 pound lean ground beef
½ pound lean ground pork
½ pound lean ground veal

6 large eggs, lightly beaten
½ cup freshly grated Romano cheese
1 clove finely minced garlic
    (about ½ teaspoon)
1 teaspoon finely chopped Italian
    flat-leaf parsley
1½ teaspoons salt
½ teaspoon freshly ground black
    pepper
¾ cup plain dried bread crumbs,
    divided

PROCEDURE

For the Sauce:

1. Seed the tomatoes, following the directions given in the Marinara Stepping-stone Technique, page 3; then chop. Reserve the juice and additional bits and pieces of tomatoes.

2. Place an extra-large nonreactive sauce pot over medium heat. When the pot is warm, add the first 2 tablespoons of olive oil. When the oil is hot, add the garlic. Stir and sauté until the garlic is just golden. Add the seeded tomatoes and puree to the pot.

3. Place 6 cups of warm water in a large bowl along with the tomato paste. Dilute the paste so there are no lumps left. Pour this into the large sauce pot.

4. Take any leftover tomato juice and bits and pieces of tomatoes and pass them through a food mill into the large sauce pot. Discard the seeds. Add salt, pepper, basil, and bay leaves.

5. When the sauce starts to boil, reduce the heat to medium-low. Stir the bottom of the pot well every 15 minutes or so with a wide spatula or spoon. (You don't want to scorch the sauce.)

6. While the sauce is cooking, rinse the chunks of meat and bones under cold running water. Drain and pat dry with paper towels. Lightly season the meat and bones with salt and pepper. Put a large skillet over medium heat; then add the second 2 tablespoons of olive oil. When the olive oil is hot, add the chunks of meat and the soup bones and brown on all sides.

7. As each piece of meat is browned, place it in the pot of sauce.

8. Do not wash the skillet. Leave the oil and drippings and use them to lightly brown the meatballs.

*Pasta, Rice,
Gnocchi,
and Polenta*

For the Meatballs:

1. In a large bowl, place the ground pork, beef, and veal. Add the eggs, cheese, garlic, parsley, salt, and pepper.

2. Using a fork or hand (hand is better), mix until all the ingredients are uniformly blended. Add ½ cup of the bread crumbs and mix again. Then let the meatball mixture rest for 5 minutes. During this resting period, the mixture will become firmer as the eggs absorb the bread crumbs. The mixture should still be a little sticky. If it is too sticky and does not hold together, add more bread crumbs, 1 tablespoon at a time, until you get the right consistency. Adding too much bread crumbs will make the meatballs tough—you want them to be light.

3. Place a sheet of wax or parchment paper on the counter. Roll the meat mixture into balls the size of a golf ball and place them on the paper. Wetting your hands lightly will prevent the mixture from sticking to them.

4. Return the skillet to the stove and turn the heat to medium. When the skillet is hot, add more oil if necessary, and when the oil is hot, add the meatballs, one at a time. Do not crowd the pan. Cook each meatball until it is lightly browned on all sides. As they are browned, place the meatballs into your pot of sauce to finish cooking.

5. Now everything should be in the sauce pot. Simmer the mixture uncovered for 4 to 4½ hours over low heat at a slow boil. Stir every 15 minutes or so, making sure you stir the entire bottom of the pot to prevent the sauce from burning and sticking. Using a flat-edged utensil, such as a long-handled metal spatula, makes it easier to stir the entire surface of the bottom of the pot.

6. Taste for seasoning and adjust accordingly. Remove bay leaves and bones before saucing pasta.

Yield: 24 servings, 16 to 17 cups sauce
(with about 25 meatballs)

NOTES

Leftovers will keep fresh in the refrigerator in covered containers for up to 5 days and freezes well for up to 6 months. Divide into meal-size portions before freezing. Defrost it overnight in the refrigerator. Place the defrosted sauce in a medium sauce pot and heat.

Bolognese Meat Sauce

....

Ragù Bolognese

Preparation Time: 20 minutes (not including preparation time for the broth)

Cooking Time: 1 hour

2 tablespoons butter, divided

2 tablespoons extra-virgin olive oil, divided

1 medium onion, finely minced

1 celery stalk, finely minced

1 large carrot, finely minced

2 ounces pancetta or bacon, finely chopped

8 ounces lean ground beef

8 ounces lean ground pork

½ cup dry white wine

A pinch of nutmeg

¼ teaspoon salt

¼ teaspoon freshly ground black pepper

1 (6-ounce) can tomato paste

2 cups Beef Broth (page 61) or commercial broth

½ cup milk

½ cup freshly grated Parmigiano-Reggiano, plus extra for the table

PROCEDURE

1. In a large skillet set over medium heat, heat 1 tablespoon of the butter and 1 tablespoon of the olive oil. When the butter has melted and stops foaming, add the onion, celery, carrot, and pancetta. Stir and sauté gently for 7 to 10 minutes.

2. Add the remaining olive oil, butter, ground beef and pork, stirring with a fork to break up the meat. Sauté over medium heat for about 7 minutes, or until the ground meat is no longer pink and starts to brown.

3. Add the wine and cook until most of the wine has been absorbed, about 2 to 3 minutes. Stir in the nutmeg, salt, and pepper. Dilute the tomato paste with 2 cups of the broth, add it to the skillet, and cook for ½ hour over low heat, stirring a few times. Add more broth if the mixture becomes too dry.

4. Add the milk and ½ cup grated cheese. Stir and cook the sauce for an additional 5 minutes. Serve hot over cooked, drained pasta. Pass extra grated cheese at the table.

Yield: more than 4 cups (sauces 1 pound pasta generously, with some left over to freeze)

Pasta, Rice, Gnocchi, and Polenta

NOTES

When stored properly, extra sauce will keep in the refrigerator, in a covered container, for up to 4 days. This sauce freezes very well and will keep for several months.

Tomato-Basil Cream Sauce

Salsa di Pomodoro con Basilico e Panna

Preparation Time: 20 minutes • Cooking Time: 1 hour and 45 minutes

This dish was presented to our family by my daughter Lisa several summers ago on vacation at Lake George. She first tasted this sauce while having lunch in Little Italy, and because the chef would not divulge his cooking secrets, she came home and experimented until she got it right. My mother-in-law, Connie, insisted that no one could make this sauce as well as her beloved granddaughter, although we've followed her recipe exactly time and time again. So try preparing this with penne for someone who adores you; I assure you that they will praise you for some time to come.

3 (28-ounce) cans whole Italian plum
   tomatoes and their juice, seeded
   (see page 3)
3 tablespoons extra-virgin olive oil,
   divided
3 garlic cloves, chopped
   (about 1½ teaspoons)
4 fresh basil leaves
¼ teaspoon freshly ground black
   pepper (plus more if needed)

¼ teaspoon salt (if needed)
½ tablespoon sugar (if needed)
½ cup vodka (optional)
1 pint heavy cream
⅔ cup freshly grated Romano cheese
20 fresh basil leaves, chopped
Freshly ground black pepper to taste

PROCEDURE

First, Make Marinara Sauce:

   Follow directions on page 5.

Then, Assemble the Tomato-Basil Cream:

   1. Add the vodka, if using, and cook for 3 minutes.

   2. Add the cream, Romano cheese, and the chopped basil leaves. Heat to almost boiling. Taste for seasonings and adjust accordingly. Keep warm until ready to use.

Yield: 6½ cups
(enough sauce for 2 to 3 pounds of pasta)

*Pasta, Rice,
Gnocchi,
and Polenta*

NOTES

Store leftover sauce in a covered container in the refrigerator; leftovers will keep for several days, or freeze in individual containers. It will keep in the freezer for several months. Defrost in the refrigerator and heat before using, but do not let it come to a boil.

If you prefer, make the marinara in advance; then assemble the rest of sauce on the day you plan to use it.

Olive Paste Sauce

Salsa di Olive

Preparation Time: 10 minutes

If you love olives, you will definitely appreciate this sauce. It is a special treat served with pasta and great as a spread over fresh or toasted bread (bruschetta). It can also be used over meat, chicken, or fish.

3 cloves garlic, minced
½ cup extra-virgin olive oil
4 canned anchovies

6 ounces Kalamata olives, pitted
⅛ teaspoon freshly ground black
   pepper

PROCEDURE

1. Heat the oil in a small skillet over medium-low heat. Add the anchovies along with the oil they are packed in. With a fork, mash the anchovies with the oil for 1 minute. Add the garlic and cook until it is just golden (about 2 minutes). Remove from the heat; it will continue to cook if left on the burner.

2. Process the garlic-anchovy mixture, olives, and pepper in a blender or food processor until finely minced. I suggest using the pulse button.

Yield: ¾ cup (enough to sauce up to 1 pound of pasta)

NOTES

You may substitute other olives of your choice.

Since this is such a quick sauce, I would suggest making it the same day you are going to use it. The anchovies always taste their best when the can is just opened. If you are using the sauce over pasta, cook the pasta while you make the sauce, and serve the sauce fresh. Drain the pasta in a colander, but reserve 1 cup of the pasta-cooking water. Pour the drained pasta back into the pasta pan. Add all the sauce—stir and toss. If you feel the pasta is too dry, add a little of the pasta liquid to moisten it. Serve with extra cheese for sprinkling on top.

Place any leftover sauce or sauced pasta in covered containers in the refrigerator; they will keep for up to 5 days. I do not recommend freezing.

Risotto alla Milanese

Risotto alla Milanese

Preparation Time: 5 minutes • *Cooking Time: 30 minutes*

This wholesome, flavorful traditional dish is really not difficult to prepare. It takes a bit of baby-sitting (which most of us are familiar with), loving care, and patience to produce a perfect risotto. It should always be cooked firm to the bite, yet creamy and moist. The butter and cheese, which are added at the very end of the cooking cycle, are beaten into the risotto with a wooden spoon just before you spoon it onto the platter. This is a special technique used in almost all risotto, imparting its traditional characteristics of richness, creaminess, and firmness. The risotto must be served steamy hot.

Remind your guests that it is very easy to overeat risotto, especially if you are eating other courses. Pace yourself or you will not be able to enjoy the rest of your meal!

5 cups Chicken or Vegetable Broth (page 60 or 62) or or substitute canned broth

8 tablespoons butter, divided

1 medium-large yellow cooking onion, chopped

2 cups Arborio, Carnaroli, or Vialone Nano rice

⅔ cup dry white wine

¼ teaspoon saffron threads, crushed with a mortar and pestle or with kitchen mallet

½ teaspoon salt

3 tablespoons cream

½ to ¾ cup freshly grated Parmigiano-Reggiano cheese

PROCEDURE

1. In a medium saucepan, heat the broth to simmering; keep hot over low to medium heat throughout the cooking process.

2. Place a large heavy-gauge skillet over medium-high heat. When the skillet is warm, add 4 tablespoons of the butter. When the butter has melted and starts to foam, add the chopped onion and sauté for 3 to 5 minutes, until the onion has softened. Stir in the rice and sauté for 2 to 3 minutes, until the rice grains are coated with butter and turn opaque.

3. Stir in the wine, crushed saffron, and salt. Cook uncovered over moderate heat, stirring continuously, until the wine has been absorbed. Add the simmering broth to the rice, about ½ cup at a time, stirring often until the rice absorbs the liquid before adding the next ½ cup.

4. After approximately 15 minutes of cooking, begin testing the rice for doneness. The rice is done when it is tender but still firm to the bite and has a creamy consistency. Not all the broth may be required. If you run out of broth, use hot water.

5. Keep the risotto on the stove on low heat and stir in the remaining 4 tablespoons butter, cream, and cheese. Place in a warm serving dish and serve immediately. People should be seated at the table before you plate the risotto—it waits for no one!

Yield: 6 to 8 servings

NOTES

Extra-virgin olive oil may be substituted for part of the butter.

Risotto tastes best when eaten immediately after it is cooked. Any leftovers should be stored in the refrigerator in a covered container; they will keep for several days. Reheat in the microwave or on the stove after adding some milk to loosen it. I do not recommend freezing risotto. Leftovers can also be used to make the Rice Balls included in the "Antipasti" chapter (page 93).

Risotto with Seafood

....

Risotto alla Pescatoro

Preparation Time: 20 minutes (not including preparation of the broth, if making your own)
Cooking Time: 45 to 50 minutes

This risotto is truly decadent—a feast for all the senses. The addition of the seafood makes it more expensive and time consuming to make, but well worth it. I recommend a very light antipasto such as marinated artichokes, mushrooms, or roasted bell peppers to precede the risotto, followed by a green salad and a fruity lemon ice dessert. Keep it simple and refreshing.

Most Italians do not believe in combining cheeses with their seafood. They feel that the cheese overshadows the delicate flavor of the seafood. This dish is an exception.

8 tablespoons butter
½ pound large shrimp, shelled deveined (see page 224), rinsed, patted dry with paper towels, and seasoned with salt and pepper
½ pound scallops, rinsed, patted dry with paper towels, and seasoned with salt and pepper; remove the tiny white muscle tab from the side of the scallop
½ pound white fish fillets, rinsed and patted dry with paper towels
1 cup dry white wine, divided
½ pound mussels, scrubbed, bearded, rinsed, and drained (see page 223)
6 cups Chicken Broth (page 60) or

Vegetable Broth (page 62) or Fish Broth (page 59)
1 medium-large yellow cooking onion, chopped
2 cups Arborio, Carnaroli, or Vialone Nano rice
¼ teaspoon saffron threads, crushed with a mortar and pestle
¼ cup whole milk, heated until hot
½ to ¾ cup freshly grated Parmigiano-Reggiano or Romano cheese

For the Garnish:
Zest from 1 lemon—in threads
2 tablespoons roasted red pepper, diced (see page 14)

PROCEDURE

1. Heat 1 tablespoon of the butter in a large skillet. Sauté the shrimp until just pink, 2 to 3 minutes, and then set aside.

2. Using the same pan, melt 1 more tablespoon butter on high heat. Sauté both sides of the scallops on high heat, for a total of 4 minutes. Set aside.

3. Using the same pan again, melt 1 more tablespoon butter and sauté the fish 2 minutes on each side. Remove from the pan and cut into 1-inch pieces.

4. Pour ½ cup of the wine into the skillet and add the mussels. Heat over high heat and steam the mussels until they open. Set aside, discarding any that don't open.

5. In a medium saucepan, heat the broth to simmering; keep hot over low to medium heat throughout the cooking process, ready to be added in stages.

6. Place a large heavy-gauge skillet over medium-high heat. When the skillet is warm, add 2 more tablespoons of the butter. When the butter has melted and starts to foam, add the chopped onion and sauté for 3 to 5 minutes, until the onion has softened. Stir in the rice and sauté for 2 to 3 minutes, until the rice grains are coated with butter and are opaque.

7. Stir in the remaining ½ cup wine and the saffron. Cook uncovered over moderate heat, stirring, until the wine has been absorbed. Add simmering broth to the rice ½ cup at a time, stirring frequently. As broth is absorbed, add more, repeating the process.

8. Add the seafood to the risotto during the last 3 minutes of cooking. The rice is done when it is tender but still firm to the bite and has a slightly creamy consistency. Not all the broth may be required.

9. Keep the risotto on the stove at medium heat and stir in the remaining 3 tablespoons butter, the heated milk, and the cheese. Place in a warm serving platter and serve immediately. Add the lemon zest and roasted pepper to garnish.

Yield: 6 to 8 servings

NOTES

Risotto tastes best when it is freshly cooked. Store any leftovers in the refrigerator in a covered container and eat the following day. To reheat leftovers, sprinkle 1 tablespoon of milk over the top, place in the microwave, and heat until just warm. I do not recommend freezing.

Pasta, Rice,
Gnocchi,
and Polenta

Risotto alla Bolognese

Risotto alla Bolognese

Preparation Time: 5 minutes, not including preparation of the Bolognese Sauce

Cooking Time: 20 minutes

6 cups Chicken Broth (page 60) or
    Vegetable Broth (page 62) or
    canned broth
4 tablespoons butter, divided
1 medium-large yellow cooking
    onion, chopped
2 cups Arborio, Carnaroli, or Vialone
    Nano rice

1 cup dry white wine
1½ cups Bolognese Meat Sauce
    (page 125)
¼ cup whole milk, heated until hot
½ to ¾ cup freshly grated
    Parmigiano-Reggiano or
    Romano cheese

PROCEDURE

1. In a small saucepan, heat the broth to simmering; keep hot over low to medium heat throughout the cooking process.

2. Place a large heavy-gauge skillet over medium-high heat. When the skillet is warm, add 3 tablespoons of the butter. When the butter has melted and starts to foam, add the chopped onion and sauté for 3 to 5 minutes, until the onion has softened. Stir in the rice and sauté for 2 to 3 minutes, until the rice grains are coated with butter and turn opaque.

3. Stir in the wine and cook uncovered over moderately high heat, stirring continuously until the wine has been absorbed. Add the hot broth to rice about ½ cup at a time, stirring often until the rice absorbs the liquid before adding the next ½ cup.

4. After approximately 15 minutes of cooking, add the Bolognese Sauce and cook for an additional 5 minutes. Test the rice for doneness. The rice is done when it is tender but still firm to the bite and has a slightly creamy consistency. Not all the broth may be required.

5. Add the remaining 1 tablespoon butter, milk, and cheese, mixing well. This risotto has a creamy and somewhat loose consistency.

6. Place in a warm serving dish and serve immediately.

Yield: 6 to 8 servings

NOTES

Store any leftovers in the refrigerator in a covered container. Reheat in the microwave or on the stove after adding a sprinkling of milk to the surface to hydrate it. I do not recommend freezing risotto. If you have a lot of leftovers, try making the Rice Balls *(Arancini)* on page 93.

Pasta, Rice, Gnocchi, and Polenta

Quick, Delicious, and Simply Elegant Rice

Riso Delizioso

Preparation Time: 5 minutes (does not include time needed to make your own broth)
Cooking Time: 20 minutes

This recipe is an American variation from the Italian-inspired risotto. It uses long-grain white rice, which is readily available. It is much simpler to prepare; very delicious. I enrich it with peas or sautéed vegetables and sometimes toasted nuts. When you become proficient at its technique, you will be able to create your own recipes.

2 tablespoons extra-virgin olive oil or butter
1 medium onion, chopped
2 cups long-grain rice
⅛ teaspoon crushed saffron threads (optional)

4 cups Vegetable Broth (page 62) or Chicken Broth (page 60)
1 sprig of fresh thyme (optional)
1 bay leaf
2 tablespoons chopped Italian flat-leaf parsley

PROCEDURE

1. Heat a medium-size heavy-gauge saucepan over medium heat. When warm, add the oil. When the oil is hot, add the chopped onion and sauté for 3 to 4 minutes, until tender and just starting to turn golden. Stir occasionally.

2. Add the rice and saffron and sauté for 2 to 3 minutes, stirring to coat all the grains with olive oil. Add the broth, thyme, bay leaf, and parsley and bring to a boil. Reduce the heat to low, cover, and continue to cook for 18 to 20 minutes. The rice is done when the grains are tender but firm and the liquid has been absorbed. Try not to remove the cover and peek during the cooking process.

Yield: About 8 cups; 6 to 8 servings

NOTES

Make more of this rice than you need. Store any leftovers in the refrigerator in a covered container; leftovers will keep for about 1 week. Leftovers can be added to enrich soups, stews, frittatas, salads, and stuffings. If you're in the mood, try making the Rice Balls *(Arancini)* on page 93.

Ricotta Gnocchi

Gnocci di Ricotta

*Preparation Time: 1 hour or more (varies according to experience),
not including preparation of sauce or ricotta*

Cooking Time: 3 to 6 minutes

1 cup Homemade Fresh Ricotta
    (page 8) or commercial ricotta
    (or fresh deli ricotta)
2 large eggs, beaten
1 cup freshly grated Romano cheese
2 cups unbleached all-purpose flour
    (more if needed)
⅛ teaspoon freshly ground nutmeg
5 quarts water
1 tablespoon salt

Toppings:
Béchamel Sauce (page 27),
    Marinara Sauce (page 5), or
    Pesto (page 25), Salmon Sauce
    (page 143), or Spinach Sauce
    (page 144)
Freshly grated Parmigiano-Reggiano
    or Romano cheese, for sprinkling

PROCEDURE

1. Line two baking sheets with parchment or wax paper. Dust lightly with flour and set aside.

2. Pass the ricotta through a food mill into a medium bowl. If you have several different disks with your food mill, use the medium-size one. Add the eggs, cheese, and flour. Mix until everything sticks together and a dough forms. If you prefer, use a mixer or food processor.

3. Dust your work surface with flour and knead the dough for 2 to 3 minutes. If the dough is sticky, add a little more flour. The dough should be moist, soft and pliable, but not sticky.

4. Divide the dough into pieces the size of a small egg. Flour your hands lightly and, using both hands, roll the pieces into coils with a ½-inch diameter, about the diameter of your little finger. Cut each roll into ½-inch pieces.

5. To form the gnocchi, use either a fork or a ridged butter press, and follow the instructions on page 138. Move the formed pieces onto the prepared baking sheets and dust with flour. Cover each layer of gnocchi with a piece of parchment paper so they don't stick together.

6. Bring the water to a boil in a large pot on high heat. When it comes to a rolling boil, add the salt. Add about half the gnocchi and stir. When gnocchi are

done they will start to rise to the surface. When all the gnocchi have risen to the surface, taste for doneness, remove with a slotted spoon, and place in a warm oven. Repeat the process with the remaining gnocchi.

7. Pour about half the sauce into an attractive serving dish. Add the gnocchi and toss lightly. Cover with the remaining sauce and sprinkle with cheese. If you like, garnish by using some of the ingredients from your chosen sauce, such as chopped parsley.

Yield: 4 to 6 servings (depending on appetite
and what else is being served)

NOTES

If you have a sushi mat, try using that to form your gnocchi.

If using purchased ricotta, make sure you allow it to drain in a sieve lined with a coffee filter or cheesecloth. Store-bought packaged ricotta always has a lot of liquid in it, if you don't drain it, you will have to use more flour in your dough, making the gnocchi heavier.

Store any leftover cooked and sauced gnocchi in the refrigerator in a covered container; leftovers will keep for several days. To reheat, sauté quickly in a skillet or heat in the microwave until hot. I do not recommend freezing cooked gnocchi.

Making Gnocchi

Gnocchi are similar to a small dumpling. They can be made with a variety of ingredients, formed into several shapes, sauced with a multitude of sauces.

Start with less flour than the recipe calls for—the less flour used, the lighter the gnocchi. You can always add more when you are kneading the dough. Unlike bread, gnocchi should not be kneaded too long. The more you knead the dough, the more flour it will absorb and, again, the more flour, the heavier the gnocchi. Using your thumbs, roll the dough into concave shell-shaped pieces.

I suggest that you have a small pot of water boiling and only prepare a couple of gnocchi at first as an experiment. They should be firm enough to hold together and not fall apart in the water or be too gooey. If they don't hold together, knead in a bit more flour. When you boil an entire batch, use a large stockpot with plenty of boiling water so the gnocchi can dance freely in the water without sticking to each other. They rise to the surface when done.

Potato Gnocchi

Gnocchi di Patate

Preparation Time: 1 hour or more (varies according to experience);
plus 45 minutes to 1 hour for baking the potatoes—can be done in advance
Cooking Time: 2 to 4 minutes

The potatoes of choice for gnocchi are the drier, more floury potatoes such as Russet or Idaho. They make for lighter, nongummy gnocchi. I prefer to bake the potatoes instead of boiling them. When potatoes are boiled, they absorb water, thereby forcing you to use more flour to form the gnocchi dough. The less flour used, the lighter the gnocchi. Plan on 1 medium potato per person for a large serving.

4 medium Russet or Idaho potatoes,
    washed and dried
1 tablespoon salt
1 egg, beaten

1¼ to 2 cups unbleached all-purpose
    flour
5 quarts water
1 tablespoon salt (additional)

PROCEDURE

1. Preheat the oven to 375°F. Line two baking sheets with parchment or wax paper, dust lightly with flour, and set aside.

2. Make an incision in each potato ½ inch deep and 2 inches long with the point of a knife. Place potatoes in a baking pan and bake until tender, 45 minutes to 1 hour.

3. When cool enough to handle, peel the potatoes. Chop into chunks and pass through a food mill or ricer into a medium bowl.

4. Add the salt, egg, and half the flour, and mix with your hands or a wooden spoon. Add the remaining flour ¼ cup at a time until the dough starts to form a ball. If the dough is too sticky, add the rest of the flour a little at a time until the stickiness is gone.

5. Turn out the dough onto a floured work surface and knead lightly for about 3 to 4 minutes, adding more flour only if necessary. Remember, if you add too much flour, the gnocchi will get tough. The gnocchi dough is ready when it is soft and pliable. Do not overwork the dough.

Pasta, Rice,
Gnocchi,
and Polenta

6. Cut the dough into equal pieces the size of a small egg. Flour your hands lightly and, using both your hands, roll each piece back and forth into a coil about ½ inch in diameter, about the diameter of your little finger. Cut each roll into ½ inch pieces.

7. To form the gnocchi, use either a fork or a ridged butter press and follow the instructions for Ricotta Gnocchi on page 137. Move the formed gnocchi onto the prepared baking sheets. Cover each layer of gnocchi with a piece of parchment paper so they don't stick together.

8. Cook the gnocchi according to the instructions on page 137 and serve with the sauce of your choice.

Yield: 4 to 8 servings (depending on appetite
and what else is being served)

NOTES

The potatoes may be baked in advance. Pass them through the food mill or ricer when you are ready to make the dough.

Store leftover cooked gnocchi in the refrigerator in covered containers; they will keep for several days. To reheat, sauté quickly in a skillet or heat in the microwave until hot. I do not recommend freezing cooked gnocchi.

Spinach Gnocchi

Gnocchi di Spinaci

Preparation Time: 1 hour or more (varies according to experience),
plus 45 minutes to 1 hour for baking the potatoes.

Cooking Time: 2 to 4 minutes

1 pound Russet or Idaho potatoes, washed and dried

1½ pounds fresh spinach, washed, drained, and spun dry

2 tablespoons extra-virgin olive oil

Salt and freshly ground black pepper (a sprinkling)

1¼ cups or more unbleached all-purpose flour

1 egg, beaten

2 tablespoons salt

5 quarts water

1 tablespoon salt (additional)

PROCEDURE

1. Preheat the oven to 375°F. Line two baking sheets with parchment or wax paper, dust lightly with flour, and set aside.

2. Make an incision in each potato ½ inch deep and 2 inches long with the point of a knife. Place the potatoes in a baking pan and bake until tender, 45 minutes to 1 hour.

3. Prepare the spinach according to the directions for Spinach with Garlic and Olive Oil (page 29), omitting the garlic. Squeeze as much water as possible from the spinach and chop *very fine* with a knife.

4. When cool enough to handle, peel the potatoes. Chop into chunks and pass through a food mill or ricer into a medium bowl.

5. Add the spinach, flour, egg, and salt to the potatoes and mix with your hands or a wooden spoon to form a soft dough.

6. Turn the dough out onto a floured work surface and knead lightly for about 3 to 4 minutes, adding more flour if necessary. Remember, if you add too much flour, the gnocchi will get tough. The gnocchi dough is ready when it is soft and pliable. Do not overwork the dough or the gnocchi will be heavy.

7. Cut the dough into equal pieces the size of a small egg. Flour your hands lightly and, using both your hands, roll each piece back and forth into a coil about ½ inch in diameter, about the diameter of your little finger. Cut each roll

Pasta, Rice,
Gnocchi,
and Polenta

into ½-inch pieces. To form the gnocchi, use either a fork or ridged butter press and follow the instructions for Ricotta Gnocchi on page 137. Move the formed gnocchi onto the prepared baking sheets and dust with flour. Cover each layer of gnocchi with a piece of parchment paper so they don't stick together.

8. Cook the gnocchi according to the instructions on page 137 and serve with the sauce of your choice.

Yield: 4 to 8 servings (depending on appetites
and what else is being served)

NOTES

The potatoes may be baked in advance. Pass them through the food mill or ricer when you are ready to make the dough.

Store any leftover cooked gnocchi in covered container in the refrigerator; they will keep for several days. To reheat, sauté quickly in a skillet or heat in the microwave until hot. I do not recommend freezing cooked gnocchi.

Antipasti tray: Rice Balls (page 93); Roasted Red, Green, and Yellow Peppers with Anchovies (page 79) mingled with rolled proscuitto; St. Joseph's Cauliflower and Broccoli Fritters (page 37); Rice Balls cut in half; assortment of olives; Stuffed Mushrooms (page 83); Red Roasted Peppers Stuffed with Capers (page 15)

Variety of antipasti: Sweet and Sour Olives (page 85); Olive Salad; Homemade Fresh Ricotta with Olives (page 8); Marinated Sun-Dried Tomatoes (page 18); Marinated Mushrooms (page 13)

Tortelloni with
Mushroom Sauce
(page 119)

Orecchiette with
Sautéed Broccoli
(page 249);
Spaghetti with
Bolognese Meat
Sauce (page 125);
Mini Rigatoni with
Olive Paste Sauce
(page 129)

Assorted Breads

Assorted pizza slices (page 188): Plain with Marinara Sauce; Marinara with Assorted Vegetables; White Pizza with Olives; Mushrooms and Ricotta

Boned Stuffed Roast Leg of Lamb (page 193); Roasted Potatoes with Cheese and Herbs (page 252)

Stuffed Pork Tenderloin (page 201); Asparagus with Pancetta and caramelized nuts (page 244)

Fresh Sausage
(page 196),
Panini (page
177), and Fried
Green and Red
Peppers (page
242)

Spinach Gnocchi
with Salmon Sauce
(pages 141 and
143); Potato Gnoc-
chi with Spinach
Sauce (pages 139
and 144); Ricotta
Gnocchi with Mari-
nara Sauce (pages
137 and 5)

Baked Chicken with
Potatoes and Vegeta-
bles (page 208)

Dad's Quick Sautéed
Steak with Mush-
rooms (page 203)

Breaded Chicken
Cutlets with
Marinara Sauce
and Mozzarella
(pages 52 and 5);
Meatless "Cut-
lets" (page 218);
Baby Peas with
Sun-Dried Toma-
toes and Toasted
Pine Nuts (page
241)

Stuffed Turkey
Breast (page 216);
Green Beans with
Balsamic Vinegar
and Oregano
(page 239)

❧❧ Elegant Shrimp with Spinach Stuffing (page 229)

Risotto with Seafood (page 132)

Mussels in Spicy Marinara (page 88)

Magnificent Stuffed Artichokes (page 90)

Chocolate Custard Cream (page 278); Ricotta Cloud Cream (page 280); Mama Rosa's Lemon Custard Cream (page 73)

Salmon Sauce

Salsa di Salmone

Preparation Time: 5 minutes • Cooking Time: 5 minutes

This elegant, creamy sauce makes a little salmon go a long way. I created it to be used over gnocchi, but it also marries well with vegetables and fish and other varieties of pasta.

¼ pound smoked salmon, flaked, divided
2 cups heavy cream
⅛ teaspoon freshly ground nutmeg

Salt and freshly ground black pepper
1 tablespoon chopped fresh chives
Leaves from 1 sprig fresh thyme

PROCEDURE

1. Place a small saucepan on medium heat. Add the cream and nutmeg and heat until very hot but not boiling. Reduce the heat. Add half the smoked salmon and simmer on low for 4 minutes. Taste for seasonings and adjust accordingly.

2. Place in a food processor or blender and puree. Return to the stove, add the herbs, and keep on warm until ready to use. To prevent a skin from forming on the sauce, place a piece of plastic wrap directly over the surface.

3. Serve immediately, while it is nice and hot.

Yield: 2 cups sauce; 4 to 6 servings—
will sauce 1 pound pasta or 1½ pounds gnocchi

NOTES

This sauce can be made the morning you plan to use it; store it in the refrigerator until needed. Heat and use. Store any leftover sauce in the refrigerator in covered containers; it will keep for several days. I do not recommend freezing this sauce.

Pasta, Rice,
Gnocchi,
and Polenta

Spinach Sauce

Salsa di Spinaci

Preparation Time: 10 minutes • Cooking Time: 10 minutes

This elegant, versatile, easy sauce has a mild favor and is well suited for any of the gnocchi recipes in this book. It is also a wonderful sauce to serve with fish, veal, or chicken or over pasta.

1 pound fresh spinach (baby spinach is best), washed, drained, and dried
2 shallots, minced
1 clove garlic, minced
2 tablespoons extra-virgin olive oil
¼ teaspoon salt

⅛ teaspoon freshly ground black pepper
⅛ teaspoon freshly ground nutmeg
2 cups heavy cream, divided
⅓ cup freshly grated Parmigiano-Reggiano cheese

PROCEDURE

1. Place the spinach, shallots, garlic, oil, salt, pepper, and nutmeg in a re-closable plastic freezer bag. Close the bag, leaving an inch of open space for ventilation. Shake the bag to evenly distribute the seasonings.

2. Place the bag in the microwave and cook on High power for 4 minutes.

3. Place in the food processor or blender and puree with ½ cup of the heavy cream.

4. In a medium saucepan, combine the rest of the cream, the pureed spinach, and the cheese. Stir and cook on medium-low until the sauce is very hot but not boiling; continue cooking on low for an additional 2 minutes. Adjust for seasoning. Serve warm. To prevent a skin from forming over the sauce, place a sheet of plastic wrap directly on the surface until ready to use.

Yield: 2½ cups; 6 to 8 servings—
will sauce 1½ pounds gnocchi or 1 pound pasta

NOTES

Store any leftover sauce in the refrigerator in covered containers for up to 2 days. It can be frozen for up to 2 months. To reheat, defrost and microwave until hot; do not boil.

Semolina Polenta with Broccoli

Polenta di Semonno con Broccoli

Preparation Time: 15 minutes

Cooking Time: 25 minutes, including boiling and sautéing the broccoli

This is an unusual way to make polenta. Our family has been making it this way for years. Most polenta is made using cornmeal as its base, but that is not the case with this old-time favorite. My dad grew his own wheat, so we used semolina to make our polenta. My mother would add various ingredients to make it more nutritious and delicious. Sometimes she would use broccoli, zucchini, or Swiss chard, and on special occasions when we had leftover cooked sausages, she would cut them up and toss them in toward the end of the cooking cycle. She would serve it with slices of bread that would be torn into large chunks and placed around the rim of the bowls. The polenta would go in the center, covering up portions of the bread. Because polenta is rather thick, we would then use the bread chunks as spoons to eat it. I continue to serve it this way.

This recipe uses the simple techniques of sautéing the broccoli in extra-virgin olive oil with a little onion and garlic, and uses the Marinara Sauce that you may already have in your freezer.

Crusty Italian bread
8½ cups of cold water
1½ tablespoons salt, divided
1 large head of broccoli, cut into
    florets, washed
¼ cups extra-virgin olive oil

1 medium onion, chopped
3 cloves garlic, chopped (about
    1½ teaspoons)
1 cup Marinara Sauce (page 5)
1¼ cups semolina

PROCEDURE

1. Cut slices of crusty bread into finger-long slices.

2. Bring the water to a boil in a large, deep, heavy-gauge sauce pot over high heat. When the water comes to a boil, add 1 tablespoon of the salt and the broccoli florets. Bring the water back to a boil and boil the broccoli for 4 to 5 minutes or until it is fork-tender. Remove the broccoli with a slotted spoon,

and place in a bowl that has been fitted with a colander. Reserve pan with broccoli cooking liquid.

3. Place a large skillet over medium-high heat. When the skillet is warm, add the oil. When the oil is hot, add the onion. Stir and sauté for 4 minutes; then add the garlic and stir and sauté for an additional 2 minutes. Add the broccoli, and stir sauté the mixture for 4 minutes.

4. While the broccoli is sautéing, bring the sauce pot with the broccoli-cooking liquid back to a boil over medium-high heat. Add the Marinara Sauce and sautéed broccoli. Stir and reduce the heat to medium-low, a gentle simmer.

5. Start adding the semolina by handfuls, in a fine, steady stream, very slowly, stirring constantly with a long-handled wooded spoon. You are trying to avoid making lumps. Cook the polenta at a simmer for another 7 to 10 minutes, until thick, stirring continuously, allowing the semolina to cook and the flavors to blend throughout. As it cooks, it will thicken, which is why you need a long-handled spoon for stirring; it has the tendency to act like an erupting volcano and bubble upward. Keep stirring, and if you see any lumps of semolina, break them up. If it is too thin, add a little more semolina. If it is too thick, add a little bit of water.

6. Place the sliced bread around the edges of the soup bowls. Ladle hot polenta into the bowls. The bread is actually half in the polenta, with half sticking out from the rim. You can use these strips of bread like spoons, spooning the polenta into your mouth as you bite the bread.

Yield: 6 servings

NOTES

If you prefer to use cornmeal, by all means do so. Use your favorite plain polenta recipe and add the rest of the ingredients on page 145.

Homemade broths (pages 59–63) can be used instead of water to cook the polenta, making for an even more nutritious dish.

Store any leftover polenta in the refrigerator in covered containers; it will keep for 3 days. To reheat the polenta, place it in the microwave or heat in a saucepan with the addition of a little broth or water. Stir and heat until hot. I do not recommend freezing polenta.

SOUPS

Soups can be simple or elegant, light or robust and substantial. Soups have always been an integral part of the Italian diet, with each region boasting its own versions and specialties. In an Italian dinner, soup is often served as the first course, or it can become the main meal when served with a salad and bread. Soup can also be served as a light lunch.

In the spring, fall, and winter months, I love preparing, serving, and eating large bowls of soup. From the moment the ingredients are placed into the boiling liquids, the fragrance begins to fill my kitchen, slowly filtering throughout the house.

The ingredients used for making most soups are modest and unpretentious. Many soups are water-based, while some draw from broths made from poultry and meat. Others are made more substantial by using rice, pasta, legumes, or a portion of their own ingredients pureed to thicken them.

For the most part, the soup recipes you will find in this

book are hearty peasant fare with basic ingredients, producing soups that are more nutritious with a great source of protein and fiber while yielding a taste that is memorable. These recipes use simple techniques that I have learned from my mother. Feel free to vary the ingredients, add the vegetables you prefer, and use what you have on hand in your refrigerator and cupboard. My hope is that you will get excited by these recipes, become familiar with them, and explore creating your own.

You may choose to make many of the soups in this chapter more nutritious and filling by converting them into main-course meals with the addition of cooked pastas, homemade or store bought. Some suggestions are the smaller-shaped varieties of dry pasta such as ditaline, tubettini, stelle, or orzo.

There are some problems to avoid when using cooked pastas in soups: 1. Do not cook the pasta in your soup, the pasta will absorb most of the liquid. 2. Do not put your cooked pasta into the soup until you are almost ready to serve; the longer it sits in hot soup the more liquid the pasta will absorb, leaving you with overcooked, mushy pasta and too little broth. 3. Place only enough pasta into the soup for your meal. Leftover pasta in soup when reheated gets mushy. Keep these three points in mind and you will produce perfect soup with pasta every time.

Using garnishes adds visual appeal and textural contrast to your soups, exciting your taste buds. Garnishes are not complicated, and often only take seconds to prepare. Some choices include chopped chives or scallions, herbs, grated or slivered cheese, zest from citrus, toasted nuts, a drizzle of extra-virgin olive oil, or freshly ground black pepper.

Chicken Soup with Meatballs

Zuppa di Pollo con Polpettine

Preparation Time: 30 minutes

*Cooking Time: 2 hours, plus 10 minutes for cooking the meatballs
and 10 minutes for making the pasta*

My mother-in-law Connie's chicken soup, which included her special pasta that she rolled out by hand, ranks among my favorite things she made for us. We would always go looking from store to store for old hens. When we were able to find them, she was almost satisfied; after all, the older the chicken, the more flavorful the broth. She would always say, no matter how many frying chickens you use, the soup will always taste like *acqua salata,* salted water. When she cooked for us, she would always apologize that it wasn't quite tasty enough, not like the good old days. We would all laugh, compliment her on the meal, and ask for seconds. What a ritual!

On the other hand, my own mother believes strongly that a good soup depends on adding extra chicken bones from the back, ribs, and neck. She had her butcher, Giuseppe, save extra bones for her. If you don't have a butcher like Giuseppe, the supermarkets sometimes have the backs packaged up and labeled for soup. So, is it bones that make a good soup or the age of the chicken? What can I say? They're both right.

The soup is traditionally served with small-shaped pasta nestled among tiny meatballs. The choice of pasta is yours. For those watching calories, eliminate the pasta or use only very little for added texture and taste. The decision is one of personal taste.

For the Soup Base:

4 quarts cold water

1½ tablespoons salt

1 whole chicken or hen (4 to 5 pounds), skin on, plus any extra bones you have saved up in the freezer (or ask your butcher for chicken backs, necks, and wings)

3 carrots, peeled and sliced into ¼-inch pieces

3 ribs celery, sliced into ½-inch pieces

1 medium onion, peeled and quartered

(cont'd)

4 whole Italian plum tomatoes,
    skinned (see page 3), seeded,
    and chopped
3 sprigs Italian flat-leaf parsley,
    washed and chopped
½ teaspoon freshly ground black
    pepper
Salt to taste

For the Meatballs:
½ pound lean ground beef
2 large eggs beaten lightly
1 tablespoon freshly grated Romano
    cheese
1 teaspoon finely chopped Italian
    flat-leaf parsley
1 scallion, white part only, minced

½ teaspoon salt
⅛ teaspoon freshly ground black
    pepper
2 to 3 tablespoons bread crumbs
1 quart water

For Finishing the Soup:
1 celery heart, including leaves,
    chopped (added during the last
    5 minutes of cooking the soup, it
    gives a wonderful fresh burst of
    flavor)
5 quarts cold water
1 tablespoon salt
Freshly grated Romano cheese, for
    the table

PROCEDURE

To Make the Soup Base:

1. Rinse the chicken under cold running water, inside and out, and drain in a colander. Rub about 2 teaspoons of the salt in the chicken's cavity and over the outside.

2. Place the chicken (along with any bits and pieces of leftover chicken you may have in the freezer) in a large stockpot and fill it with the 4 quarts of water, making sure the chicken is completely submerged in water by at least 1 to 2 inches. Add more water if necessary. Place the stockpot on high heat. When the water comes to a boil, skim off any foam that comes to the surface with a slotted spoon.

3. Add the carrots, celery, onion, tomatoes, parsley, and pepper and the rest of the salt. Bring back to a boil, reduce the heat to medium-low, and simmer for 2 hours

To Make the Meatballs:

1. While the soup is cooking, make the meatballs. In a medium bowl, combine the meat, eggs, cheese, parsley, scallion, salt, and pepper. Add the bread crumbs and mix. The mixture will be sticky and semi-firm. The mixture *should* be sticky but hold together, adding the minimum of bread crumbs will make the meatballs more tender. Let the mixture rest for 5 minutes to firm up.

2. Place a sheet of wax or parchment paper on your work surface. Wet your hands lightly with water, roll a small amount of the meat mixture into a ball the diameter of a quarter, and place the meatball on the wax paper. Repeat until all the mixture has been used. You should have about 40 meatballs. Wetting your hands periodically will allow you to roll them more easily!

To Assemble the Soup:

1. After the soup has cooked for 2 hours, remove the chicken and reserve for another use. (When you have a chance, remove the chicken from the bones and store in the refrigerator in a covered container.) Strain the soup through a sieve, discard the solids, and bring the soup back to a low boil. Add the celery heart and leaves and reduce the heat to warm. Taste for seasonings and adjust accordingly.

2. In a separate pot, bring the 1 quart water to a rolling boil. Add the meatballs one at a time to the boiling water, reduce the heat to medium, and cook for 7 to 10 minutes. The meatballs will rise to the surface when cooked. Remove with a slotted spoon and drop into the soup.

3. You need to remove all the fat that has risen to the surface of the soup. If you are going to eat the soup the same day you make it, defat the soup by putting a paper towel on the surface and allowing it to soak up any fat floating on the surface. Repeat with fresh pieces of paper towel until all the fat has been removed. If you are making the soup in advance, refrigerate it. By the next day the fat will have solidified on the surface like a disk. Simply lift it off and discard it.

4. If using pasta, prepare it now. Bring a large pot of water to boil. Add 1 tablespoon salt and the pasta. If you're using homemade pasta, boil for 1 to 2 minutes, just until tender. If using dry pasta, follow the instructions on the package, but check for doneness *2 minutes earlier* than directed. Drain and add to the soup.

5. Serve the soup piping hot, and sprinkle with freshly grated Romano cheese on top, if desired.

Yield: 8 main-course servings (about 16 cups)

Soups

NOTES

This soup can be stored in the refrigerator for 3 days or in the freezer for up to 2 months. Remove the cooked chicken from the bones. Use the cooked chicken for another meal, such as in the Chicken Salad on page 215, or reserve it for sandwiches or other dishes. If you prefer, you can shred some of it and place it back in the soup. Although the soup itself freezes well, I do not recommend freezing the chicken from the soup.

Chicken and meatball soup can be transformed into the traditional Italian Wedding Soup by following these simple instructions: 1. Take 1 head of escarole, disengage the leaves, and wash them until all the sand and soil have been removed. Drain and chop the leaves into large pieces. Boil them in 4 quarts water until wilted and tender, about 3 minutes. Then drain and set aside. 2. In a medium bowl, lightly beat 4 eggs along with ¼ cup freshly grated Romano cheese, 2 tablespoons chopped fresh Italian flat-leaf parsley, ¼ teaspoon salt, and ¼ teaspoon freshly ground black pepper. 3. Add the escarole to the soup along with 2 cups of cooked small pasta. Take your egg mixture and add to the soup in a steady stream, stirring as you go. The egg will cook almost instantly as it hits the soup. Serve immediately.

Soup with Kohlrabi

Minestra di Cavoli

Preparation Time: 20 minutes • Cooking Time: 30 to 45 minutes

This soup always reminds me of my dad, who enjoyed eating it so much. It is simple, prepared with basic ingredients that are easily available. It's the combination of ingredients, with their unique flavors, textures, and colors that gives this soup its outstanding taste and appearance.

Kohlrabi is available sporadically all year round in most supermarkets. The peak growing season runs from May to August. When purchasing kohlrabi, look for small to medium bulbs that are firm and light green in color. Stalks and leaves should be firm, moist, crisp, and green. Refrigerate kohlrabi in plastic bags for up to 1 week.

2 bunches kohlrabi (about 3 pounds)
¼ cup extra-virgin olive oil
1 large yellow cooking onion, chopped
4 cloves garlic, chopped (about 2 teaspoons)
1½ tablespoons salt, divided
½ teaspoon freshly ground black pepper, divided

12 cups cold water
2 cups Marinara Sauce, from your freezer (page 5)
1 tablespoon Pesto from your freezer (page 25) or 5 leaves fresh basil
½ pound pasta (small variety)
Freshly grated Romano cheese, for the table

PROCEDURE

1. Cut the stems and leaves from the kohlrabi bulbs. Discard any leaves that are old, wilted, yellow, or damaged. Wash the leaves and stems in a large bowl of cold water, swishing the leaves around to disengage any soil or dirt. Remove the water and drain in a colander. Repeat until the water in the bowl is clear.

2. Cut the leaves from the stalks and place in separate piles. Chop the leaves into bite-size pieces and either spin or towel-dry and place in large bowl. Cut the stalks into ½-inch pieces, and place in the bowl with the leaves. Set aside.

3. Peel the kohlrabi bulbs with a paring knife, cut in half, and then into ½-inch diced pieces. Place in a separate bowl and set aside.

4. Place a large, heavy-gauge nonreactive sauce pot over medium-high heat. When the sauce pot is warm, add the oil. When the oil is hot, add the onion, and stir and sauté for 4 minutes. Add the garlic, and stir and sauté for an additional 2 minutes.

5. Add the kohlrabi bulbs to the onion-and-garlic mixture. Stir and season with ½ teaspoon of the salt and ½ teaspoon of the pepper. Continue to sauté for another 5 minutes. Add the stalks and leaves; stir and sauté for another 4 minutes.

6. Add the water, the remaining 1 tablespoon salt, and the Marinara Sauce and Pesto. Stir and bring to a boil. Reduce the heat to medium-low. Put the cover on slightly askew and cook the soup for an additional 20 minutes or so, until the kohlrabi is tender and the soup is flavored throughout. Taste for seasoning and adjust accordingly.

7. If you are going to add pasta to the soup, follow the directions on page 148.

8. Serve the soup piping hot, with a small sprinkling of freshly grated cheese.

Yield: 16 cups; 8 servings as a main course

NOTES

Sometimes you will see kohlrabi with their bulbs and stalks a violet-purplish color. Don't let this confuse you; the flavor is the same.

Store any leftovers in the refrigerator in covered containers; this soup will keep for up to 5 days. It freezes very well and will keep in the freezer for up to 4 months.

Lentil and Pumpkin Soup

Minestra di Lenticchie e Zucca

Preparation Time: 15 minutes • Cooking Time: 1 hour

Lentils are tiny, lens-shaped legumes that grow in pods and are sold podded and dried. They may be purchased in grocery stores, natural foods markets, and specialty stores. The most common variety, and the least expensive, is grayish brown, but they are also available in yellow and red.

I have eaten lentil soup ever since I can remember, and no matter how many times I prepare it in its many variations, I always get the same feeling of wholesomeness and goodness. This is one of my favorite vegetarian recipes. Lentils are inexpensive, nutritious, hearty, filling, and, when prepared properly, absolutely delicious.

1 pound lentils (2 cups)
4 quarts cold water
¼ cup extra-virgin olive oil, divided
1 medium-large yellow cooking
   onion, coarsely chopped
4 cloves garlic, chopped
   (about 2 teaspoons)
2 carrots, peeled and cut into
   ¼-inch slices
2 celery stalks, cut into ¼-inch
   slices
1 tablespoon salt, divided
1½ teaspoons freshly ground black
   pepper, divided
½ cup canned Italian plum

tomatoes, seeded (see page 3)
   and chopped
Several sprigs parsley and thyme,
   leaves only
1 bay leaf
2 (28-ounce) cans pumpkin (or
   equivalent fresh if in season)

Optional:
1 lemon, cut into 1/16-inch slices
Extra-virgin olive oil, to drizzle on
   soup
Freshly grated Romano cheese, to
   sprinkle on the soup

PROCEDURE

1. Remove any foreign material from the lentils. Sort and rinse them under cold water and then drain, before cooking.

2. Place the washed lentils in a large stockpot along with the 4 quarts cold water. Heat on medium-high until the water starts to come to a boil, reduce the heat, and, with a slotted spoon, remove any foam and lentils that come to the surface. Continue to simmer on medium heat, covered, but with the lid tilted to allow some steam to escape, making sure that the soup is on a slow boil, for 30 minutes.

3. While the lentils are cooking, place a large skillet over medium-high heat. When the skillet is warm, add 2 tablespoons of the olive oil. When the olive oil is hot, add the onion and garlic and cook for 3 minutes, until tender. Add the carrots, celery, 1 teaspoon of the salt, and ½ teaspoon of the pepper and cook for 5 to 7 minutes. Set aside.

4. After the lentils have cooked for 30 minutes, add the sautéed vegetables mixture, tomatoes, herbs, 2 teaspoons of the salt, and ½ teaspoon of the pepper and continue to cook over medium heat for another 30 minutes, or until the vegetables and lentils are tender and cooked. Be sure to stir soup occasionally to prevent it from scorching.

5. During the last 5 minutes of cooking, add the pumpkin and the remaining salt and pepper, stirring well. Taste for seasonings and adjust accordingly. (You may need to add more salt.) Remove the bay leaf and discard.

6. Ladle the hot soup into individual bowls, drizzle 1 teaspoon extra-virgin olive oil over the top of each bowl and sprinkle with Romano cheese. Garnish with a lemon slice on the edge of the bowl. Serve with homemade bread and a green salad. Enjoy!

Yield: 8 servings, plus leftovers to freeze

NOTES

Because of the starchiness of the lentils and pumpkin, this soup will thicken considerably as it sits. Thin leftover soup or frozen soup with some broth or water. To alter this recipe just a bit, try sautéing ¼ pound of pancetta with the onions and garlic.

Store soup in the refrigerator in covered containers; it will keep for up to 5 days. It freezes very well and will keep in the freezer for up to 4 months. To serve frozen soup, defrost overnight in the refrigerator and heat in the microwave or on the stove.

For a wonderful lentil salad, try cooking them in vegetable broth and adding a combination of fresh herbs such as mint, thyme, oregano, marjoram, basil, or parsley. Drain and serve warm or at room temperature with oil and vinegar as a side dish. You will be surprised what a nice addition it makes to a meal.

Split Pea and Barley Soup

Minestra di Piselli Secchi con Orzo

Preparation Time: 20 minutes • Cooking Time: 1 hour

This is a thick, nutritious, stick-to-the-ribs soup, with the barley adding a silky, chewy texture. It is perfect for hearty appetites on cold winter nights, warming the body and enriching the soul. Serve with crusty bread if available. (This is where having bread in the freezer comes in handy.)

Split peas are a variety of field peas that are grown specifically for drying. The whole pea is dried and then split along a natural seam (hence its name). Green or yellow split peas are sold in 1-pound packages or in bulk. I do not find a noticeable difference in the taste between the green or yellow, although the green peas are the most common. Before using split peas, you should look them over carefully and pick out any foreign materials such as soil particles or tiny stones. Discard any peas that are discolored, shriveled, or have tiny holes in them.

Add salt to the split peas only when they are nearly tender. Salt toughens the skins and slows down the cooking process.

Although this recipe has many ingredients it is very easy to make.

1 pound yellow or green dried split peas, cleaned, rinsed, and drained

3 quarts cold water

2 bay leaves

2 tablespoons chopped fresh Italian flat-leaf parsley

3 sprigs fresh thyme (leaves only, discard stem)

¼ cup extra-virgin olive oil, divided

2 large yellow cooking onions, chopped

4 cloves garlic, chopped (about 2 teaspoons)

4 medium carrots, peeled and cut into ¼-inch slices

3 ribs celery, cut into ¼-inch slices

½ teaspoons salt, divided

¾ teaspoon freshly ground black pepper, divided

4 whole (fresh or canned) Italian plum tomatoes, skinned (see page 3), seeded, and chopped into small pieces

3 tablespoons tomato paste diluted in ½ cup tomato juice from the canned tomatoes

1 cup sherry or dry white wine (optional, but it is a delicious addition)

3 cups cooked barley (see Notes)

PROCEDURE

1. After the peas have been picked over, washed, and drained, place them in a large stockpot. Add the 3 quarts cold water and place on moderate heat. When the pot comes to a full boil, remove any foam that comes to the surface with a slotted spoon. Add the bay leaves, parsley, and thyme. Continue to cook at a slow boil for 30 minutes.

2. While the peas are cooking, place a large skillet over medium-high heat. When the skillet is warm, add 2 tablespoons of the olive oil. When the oil is hot, add the onion and garlic and stir and cook for 4 minutes. Add the remaining 2 tablespoons olive oil, and the carrots and celery. Sauté for 4 minutes. Season with ¼ teaspoon of the salt and ½ teaspoon of the pepper. Add the tomatoes, diluted tomato paste, wine (if using), and the remaining salt and pepper and cook for another 5 minutes.

3. After the peas have cooked for 30 minutes, add the sautéed vegetables to the pot and cook at a low boil for another 30 minutes, stirring occasionally, being careful not to scorch the soup. Taste for seasoning and adjust accordingly. Remove the bay leaves. Add the cooked barley. Stir, and serve piping hot with a nice chunk of homemade bread.

Yield: 14 cups; 8 servings as a main course

NOTES

You can use quick-cooking barley, the 10-minute variety; cook according to the package directions.

Because of the starchiness of the split peas and barley, this soup will thicken considerably as it sets. Thin leftover soup or frozen soup with broth or salted water.

Store leftovers in the refrigerator in a covered container; any leftover soup will keep for up to 5 days. This soup freezes beautifully and will keep in the freezer for up to 6 months. It will come in handy when you're hungry and too tired to cook. Defrost in the refrigerator overnight or in the microwave. Have some crusty bread ready, heat, and eat.

White Kidney Bean Soup

Zuppa di Cannellini

Preparation Time: 10 minutes • Cooking Time: 15 minutes

I developed this recipe as I was searching for a rich-tasting, thick, nutritious vegetarian soup resembling a bisque, but with no butter or heavy cream. Cannellini are a white Italian bean similar to the red kidney bean, but with a more delicate flavor and a more tender skin. The sun-dried tomatoes are added at the very end, when the soup is removed from the stove and you are ready to ladle out the portions. Their highly concentrated flavor, vibrant red color, and unique texture gives a last-minute dazzle to this quick-and-easy recipe.

5 (19-ounce) cans white kidney beans (cannellini), divided
¼ cup extra-virgin olive oil
1 medium yellow cooking onion, chopped
6 cloves garlic, finely chopped (about 1 tablespoon)
2 tablespoons Pesto from your freezer (page 25)
2 sprigs fresh thyme (leaves only)
2 tablespoons chopped Italian flat-leaf parsley

1 cup dry sherry or dry white wine
4 cups whole milk (see Notes)
1 teaspoon salt
¼ teaspoon freshly ground black pepper
6 marinated Sun-Dried Tomato halves, chopped (page 18)
½ cup freshly grated Romano or Parmigiano-Reggiano cheese

PROCEDURE

1. Drain, rinse, and puree 2 of the cans of beans. Drain and rinse the other 3 cans and leave the beans whole.

2. Place a medium-size saucepan over medium heat. When the saucepan is warm, add the oil. When the oil is hot (indicated by ripples on the surface of the oil), add the onion and cook until tender, about 4 minutes. Add the garlic and cook until golden, 2 to 3 minutes. Add the pesto, thyme, parsley, and sherry and cook for another minute.

3. Add the pureed beans, whole beans, milk, salt, and pepper and heat to

boiling, stirring frequently. Turn the heat to low and simmer for 5 minutes, stirring occasionally. Taste for seasoning and adjust accordingly. Remove from the heat and serve immediately, or keep warm until ready to serve.

4. When ready to serve, make sure the soup is nice and hot, remove from the stove, and stir in the sun-dried tomatoes. Ladle into individual soup bowls, sprinkle with cheese, and serve piping hot with homemade bread or focaccia.

Yield: about 10 cups; 8 servings

NOTES

Use any leftover soup to sauce pasta for an impromptu meal.

In this recipe I have used canned beans. You may use dried beans if you wish. To prepare them for this recipe, follow the instructions on the package, using the whole package (1 pound), adding 1 bay leaf, several thyme sprigs, and 2 crushed cloves garlic. Puree half the cooked beans and follow the instructions on page 159. Dry cannellini beans can be purchased at specialty markets, natural foods stores, and at some grocery stores. If you cannot find dry cannellini beans, substitute Great Northern beans.

For a leaner version of this dish, substitute chicken broth or vegetable broth for all or part of the milk. It still tastes delicious. For a richer version, substitute 4 cups half-and-half for the whole milk.

Store the soup in the refrigerator in covered containers; it will keep for 4 days or in the freezer for up to 2 months.

Squash and Potato Stew

Spezzatino con Zucca e Patate

Preparation Time: 15 minutes

Cooking Time: 45 minutes to 1 hour, depending on the size of the vegetable pieces

This dish is inexpensive to make, very tasty, filling, and satisfying—perfect to serve in the fall, winter, and early spring. Whenever I make this dish, I think of my mother, who loved to make it for me, and of my mother-in-law, for whom I in turn made it during the last years of her life.

This soup can be made with zucchini, but if you can get it when it is in season, try using a type of squash called *cucuzza*. It is light green in color with a diameter of about 3 to 4 inches. They grow quite long, between 16 and 20 inches, and most always have an unusual curve. The skin is a little thicker than the zucchini and the flesh firmer, with fewer seeds in the center. Cucuzza is grown throughout Italy but is very popular in Sicily. It is also harvested in the U.S. and has become popular in many upscale restaurants. Last summer at our local outdoor farmers' market, I spotted a vendor selling cucuzza at his booth. I was not the only one delighted at finding cucuzza that day; there were five other women of different backgrounds: Indian, Mexican, Spanish, and Asian. Among us, we bought the whole case. If you garden, you might try growing your own! The seeds are now available in many seed catalogs.

¼ cup extra-virgin olive oil

1 large yellow cooking onion, cut in half and sliced

1 clove garlic, minced (about ½ teaspoon)

1½ pounds potatoes, peeled and cut into large bite-size chunks

2 carrots, peeled and cut into ½-inch slices

2 to 2½ pounds cucuzza, peeled and cut into large bite-size chunks (or substitute zucchini if unavailable—see Notes)

1½ teaspoons salt

½ teaspoon freshly ground black pepper

1 (16-ounce) can Italian plum tomatoes with juice, seeded (see page 3) and chopped (pass the juice through a strainer to remove seeds)

½ cup water

1 tablespoon chopped Italian flat-leaf parsley

6 basil leaves, chopped, divided

1 cup frozen baby peas

PROCEDURE

1. Place a large, heavy-bottomed saucepan over medium-high heat. When the saucepan is warm, add the oil. When the oil is hot (indicated by ripples on the surface of the oil), add the onions and garlic and sauté for 3 minutes. Add the potatoes and carrots and stir to coat with oil. Cook for 5 minutes, stirring occasionally.

2. Add the squash, salt, and pepper, and stir and cook for another 5 minutes. Add the tomatoes and juice, water, parsley, and half the basil. Bring to a boil, reduce the heat, cover, and cook gently over low heat for another 20 to 30 minutes, or until the vegetables are tender.

3. Add the peas and the rest of the basil. Taste for seasoning and adjust accordingly. Cook, covered, for an additional 5 minutes, until the peas have defrosted. Serve hot, with homemade bread.

Yield: 8 servings for main course

NOTES

If you cannot find cucuzza, use zucchini or yellow squash and allow 10 minutes less cooking time.

To serve this as a vegetable course, omit the tomato juice. It will be too runny on the plate.

Store squash stew in the refrigerator in covered containers; it will keep for up to 5 days. If making batches to freeze, undercook it a little; it will keep in the freezer for several months.

BREADS, PIZZA, AND FOCACCIA

For me, nothing comes close to the joy, pleasure, and sense of satisfaction I receive from the total process of bread-making. I venture to say that it can be a spiritual and sensual experience to witness how the combinations of such elemental ingredients as flour, water, yeast, and salt can transform into beautiful tableaux of loaves whose aroma and shapes evoke associations of home, love, and nurturing.

Pizza is a very simple food made from a basic bread dough. The dough is flattened and stretched and then flavored with a variety of fresh sauces, seasonings, and toppings. Focaccia is a much humbler form of pizza; it is a flatbread adorned with only a few seasonings. A variety of ingredients can be worked into the dough or, like pizza, used as toppings.

The decision to bake bread requires a commitment of time and energy, so attempt it only when you have the freedom to truly enjoy the experience. Eventually, you will become so confident that you will in turn teach your family and friends.

About Bread-Making

There are only a few basic ingredients in bread. Some are constant and others you can choose to vary if you like.

FLOUR

The best loaves of bread are made using flour from hard wheat kernels. Hard wheat flour has a higher protein content. In the protein is the gluten, which, along with the yeast, aids in the rising process.

All-purpose unbleached flour, a blend of hard and soft wheat flour with a protein content of 12 to 14 percent, is very good for bread-making. For a more substantial, nutritious loaf of bread, combine unbleached all-purpose flour with various grains, oats, seeds, and nuts. You will get a denser bread. It usually takes more yeast per cup of flour to raise multigrain breads.

YEAST

Yeast is a living microscopic organism that is in the air and thrives on the natural sugars in starch. When yeast combines with moisture and warmth, it begins to ferment, which is necessary for rising, converting the flour's starchy nutrients into alcohol and carbon dioxide gas. Gas bubbles trapped in the protein part of the flour make it rise. As the liberated carbon dioxide expands, the bread rises. When the bread is baked in the oven, the heat of the oven stops the fermentation process, and the carbon dioxide gases are passed off as a vapor.

Active dry yeast, which can be found in most supermarkets, natural foods stores or baking supply outlets, can be purchased in small ¼-ounce packets (each containing a scant tablespoon) or in bulk packages. Dry yeast comes in two forms—regular (as required for recipes in this book) and quick-rising. All active dry yeast has been dehydrated; its cells are still alive but in a dormant state. It is activated by the addition of warm liquid, usually water. Quick-rising yeast works more rapidly than active dry yeast, leavening bread 30 to 50 percent faster. However, keep in mind that the best breads are usually the result of a slower rise process.

Store dry yeast in the refrigerator or freezer. The dry yeast sold in small packets is dated on the envelope and should be used before that time. Dry yeast will last longer stored in the refrigerator, and when placed in the freezer will last for at least a year. Always store fresh compressed yeast in the refrigerator or freezer. It will keep for up to 2 weeks in the refrigerator and up to 6 months in the freezer.

Some important items to remember:

- One package of yeast will leaven 5 to 7 cups of all-purpose flour.
- Doughs that are rich in eggs, butter, sweeteners, fruit, or nuts usually require double the amount of yeast.
- Too much yeast will produce a porous texture and an overly yeasty flavor.
- Too little yeast with a short rising time creates a heavy, dense bread.
- Yeast dough that is allowed to rise and fall a couple of times during the dough-making will have an improved texture and a wonderful nutty flavor. Better breads are often the result of a slower rising process.

LIQUIDS

More often than not, water is the liquid used in bread-making. Milk makes the dough richer and stronger. The amount of liquid varies depending on the type of grains used and their absorbency. For plain Italian bread, water alone is sufficient and gives the bread a better texture.

SALT

Salt improves the flavor.

FAT

Butter or oil may be added to give a richer flavor and a softer crumb.

EGGS

Eggs create a tastier, richer, more nutritious loaf.

SUGAR

A small amount of sugar added to the yeast-proofing mixture speeds up the fermentation process.

PROOFING YEAST

Proofing is the process of activating dry yeast. To proof yeast, add the yeast and sugar to warm water (105° to 115°F; use an instant-read thermometer to determine the temperature if you are not sure), stir briefly with a fork, and let dissolve 3 to 5 minutes. The mixture will bubble and foam if the yeast is alive and usable. If it doesn't, the yeast is no longer alive and should be discarded. Start again with new yeast. Proofing your yeast prevents you from mixing all the dough only to find out that it will not rise, thus saving you a lot of time and frustration.

MAKING THE DOUGH

Put the flour into a large bowl, make a well in the center, and add the proofed yeast, liquids, salt, and any other ingredients. With one hand holding the edge of the bowl, use the other hand to incorporate and mix the ingredients until all is well blended. If the dough is sticking to your hand, add more flour a little at a time until the dough pulls away from the sides of the bowl. Be careful; many beginners add too much flour, resulting in drier, dense loaves of bread. A lighter loaf will be formed by a slightly tacky dough. This might be a little messy at first, but don't give up.

KNEADING

Turn the dough out onto a lightly floured surface to knead. Kneading is a technique used to work the dough into a cohesive pliable mass.

There are many acceptable ways to knead bread. Here is my way. I like to think of kneading as a dance, a rhythmic process done by pressing, folding, and turning the mass. If you are using 5 pounds of flour, divide the dough into two pieces to make it more manageable. Push down with the heel of your hand, pulling it over toward you with your fingers. Use the weight of your upper body to put more pressure on the mass of dough, pushing away from the body. Pull and fold half of the dough onto itself, turning the dough a quarter turn (90 degrees) each time. Continue to knead in a rhythmic, rocking motion. If the dough is sticking to the work surface, sprinkle it lightly with flour. Kneading the dough usually takes from 7 to 15 minutes, depending on your experience. You will know when the dough is kneaded enough when it is smooth and elastic and has a nice bounce to it. Place 1 tablespoon of oil in the palm of your hand and rub the dough all over with it.

RISING

Let the dough rise in white unscented plastic bags or in a large bowl covered with plastic wrap until doubled in bulk, about 1½ to 2 hours, in a warm, moist, draft-free atmosphere. One place to consider for this purpose is your oven. If you have a gas stove, the pilot light alone will give a gentle warmth. If you have an electric oven, turn the oven light on, and that works just as well. There is always the furnace room when the furnace is on, or when all else fails simply cover your bowl with a blanket. Once the dough has doubled in bulk, give it a few good punches with your fist and knead briefly to let the gas bubbles escape.

SHAPING THE LOAVES

Form the loaves after the first rising. Sprinkle a baking sheet generously with cornmeal. Form the dough into whatever shape you desire—long thin baguettes, flat round loaves, chunky rectangular loaves, individual rolls, or flat bread—and place on the prepared baking sheet to rise again.

BAKING THE BREAD

After the loaves have doubled in bulk (which usually takes about 45 minutes), position the oven racks, one on the bottom and the other on the second from the top. Preheat oven to between 400°F and 450°F. Place the bread on bottom rack for 15 minutes and then move to the upper rack and continue to bake for an additional 15 minutes, or until the bread is cooked. The crust should be golden brown and the loaf should sound hollow when tapped. Remove from the oven immediately. Transfer the bread from the baking sheet to a wire rack or place on several layers of kitchen towels, to cool.

To store bread for a day or two, place baked, completely cooled loaves in paper bags to help retain a good crust. Any bread that you know you will not be eating in a day or two should be frozen. Bread will keep in the freezer for up to 3 months. To freeze bread, wrap completely cooled bread in aluminum foil and then place in reclosable plastic freezer bags. To serve frozen bread, defrost at room temperature and bake in a preheated 350°F oven for 7 to 10 minutes.

IDEAS FOR SHAPING AND DECORATING

Once you have mastered the technique for making bread, feel free to indulge your artistic side by forming your bread dough into creative shapes. Here are a few suggestions:

- Slash the top of shaped loaves with a very sharp knife. Be assertive and quick, cutting ½ inch into the dough in parallel lines. This creates a simple decorative effect.

- Make a braided loaf. Roll out three or four coils of equal length; then braid the coils.
- Snip and cut the edges of the loaf with pointed scissors. This cutting and shaping also helps the bread release excess gas during baking and will give a better texture.
- Form the loaves into shapes of birds, animals, or fish.
- Turn to the bread photograph for a visual treat.

DIFFERENT CRUSTS

If you want to add flavor, color, shine, or texture to your crust, coat the top of the loaves with a glaze before baking. A pastry brush is useful for applying the following glazes:

- *Water:* Brushing or misting water on the dough creates a crispy, crunchy crust.
- *Egg Wash:* Brushing on 1 whole egg beaten with 1 tablespoon water will add shine and color.
- *Egg Yolk:* Brushing on 1 beaten yolk with 1 teaspoon water will give a brown, shiny crust.
- *Egg White:* Brushing on 1 beaten white with 1 teaspoon water will give a shiny crust.
- *Milk, Oil, or Melted Butter:* Brushing the loaves with milk or butter creates a soft and tender crust.
- *Pizza Stones, Bread Stones, or Tiles:* Using these creates a good, crunchy crust.

While the glaze is still moist, you can sprinkle the dough with seeds, nuts, cornmeal, oatmeal, cracked wheat, or ground oats. For example, misting the bread with water and rolling it in a combination of cornmeal and sesame seeds creates a crispy, crunchy crust. Wetting the bread with a glaze helps the toppings adhere to the loaves.

Use your imagination.

Multigrain Peasant Bread

Pane Casareccio

Preparation Time: 30 minutes

Rising Time: first, 2 hours; second, 1 hour

Baking Time: 30 minutes

Proofing Mixture:
1 cup warm water (105° to 115°F)
2 tablespoons active dry yeast
1 teaspoon sugar

For the Dough:
13⅓ cups (4 pounds) unbleached
    all-purpose flour
3⅓ cups—(about 1 pound) grains
    (semolina, cracked wheat, steel-
    ground oats, oatmeal, oat bran,
    wheat flakes, cornmeal, whole

wheat flour—in any combination
    you prefer)
2 tablespoons salt
5 cups warm water
¼ cup extra-virgin olive oil plus
    1 tablespoon

**For the Work Surface and
Baking Sheets:**
Extra flour for work surface and
    kneading (if necessary)
½ cup yellow or white cornmeal

PROCEDURE

1. To proof the yeast, pour 1 cup warm water into small bowl. Sprinkle the yeast and sugar over the surface, and stir with a fork briefly (about 30 seconds). Let stand for 5 minutes, until the mixture is frothy. (If the yeast does not froth, it is no longer active and should be discarded.)

2. While the yeast is proofing, place the flour, grains, and salt in a large bowl and stir to combine. Make a deep well in the center of the flour by pushing the flour up the sides of the bowl. Pour the proofed yeast mixture, the 5 cups water, and ¼ cup of the olive oil in the well in the flour.

3. Holding the edge of the large bowl with one hand, use the other hand to mix the liquid with the flour. Starting from the center, slowly work your way around the bowl, incorporating a little of the flour at a time. Keep going around until all the flour and liquid is combined to form a soft dough. Rub the extra dough clinging to your hand into the mixture. If the dough is too sticky, add a little more flour, 1 tablespoon at a time, until the stickiness is gone. If

*Breads,
Pizza, and
Focaccia*

there is flour left in the bowl, add a little more water, a tablespoon at a time, until all the ingredients are combined into a nonsticky mound of dough.

4. For kneading, you will work with half of the dough at a time. Turn the dough out onto a lightly floured work surface. Lightly oil your hands to prevent the dough from sticking. Following the instructions on page 166, knead for about 10 or 15 minutes, alternating between the two halves of dough. The dough will become smooth, elastic, and satiny.

5. Place 1 tablespoon olive oil in the palm of your hand and rub the oil over the entire surface of the dough. Place the dough in a large, unscented plastic bag. Push all the air out of the bag and close it at the top with a twist tie, leaving room from the dough to rise and double in bulk inside the bag. Place in a draft-free, warm spot (about 80°F). This is the first rise.

6. In about 2 hours, the dough should be ready. To check its progress, press two fingertips about ½ inch into the dough. If the indentations remain when your fingertips are removed, the dough is ready. Punch the dough down and knead briefly to distribute the air bubbles, about 30 seconds.

7. Sprinkle the cornmeal on two or three 17 × 11–inch baking sheets, depending on the shape of your loaves. Divide the dough equally into six parts and shape into loaves. Place the loaves on the baking sheets, allowing enough room for each to double in size. The second rising will take about 1 hour.

8. Prepare the oven by arranging one oven rack on the bottom shelf and the other on the second from the top shelf. Preheat the oven to 400°F.

9. Place one baking sheet on the bottom rack and bake for 15 minutes; then transfer it to the upper rack and bake an additional 15 minutes. Place another baking sheet on the bottom rack. This staggering technique makes best use of the oven space, allowing you to be more efficient. The loaves take about 30 minutes total to bake. You will know the bread is done if the loaves make a hollow sound when you tap on them and by their golden brown color.

10. When done, remove the bread from the baking sheets *immediately* and place on wire racks or kitchen towels to cool. This allows the moisture from the bottom of the loaves to evaporate, keeping the crust crispy.

Yield: 6 loaves, 1⅓ pounds each

NOTES

If you are going to use the bread the same day, or the day after, store the loaves at room temperature in a brown paper bag. This will help retain a good crust. The bread will keep fresh this way for up to 2 days. I feel that it is better to freeze bread that you are not going to eat within 2 days. It actually tastes better than bread stored fresh in plastic bags.

This bread freezes very well and will keep in the freezer for up to 3 months. Wrap individual loaves in heavy-duty aluminum foil and place in reclosable plastic freezer bags. To reheat frozen bread, allow it to defrost at room temperature. Place unwrapped bread in a preheated 350°F oven directly on the oven racks for 7 to 10 minutes.

St. Joseph's Bread

Pane di San Giuseppe

Preparation Time: 30 minutes
Rising Time: first, about 2 hours; second, about 1 hour
Baking Time: 30 minutes

St. Joseph's Bread is a traditional bread served on St. Joseph's Day, March 19. It is an egg bread with a crumb that has a tighter, denser weave, allowing the dough to be used for fancy bread-sculpting designs. Breads in the form of crosses, staffs, wheat sheaves, images of St. Joseph, and braids of the Blessed Mother adorn the St. Joseph table and are eaten throughout the feast day. I make this bread throughout the year when I am in a sculpting mood.

Proofing Mixture:
½ cup warm water (105° to 115°F)
1 tablespoon active dry yeast
1 teaspoon sugar or honey

For the Dough:
7 cups unbleached all-purpose flour
1 tablespoon salt
2 cups water
3 tablespoons extra-virgin olive oil,
　　divided

4 large eggs, beaten slightly

For the Work Surface and
Baking Sheets:
Extra flour for work surface and
　　kneading (if necessary)
½ cup yellow or white cornmeal

For the Egg Wash:
1 whole egg
1 tablespoon water

PROCEDURE

　　1. To proof the yeast, pour ½ cup warm water into a small bowl. Sprinkle the yeast and sugar over the surface, and stir with a fork for about 30 seconds. Let stand for 5 minutes, until the mixture is frothy. (If the yeast does not froth, it is no longer active and should be discarded.)

　　2. While the yeast is proofing, place the flour and salt in a large bowl and stir to combine. Make a deep well in the center of the flour by pushing flour up the sides of the bowl. Pour the proofed yeast mixture, the 2 cups water, 2 tablespoons of the olive oil, and eggs into the well in the flour.

3. Holding the edge of the large bowl with one hand, use the other hand to mix the liquid into the flour. Starting from the center, slowly work your way around the bowl, incorporating *a little* of the flour at a time. Keep going around until all the flour and liquid is combined to form a soft dough. Rub the extra dough clinging to your hand into the mixture. If the dough is too sticky, add a little more flour, a tablespoon at a time, until the stickiness is gone. If there is flour left in the bowl, add a little more water, 1 tablespoon at a time, until all the ingredients are combined into a nonsticky mound of dough.

4. Turn the dough out onto a lightly floured surface. Lightly oil your hands to prevent the dough from sticking. This dough needs to be firmer than the other bread doughs; knead more flour into it. The firmer the dough, the easier it is to get more definition in your sculpted bread. It will not rise as much, allowing you to make more intricate designs.

5. To knead, divide the dough in half. Following the instructions on page 166. Knead for about 10 to 15 minutes. The dough will become smooth, elastic, and satiny.

6. Place 1 tablespoon olive oil in the palm of your hand and rub the oil over the entire surface of the dough. Place the dough in a large, unscented plastic bag. Push all the air out of the bag and close it at the top with a twist tie, leaving room for the dough to rise and double in bulk inside the bag. Place in a draft-free, warm spot (about 80°F) to rise.

7. In about 1½ hours, the dough should be ready. To check on its progress, press two fingertips about ½ inch into the dough. If the indentations remain when your fingertips are removed, the dough is ready. Punch the dough down and knead briefly to distribute the air bubbles, about 30 seconds.

8. Sprinkle 2 tablespoons cornmeal on each of two 17 × 11–inch baking sheets. Divide the dough into two portions and form loaves. Place the loaves on the baking sheets. Brush top with egg wash. Allow enough room for each to double in size. The second rising will take about 1 hour.

9. Prepare the oven by arranging on oven rack on the bottom shelf and the other on the second from the top shelf. Preheat the oven to 400°F.

10. Place one baking sheet on the bottom rack and bake for 15 minutes; then transfer it to the upper rack, baking for an additional 15 minutes. Place another baking sheet on the bottom rack. This is my staggering technique of baking, making the best use of the oven space, allowing you to be more efficient. The loaves will take 30 minutes to bake. You will know the bread is done if it makes a hollow sound when you tap on it or by its golden brown color.

11. When done, remove the bread from the baking sheets *immediately* and place on wire racks or kitchen towels to cool.

Yield: 2 loaves, 1⅓ pounds each

NOTES

If you are going to use the bread on the same or following day, store the loaves at room temperature in a brown paper bag. This will help retain a good crust. The bread will keep fresh this way for up to 2 days.

This bread freezes very well and will keep in the freezer for up to 3 months. Wrap individual loaves in heavy-duty aluminum foil and place in reclosable plastic freezer bags. To reheat frozen bread, remove plastic bag and allow to defrost at room temperature. Place unwrapped bread directly on the oven rack in a preheated 350°F oven for 7 to 10 minutes.

Turn to the photograph to see how these loaves can be sculpted.

Italian Bread
(Food Processor Method)

....

Preparation Time: 5 minutes
Rising Time: first, 1 to 1½ hours; second, 30 to 45 minutes
Baking Time: 30 minutes

Want a quick honest loaf of bread? Try this!

Proofing Mixture:
⅓ cup warm water (105° to 115°F)
1 tablespoon active dry yeast
1 teaspoon sugar

For the Dough:
2 cups warm water
2 tablespoons extra-virgin olive oil,
    divided

6 cups unbleached, all-purpose flour
1 tablespoon salt

**For the Work Surface and
Baking Sheets:**
Extra flour for the work surface
⅓ cup cornmeal

PROCEDURE

   1. Place the warm water in a medium bowl. Sprinkle the yeast and sugar over the surface, and stir with a fork for about 30 seconds. Let stand for 5 minutes, until the mixture is frothy and bubbly. (If the yeast does not froth, it is no longer active and should be discarded.)

   2. Add the other 2 cups water and the 1 tablespoon of oil to the proofing mixture.

   3. Fit the food processor with the plastic blade (called a dough blade). Add the flour and salt to the food processor bowl. Cover and process for 30 seconds. With motor on, add the liquid mixture in a slow, continuous stream through the feed tube. The dough will go through different stages, starting in a mealy dry stage, then forming pea-shaped pellets, and finally progressing to a ball stage. When the ball starts to form, process for 1 more minute; then turn off the machine.

   4. Rub your hands with a small amount of oil. Remove the dough onto a lightly floured work surface and form it into a ball.

5. Place 1 tablespoon olive oil in the palm of your hand and rub oil over the entire surface of the dough. Place the dough in a large, unscented plastic bag. Push all the air out of the bag and close it at the top with a twist tie, leaving room for the dough to rise and double in bulk. Place in a draft-free, warm spot (about 80°F).

6. In about 1½ hours, the dough should have risen and doubled in bulk. To check on its progress, press two fingertips about ½ inch into the dough. If the indentations remain when your fingertips are removed, the dough is ready. Punch the dough down and knead briefly to distribute the air bubbles, about 30 seconds.

7. Grease one or two baking sheets with vegetable shortening and sprinkle 2 tablespoons of cornmeal on each sheet. Divide the dough equally into two parts and shape into loaves, or if you prefer, divide into four parts to make four loaves. Place the loaves on the baking sheets, allowing enough room for each to double in size. This second rising will take about 45 minutes.

8. Prepare the oven by arranging one oven rack on the bottom shelf and the other on the second from the top shelf. Preheat the oven to 400°F.

9. Place one baking sheet on the bottom rack and bake for 15 minutes; then transfer to the upper rack. Place the other baking sheet on the bottom. This is my staggering technique of baking, making best use of the oven spaces, allow you to be more efficient. Continue baking from another 15 minutes. The loaves will take 30 minutes to bake. You will know the bread is done if the loaves make a hollow sound when you tap on them or by their golden brown color.

10. When done, remove the bread from the baking sheets *immediately* and place on wire racks or kitchen towels to cool.

Yield: 2 large loaves or 4 medium loaves

NOTES

The bread will keep fresh for a couple of days at room temperature. Store the loaves in a brown paper bag. This will help retain a good crust. This bread freezes very well and will keep in the freezer for up to 3 months. Wrap individual loaves in heavy-duty aluminum foil and place in reclosable plastic freezer bags. To reheat frozen bread, remove from plastic bag and allow to defrost at room temperature. Place unwrapped bread directly on the rack in a preheated 350°F oven for 7 to 10 minutes.

Panini

....

Panini

Preparation Time: 15 minutes
Rising Time: first rising, 1 hour; second rising, 45 minutes
Baking Time: 20 minutes

My husband says rolls just don't get any better than this. These little breads are the ultimate sandwich. Anyone who loves a great sandwich is likely to agree. They have a tremendous combination of being crusty with a good crumb that is light, airy, and so tasty. To make these rolls, use a stand-up electric mixer with a dough hook or a large bowl with a wooden spoon. This dough is very much like a batter, very sticky.

Build your sandwiches just before you are ready to eat them. Fill them with sandwich ingredients that add taste, texture, aroma, and color.

Proofing Mixture:
½ cup warm water (105° to 115°F)
1½ tablespoons active dry yeast
1 teaspoon sugar or honey

For the Dough:
2½ cups warm water
1 tablespoon salt
2 tablespoons extra-virgin olive oil

6½ cups unbleached all-purpose
    flour, divided

For the Baking Sheets:
Cornmeal

For the Topping:
½ cup yellow cornmeal
¾ cup sesame seeds

PROCEDURE

1. To proof the yeast, put the warm water into a small bowl. Sprinkle the yeast and sugar over the surface, and stir with a fork briefly (about 30 seconds). Let stand for 5 minutes, until the mixture is frothy and bubbly. (If the yeast does not froth, it is no longer active and should be discarded.)

2. While waiting for the yeast to proof, attach a bowl and dough hook to the electric mixer. Add the proofed yeast mixture, the 2½ cups warm water, and the salt and oil. Turn the mixer to low speed and add the flour ½ cup at a time until 6 cups flour have been used. Continue on low speed for 5 more minutes, or until the dough is smooth. It will be very sticky.

3. Remove the bowl from the mixer and, with a wooden spoon, mix the last ½ cup flour into the dough. The dough will be sticky—don't worry; that's the way it is supposed to be.

4. Oil a large bowl. Remove the dough with a rubber spatula and place in the oiled bowl. Cover top of bowl with plastic wrap.

5. Place in a draft-free, warm spot (about 80°F) and allow to rise undisturbed for 1 hour, or until double in bulk.

6. In the meantime, dust two 17 × 11–inch baking sheets generously with cornmeal. Combine cornmeal and sesame seeds on your work surface. When bread has gone through the first rising, deflate the bread by pushing it down with the back of the spoon. Grease a large spoon and your fingers generously. With the greased spoon, spoon up pieces about the size of tangerines and drop into the cornmeal and sesame seed mixture. Roll gently until the whole roll is covered. This dough is *sticky*. Keep dipping your fingers in flour; this will help you form the rolls.

7. Place the rolls on the baking sheets, six to eight a sheet, leaving rising space between them. Continue until all the dough is used. You should get 12 to 14 rolls.

8. Cover the rolls with a kitchen towel and allow to rise is a warm, draft-free place for about 45 minutes.

9. Prepare the oven by arranging one oven rack on the bottom shelf and the other on the second from top shelf. Preheat the oven to 400°F.

10. These rolls will bake for a total of 20 to 30 minutes. Spritz the top of the rolls on one baking sheet with water and place immediately in the preheated oven on the bottom rack and bake for 10 minutes. Spritz twice in the next 10 minutes. After 10 minutes are up, place this sheet of rolls on the upper rack and continue to cook for another 10 minutes or so. When you move the first sheet of rolls to the top shelf, spritz the second sheet and place it on the bottom shelf, so you have two sheets going at the same time, Spritz this sheet as you did the first. Remove the rolls on the upper rack after allotted time. Move the sheet from the bottom rack to the top rack, and place another spritzed baking sheet on the bottom. Continue in this manner until all the rolls are baked.

11. As soon as the rolls are taken from the oven, remove them from the baking sheets onto a wire rack.

Yield: 12 to 14 (5-inch) rolls

NOTES

These rolls taste best when eaten the same day or the day after they are baked. When completely cool, put the rolls in paper bags to maintain freshness.

These rolls freeze very well and will keep in the freezer for up to 3 months. Wrap completely cooled rolls individually in heavy-duty aluminum foil and place in reclosable plastic freezer bags. To reheat frozen rolls, remove from plastic bag and allow to defrost at room temperature. Place unwrapped rolls in a preheated 350°F oven for 7 to 10 minutes.

Ladder Bread with Olives and Onion

....

Pane a Scala con Olive e Cipole

Preparation Time: 30 minutes

Rising Time: first, 1½ hours; second, 45 minutes to 1 hour

Baking Time: 15 to 20 minutes

This is a wonderful bread to serve with your antipasto or soup course, or just to nibble on as a snack. Think of it as individual large breadsticks joined together to form a large ladder. This bread is passed around the table with each person breaking off one or two rungs.

Proofing Mixture:
⅓ cup warm water (105° to 115°F)
1 tablespoon active dry yeast
1 teaspoon sugar or honey

For the Dough:
6 cups unbleached all-purpose flour
1 tablespoon salt
2 cups water
3 tablespoons extra-virgin olive oil, divided
1 cup chopped onion
⅔ cup pitted Kalamata or Gaeta olives

For the Work Surface and Baking Sheets:
Extra flour for work surface and kneading (if necessary)
½ cup yellow or white cornmeal

For the Topping:
Olive oil to brush on the loaves
Sesame seeds
Freshly grated Romano cheese
Coarse salt

PROCEDURE

1. To proof the yeast, pour ⅓ cup warm water into a small bowl. Sprinkle the yeast and sugar over the surface, and stir with a fork for about 30 seconds. Let stand for 5 minutes, until the mixture is frothy. (If the yeast does not froth, it is no longer active and should be discarded.)

2. While the yeast is proofing, place the flour and salt in a large bowl. Make a deep well in the center of the flour by pushing flour up the sides of the

bowl. Pour the proofed yeast mixture, the 2 cups water, 2 tablespoons of the olive oil, onion, and olives into the well in the center of the flour.

3. Holding the edge of the large bowl with one hand, use the other hand to mix the liquid into the flour. Starting from the center, slowly work your way around the bowl, incorporating a little of the flour at a time. Keep going around until all the flour and liquid is combined to form a soft dough. Rub the extra dough clinging to your hand into the mixture. If the dough is too sticky, add a little more flour, 1 tablespoon at a time, until the stickiness is gone. If there is flour left in the bowl, add a little more water, a tablespoon at a time, until all the ingredients are combined into a nonsticky mound of dough.

4. Turn the dough out onto a lightly floured surface. Lightly oil your hands to prevent the dough from sticking. Knead for about 10 or 15 minutes. The dough will become smooth, elastic, and satiny.

5. Place 1 tablespoon olive oil in the palm of your hand and rub the oil over the entire surface of the dough. Place the dough in a large, unscented plastic bag. Push all the air out of the bag and close it at the top with a twist tie, leaving room for the dough to rise and double in bulk inside the bag. Place in a draft-free, warm spot (about 80°F).

6. In about 1½ hours, the dough should be ready. To check on its progress, press two fingertips about ½ inch into the dough. If the indentations remain when your fingertips are removed, the dough is ready. Punch the dough and knead briefly to distribute air bubbles, about 30 seconds. Divide the dough into three pieces.

7. Sprinkle each baking sheet with 2 tablespoons cornmeal. Flatten and spread out each piece of dough as though you were making a pizza about ¼ inch thick, stretching the shape to fit only two thirds of the baking sheet. With scissors or a sharp knife, cut slits through the dough at 1½-inch intervals, making sure not to cut through to the edges. Spread the slits open so the bread looks like a ladder using the whole bottom of your pan. (See the photo of the finished bread.)

8. Brush the tops with olive oil and sprinkle immediately with sesame seeds, Romano cheese, and coarse salt.

9. Prepare the oven by arranging one oven rack on the bottom shelf and the other on the second from the top shelf. Preheat the oven to 400°F.

10. Place one baking sheet on the bottom rack and bake for 10 minutes; then transfer it to the upper rack and place another baking sheet on the bottom rack. This staggering technique makes the best use of the oven space, allowing you to be more efficient. Ladder bread takes 15 to 20 minutes to bake. You will know the bread is done by its golden brown color. Do not overcook unless you want it dry like breadsticks.

11. As soon as the bread comes from the oven, remove it and place on wire racks or kitchen towels to cool. This allows the moisture from the bottom of the loaves to evaporate, keeping the crust crispy.

Yield: 3 to 4 ladder breads, depending on size

NOTES

A variation of this bread can be made by substituting 12 sun-dried marinated tomato halves (page 18), along with the oil that is clinging to the tomatoes, plus 1 tablespoon minced garlic, for the olives and the onions.

If you are going to use the bread the same day, store it at room temperature in a brown paper bag. This will help retain a good crust. The bread will keep fresh this way for up to a day.

This bread freezes very well and will keep in the freezer for up to 3 months. Wrap individual loaves in heavy-duty aluminum foil and place in individual reclosable plastic freezer bags. To reheat frozen bread, remove the plastic bag and aluminum foil and allow to defrost at room temperature. Place unwrapped bread in a preheated 350°F oven for 7 to 10 minutes.

Stuffed Bread with Spinach and Olives

Pane Ripieno con Spinaci e Olive

Preparation Time: 15 minutes, not including preparation and rising of dough
Baking Time: 30 to 35 minutes (the more stuffing used the longer the baking time)

Often, when I make a large batch of bread, I set aside 1⅓ pounds of the bread dough to make this. Try it and see how flavorful and filling it can be.

2 tablespoons cornmeal, for the baking sheet

1⅓ pounds bread dough, risen and punched down (pages 166–167)

1 tablespoon extra-virgin olive oil

⅓ cup Homemade Fresh Ricotta (page 8)

1 recipe Spinach with Garlic and Olive Oil (page 29)

1 medium onion, sliced and sautéed in 1 tablespoon extra-virgin olive oil

12 Kalamata or Gaeta olives, pitted and sliced

Egg wash (1 large egg mixed with 1 teaspoon water), to brush over loaf

PROCEDURE

1. Sprinkle the baking sheet with cornmeal. Place the dough on the prepared baking sheet and flatten with your hand—just like for Pizza (page 188).

2. With kitchen scissors, make diagonal cuts 1 inch apart and 2½ inches deep on both of the longer edges.

3. In the center of the dough, vertically, spread the ricotta, the spinach mixture, and the onions. Dot with the sliced olives.

4. Fold the side flaps up and over the stuffing by 1 inch. Then, alternating top and bottom strips, fold the flaps to the center, overlapping, and tucking the edges of the flaps and covering the filling. The effect is that of a braid or a herringbone pattern.

5. Allow the loaf to rise for about 45 minutes.

6. Preheat the oven to 400°F. Brush the egg wash over the top of the loaf, and bake for about 30 minutes.

Yield: Serves 8

NOTES

Be creative with the stuffing. Instead of the olives, ricotta, and spinach, substitute a combination of some of these ingredients—sautéed ground meats; cold cuts; a variety of soft and hard cheeses; broccoli, zucchini, and yellow squash; sautéed onions or shallots or garlic; just to mention a few.

Store any leftovers in a plastic bag in the refrigerator; they will keep for a couple of days. This stuffed bread may be frozen. To reheat, place the defrosted bread in a preheated 350°F oven and heat for about 10 minutes.

Onion, Garlic, and Cheese Focaccia (Food Processor Method)

Focaccia con Cipolla, Aglio, e Formaggio

Preparation Time: 20 minutes

Rising Time: first rising, 1½ hours; second rising, 30 minutes

Baking Time: 25 to 30 minutes per sheet

Proofing Mixture:
⅓ cup warm water (105° to 115°F)
1 tablespoon active dry yeast
1 tablespoon sugar

Dough Mixture:
2 cups warm water
¼ cup extra-virgin olive oil, divided
3 cups whole wheat flour
4 cups unbleached all-purpose flour
⅓ cup cornmeal
1½ tablespoons coarse salt
1 tablespoon extra-virgin olive oil

For the Toppings:
2 tablespoons extra-virgin olive oil
2 large sweet onions, cut in half and
  then sliced thin
4 cloves of garlic, peeled and slivered
  (sliced very thin)

¼ teaspoon salt
¼ teaspoon freshly ground black
  pepper
½ cup freshly grated Romano cheese
1 tablespoon rosemary
Extra freshly ground black pepper
  (if desired)

*To Prepare the Baking Sheets
and Work Surface:*
1 tablespoon vegetable shortening
¼ cup cornmeal
Extra flour for work surface and
  kneading, if necessary

PROCEDURE

1. To proof the yeast, pour ⅓ cup warm water into a small bowl. Sprinkle the yeast and sugar over the surface, and stir with fork for about 30 seconds. Let stand for 5 minutes until mixture is frothy. (If the yeast does not froth, it is no longer active and should be discarded.)

2. Add the other 2 cups of water and 3 tablespoons of the oil to the proofing mixture.

3. Fit the food processor with the plastic blade (called a dough blade). Add flours, ⅓ cup cornmeal, and salt to the food processor's bowl. Cover. Turn it on for 30 seconds. With motor on, add the liquid in a slow, continuous stream through the feed tube. The dough will go through different stages, starting in a mealy dry stage, then forming pea-shaped pellets, and finally on to a ball stage. When the ball starts to form, time it for 1 minute, then turn off the machine. If the dough is too dry, add water, 1 teaspoon at a time. If it is too wet, add a little flour, 1 teaspoon at a time.

4. Remove the dough to a lightly floured work surface, knead for 30 seconds, and then form into a ball.

5. Place 1 tablespoon of olive oil in the palm of your hand and rub the oil over the entire surface of the dough. Place dough in a large, unscented plastic bag. Push all the air out of the bag and close it at the top with a twist tie, leaving room for the dough to rise and double in bulk inside the bag. Place the bag in a draft-free, warm spot (about 80°F).

6. While the dough is rising, prepare the topping. Heat a large skillet over medium-high heat until warm. Add the oil. When the oil is hot, add the onions. Stir and cook for 3 minutes. Add the garlic, rosemary, salt, and pepper. Stir and continue to cook for 2 minutes. Remove from stove and cool.

7. The first rising will take about 1½ hours. To check on the dough's progress, press two fingertips about ½ inch into the dough. If the indentations remain when the fingertips are removed, the dough is ready. Punch the dough down and knead briefly to distribute air bubbles, about 30 seconds.

8. Prepare the oven by arranging oven racks with one rack on the bottom shelf and the other on the second from the top shelf. Preheat the oven to 400°F.

9. Lightly grease three 17 × 11–inch baking sheets with vegetable shortening. Divide the dough equally into three parts. Place dough on baking sheets and flatten each piece into a rectangular shape using your hands. Start from the center of the dough, pushing outward.

10. Allow dough on baking sheets to sit for ½ hour.

11. With your *fingertips,* press all over the top of the focaccia to make a dimpled surface. Spread a generous amount of sautéed garlic and onion over the surface to fill these indentations. Sprinkle with Romano cheese and freshly ground black pepper.

12. Total baking time is about 30 minutes. Place one sheet on the bottom rack and bake for 15 minutes, then transfer it to the upper rack. Place another baking sheet on the bottom rack and continue to bake for an additional 10 to 15 minutes.

13. Bake until it is crusty and golden. Immediately remove from baking sheets to a wire rack and allow to cool for a few minutes. Slice or cut with scissors into individual portions and serve.

Yield: three 17 × 11–inch rectangular pieces

NOTES

Fresh rosemary can be added to the focaccia when you add the onion.

If desired, unbleached all-purpose flour can be substituted for whole wheat flour.

Focaccia is best when eaten warm or at room temperature. It will stay fresh overnight in a brown paper bag.

Focaccia freezes very well. Wrap it tightly with aluminum foil and then place in heavy-duty freezer bags and keep in the freezer for up to 2 months. To reheat, remove plastic bag and aluminum foil and allow to defrost at room temperature. Place unwrapped bread in a preheated 350°F oven for 10 minutes.

Pizza

Preparation Time: for the dough, 30 minutes, not including rising time
For the toppings, time varies depending on what and how much you plan on using
Rising Time: first, about 1½ to 2 hours; second, about 45 minutes
Baking Time: 25 to 30 minutes (the more toppings used,
and the wetter the toppings, the longer it takes to cook)

Pizza to me always conjures memories of long trips and of picnics with family and friends. When we were married and living in New York City, our visits back home to Rochester would always find my mother making her special simple pizza for us. She always made more than we could possibly eat so we could have some to take back. We would stop at a park or lovely spot, lay out our blanket, and have a picnic with all the treats from home. Most of the goodies never made it back to New York City. As we started to have our own family and go on trips and vacations, this tradition was anticipated by our children, and now our grandchildren. What would we do without memories!

My family's favorite pizza is very simple to make. It has a thin layer of marinara sauce and generous sprinklings of sautéed onion, fresh cracked pepper, and Romano cheese. This pizza does not need to be refrigerated after being cooked. It travels very well and tastes great at room temperature. At our house, one of the three pizzas that this recipe makes is always done in this fashion. The other two are topped with a variety of ingredients, depending on who is over for dinner and what is in the refrigerator.

For the Crust:
PROOFING MIXTURE
½ cup warm water (105° to 115°F)
1 tablespoon active dry yeast
1 teaspoon sugar

DOUGH
8½ cups (about 2½ pounds)
    unbleached all-purpose flour
1 tablespoon salt
2¾ cups warm water
3 tablespoons extra-virgin olive oil,
    divided

For the Baking Sheets:
½ cup cornmeal

For the Toppings:
**ANY OF THE FOLLOWING
(OR OTHERS, AS PREFERRED)—
LET YOUR IMAGINATION CARRY
YOU AWAY!**
Cheese: Grated Romano or
    Parmigiano-Reggiano, fresh
    shredded mozzarella, crumbled
    goat cheese or ricotta

Marinara Sauce (page 5)
Spinach with Garlic and Olive Oil
   (page 29)
Marinated Roasted Peppers (page
   15)
Broiled Eggplant Slices (page 20)
Sautéed Swiss Chard (page 31)
Olive Paste Sauce (page 129)
Black olives, chopped and pitted

Pepperoni, salami, or prosciutto,
   sliced thin
Anchovies
Onions: sliced or chopped and
   sautéed lightly
Garlic: slivered, sliced, chopped, or
   minced (used raw or sautéed for
   1 minute)

PROCEDURE

1. To proof the yeast, pour ½ cup warm water into a small bowl. Sprinkle the yeast and sugar over the surface, and stir with a fork for about 30 seconds. Let stand for 5 minutes until the mixture is frothy. (If the yeast does not froth, it is no longer active and should be discarded.)

2. While the yeast is proofing, place the flour and salt in a large bowl. Make a deep well in the center of the flour by pushing flour up the sides of the bowl. Pour the proofed yeast mixture, the 2¾ cups water, and 2 tablespoons of the olive oil into the well in the flour.

3. Holding the edge of the large bowl with one hand, use the other hand to mix the liquid with the flour. Starting from the center, slowly work your way around the bowl, incorporating a little of the flour at a time. Keep going around until all the flour and liquid is combined to form a soft dough. Rub the extra dough clinging to your hand into the mixture. If the dough is too sticky, add a little more flour, a tablespoon at a time, until the stickiness is gone. If there is flour left in the bowl, add a little more water, 1 tablespoon at a time, until all the ingredients are combined into a nonsticky mound of dough.

4. Place the dough on a lightly floured work surface and divide in half. Following the instructions on page 166, knead for about 10 minutes, using as little of the flour as possible, to form a pliable, elastic dough that does not stick to your hands or the work surface.

5. Place 1 tablespoon olive oil in the palm of your hand and rub the oil over the entire surface of the dough. Place the dough in a large, unscented plastic bag. Push all the air out of the bag and close it at the top with a twist tie, leaving room for the dough to rise and double in bulk inside the bag. Place in a draft-free, warm spot (about 80°F).

6. While the dough is rising, prepare the sauce and toppings. Lightly grease three 17 × 11–inch baking sheets with vegetable shortening.

*Breads,
Pizza, and
Focaccia*

7. In about 1½ hours, the dough should be ready. To check on its progress, press two fingertips about ½ inch into the dough. If the indentations remain when your fingertips are removed, the dough is ready. Punch the dough down and knead briefly to distribute air bubbles, about 30 seconds.

8. Divide the dough into three fairly equal portions. Flatten the dough into rectangular shapes to fit the baking sheets. You may use a rolling pin or your hands. Stretch and pat the dough out to the edges of the pan. If the dough tends to spring back away from the edges (this happens because of the elasticity of the dough, which comes from its glutens), let it rest for 10 to 15 minutes; you should have no trouble making it stay at the edges then. Let it rise again for about 30 minutes.

9. While dough is rising, prepare the oven by arranging one oven rack on the bottom shelf and the other on the second from the top shelf. Preheat the oven to 400°F. Spread cooled sauce evenly over the pizza dough, add your choice of toppings, and sprinkle with freshly ground black pepper and Romano cheese. (Note: If using fresh mozzarella cheese, place it on the pizza during the last 10 minutes of cooking.)

10. Bake the pizza the same as bread, 12 to 15 minutes on the bottom rack; then switch and bake for an additional 12 to 15 minutes on the top rack, for a total of 25 to 30 minutes. The bottom of the pizza should be light golden brown and completely cooked.

11. Remove the pizza from the baking sheet *immediately* and cool on a wire rack for a few minutes so it will be easier to slice. Serve hot, warm, or at room temperature, depending on what toppings you use. Use a scissors to slice your pizza!

Yield: 3 extra-large rectangular pizzas, 17 × 11 × ½ inch

NOTES

This recipe could be made with an electric mixer using a dough hook or a food processor fitted with the plastic blade.

The cooked pizza will keep fresh in the refrigerator for several days wrapped in aluminum foil. To reheat, place uncovered in a 350°F oven or toaster oven for 7 to 10 minutes, or eat at room temperature.

Pizza will keep in the freezer for up to 2 months. To reheat frozen pizza, defrost in the refrigerator overnight and then bake in a preheated 350°F oven for 7 to 10 minutes.

MEATS AND POULTRY

In the past, meat was too expensive and hard to obtain for a majority of the Italian people and was either not used in their everyday diet or used sparingly. People relied more heavily on the wonderful pasta and vegetables. It is only recently, as the country has become prosperous, that more people have been able to add meat and poultry to their everyday diet.

A variety of animals are farmed throughout Italy, depending on the terrain. Beef and veal come from the northern part of Italy, where there are spacious flat plains with lush green pasturelands with good irrigation systems. Lamb and sheep are raised in the south, where the land is more rocky and mountainous and the soil is not as fertile. Pork is produced throughout Italy and is readily available to all. Pigs are a good choice for farmers to have on their farms; they take very little space, eat scraps from vegetables, and are fed the whey from cheesemaking. Pigs are butchered in the fall and much of the meat is cured and preserved to last the winter. The chickens raised in Italy are used for their eggs as well as for their meat.

They are, for the most part, free-range chickens, roaming the outdoors to peck and scratch and be nurtured by the sun's rays. The color, texture, and taste of these chickens are worlds apart from more cultivated fowl; their flavor can't be beat.

In this chapter you will find the meat and poultry dishes that are closest to my heart. There are traditional simple dishes from my Italian American childhood that were made in our home in Rochester, New York, as well as dishes I created in my kitchens in New York City and in Pennsylvania. Some are simply prepared and simply presented. These are uncomplicated, inexpensive, and unpretentious everyday fare. Others are very special, more elaborate, and take more time to prepare. Make these when you have time on a weekend for family and friends or for a special dinner party, and by all means enjoy yourself in the process.

Boned Stuffed Roast Leg of Lamb

Agnello al Forno Disossato e Ripieno

Preparation Time: 15 minutes; marinate lamb overnight for best results

*Baking Time: 15 to 20 minutes per pound (to an internal temperature
of 145°F for medium-rare and 160°F for medium)*

Approaching our first Easter together, Guy and I had already been living in the
heart of New York City for over six months and were taking bimonthly trips
into Little Italy. Those Saturday trips to the Italian section of the city were a
source of great joy: going from shop to shop—to the cheese store for the best
imported cheeses and wonderful made-on-the-spot mozzarella and ricotta; to
the pork store for dried sausages, fresh pork chops, and fresh sweet Italian
sausage; to the baker to behold all the beautiful shaped breads and to smell the
aroma of large quantities of bread that had just come out of the oven; and to the
pastry shops for my favorite almond paste cookies with pine nuts. One of our
favorite butcher shops, Di Santi's Father and Sons, is no longer there, but it is
the place where I learned my first butchering skills. They instructed me on the
importance of the best cuts of meat, of cutting against the grain, and, of course,
the need for those perfectly sharpened knives. On this particular Easter the
Di Santi brothers convinced me to buy half a spring-fed baby lamb, called *abbacchio*. Abbacchio is very expensive and is prized for its pale pink flesh, which
is meltingly tender. We've never forgotten it.

Lamb is a uniquely flavorful but somewhat fatty meat. The marbleing in the
meat makes it tender, moist, and juicy. Allow ½ to ¾ pound of meat per person for on-the-bone meat or ¼ to ½ pound for boned lamb per serving. I prefer to purchase boned leg of lamb for stuffing and rolling. If you give your
butcher ample time, he will probably debone it for you free of charge.

4 pounds boned leg of lamb

For the Stuffing:
1 teaspoon salt
**½ teaspoon freshly ground black
    pepper**
3 tablespoons extra-virgin olive oil

**2 teaspoons minced fresh mint
    leaves, divided**
**2 teaspoons minced Italian flat-leaf
    parsley, divided**
**2 cloves garlic, minced
    (about 1 teaspoon)**

(cont'd)

2 scallions (white to light green part
    only), chopped (reserve dark
    green sections for making broth)
¼ pound imported Romano cheese,
    cut into ¼-inch-wide by ½-inch-
    long pieces
4 tablespoons plain dried bread
    crumbs

*For the Marinade and
Basting Liquid:*
1 cup dry red wine
1 cup meat broth
¼ cup balsamic vinegar
¼ cup honey
1 bay leaf

PROCEDURE

1. Unroll the deboned leg of lamb and rub it inside and out with salt and pepper, olive oil, 1 teaspoon mint, and 1 teaspoon parsley. With the inside of the meat facing upward, distribute the garlic, scallions, and cheese over all. Sprinkle with bread crumbs, roll into a tight bundle, and tie to keep the stuffing in place.

2. Place all the marinade ingredients in a nonreactive roasting pan. Stir, and then add the stuffed leg of lamb, rolling it in the marinade. Marinating heightens the flavor, imparts depth, gives the meat a more delicate texture, and reduces cooking time. Place in the refrigerator overnight, turning and basting occasionally.

3. When ready to roast, preheat the oven to 450°F. Remove all but ½ cup marinade from the roasting pan, reserving the excess for basting. Place the meat rack in the roasting pan and the lamb on the meat rack. Roast at 450°F for ½ hour. (This sears in the juices and preserves the flavors.) Reduce the heat to 325°F. Baste with marinade every 15 minutes. Bake until the lamb reaches an internal temperature of 145°F for medium-rare or 160°F for medium. Be careful not to overcook. Lamb cooked medium-rare will be much more tender and succulent. Overcooking lamb makes it dry, tough, and not too tasty.

4. Remove from the roasting pan and place on a cutting board. Allow to sit for 10 to 15 minutes before slicing. Slice into ⅛- to ¼-inch slices and arrange on a warmed platter. Strain and defat the pan juices and keep hot in a saucepan. Moisten the meat with some of the pan juices; then place the remainder of the juices in a gravy boat. Bring all to the table and serve hot.

Yield: 8 to 10 servings

NOTES

Get your defatting cup out and, after the meat is cooked, take all that fat out of the juice and discard it. The Roast Potatoes with Cheese and Herbs (page 252) are a wonderful accompaniment to this roast.

Feel free to substitute fresh rosemary for the mint.

If using a whole leg of lamb with the bone in, make slits all over the leg of lamb with a paring knife, filling the slits with the stuffing. Proceed to bake in the same manner, remembering it takes longer to cook per pound with the bone in. Use an instant-read thermometer to check the internal temperature.

Store any leftovers in the refrigerator in a covered container; they will keep in the refrigerator for several days. Consider grinding any leftover lamb and adding it to Marinara Sauce (page 5) for a quick pasta meal that uses leftovers. Lamb can be frozen, but I do not recommend it; it will lose some of its flavor and texture.

Fresh Sausage

Salsiccia Fresca

Preparation Time: varies depending on the method; allow 1 to 2 days for seasoning the meat if possible. If you are grinding your own meat and stuffing it manually, allow about 2 hours. If you are using a machine to grind and stuff in one process, allow 30 minutes.
Cooking Time: 20 to 30 minutes

When I was a little girl in Italy, my mom was in charge of the slicing and seasoning of the pork for sausages. My dad was in charge of the grinding machine and I have vivid memories of popping all the bubbles in the casing with a needle. For me, the process of making the sausage is more of a delight than eating them. When my children were little, they too helped with this process and I hope my grandchildren will get excited about their up-and-coming responsibilities—at least the ones who are not vegetarians.

I teach sausage-making in my intermediate cooking classes. The students are always surprised at the few ingredients it takes to make true Italian sausage. If you want to simplify the process, ask your butcher to debone the pork butt and cut it up into 1-inch cubes for you. When you get home, season the pieces well, place them in a large reclosable plastic freezer bag, and allow them to rest in the refrigerator for a day or so until you are ready to make the sausage. Many of the heavy-duty stand-up mixers have grinding attachments with funnels that actually grind the meat and push it into the sausage-stuffing funnel that you have placed the casing on at the same time. It's a one-step process, and the machine does most of the work for you. If you choose to do it manually and experience the total process, you only need an old-fashioned grinding machine or a food processor and a sausage-stuffing funnel.

5 pounds boneless pork butt with
  some fat on it (see Notes)
2 tablespoons coarse salt or regular
  salt (to taste)
2 tablespoons coarsely ground black
  pepper

3 tablespoons fennel seeds
  (for medium to hot sausage),
  optional
1 tablespoon red pepper flakes (for
  medium to hot sausage), or more
  to taste

1 package natural hog casings (see Notes)

To Cook the Sausage:
1 tablespoon extra-virgin olive oil
¾ cup dry red or white wine

PROCEDURE

1. Cut up the pork into 1-inch cubes, sprinkle with the seasonings, and toss. If you have the time, place in a reclosable plastic bag in the refrigerator for 1 to 2 days to allow the seasonings to seep into the meat; this will make for a more flavorful sausage.

2. Place the seasoned pork in the freezer for ½ hour before you are ready to grind the meat; it will solidify the fat and make grinding easier. If you are using a meat grinder, grind with the *coarse* grinding disk. If using a food processor, pulse to grind. Do not overprocess; you want a coarse grind. Set aside.

3. Wash the casings under cold water to remove any extra salt. Cut the casings into 2-foot lengths.

4. Slip one end of casing onto the throat of a sausage funnel, bringing up the rest of the casing onto the funnel, just like putting on a sock. Knot the end of the casing. Push the sausage meat a little at a time through the funnel with your thumbs, pushing your thumb and the meat as deep into the funnel as possible. The casing gradually comes off the funnel as it fills.

5. Pop any large air pockets with a needle.

6. At this point, you can cook the sausage immediately or refrigerate for up to 2 days before cooking. Cook only as much sausage as you need, freezing the rest for another time.

7. To cook the sausage, place a large, heavy, nonstick skillet over medium-high heat. When the skillet is warm, add the oil. When the oil is hot, add the sausage, being careful not to overcrowd the skillet. As the fat renders, the sausages will start to turn brown. Turn the sausages with tongs as they brown. Continue to cook until all sides have browned, about 10 to 15 minutes. Add ¾ cup dry red or white wine, cover the skillet, reduce the heat to medium, and continue to cook for 5 minutes. Remove the cover and continue to cook for a few more minutes, until the wine has been reduced. Be careful not to overcook and dry out the sausage.

Yield: 5 pounds sausage
(1 pound sausage yields 4 to 5 large links)

Meats and Poultry

NOTES

Select a pork butt that is not too lean or the meat, and consequently the sausage you make, will be dry. If the pork butt has a bone in it, ask the butcher to remove it for you, and save it in the freezer until you make Sunday Tomato Sauce with Meatballs, page 122.

Alternatively, these sausages may be baked or broiled in the oven or cooked slowly on the grill.

To make sweet sausage (my favorite), omit the fennel and red pepper.

Store leftovers in the refrigerator in a covered container, where they will keep for several days; heat in a skillet until warm or hot. To use frozen cooked sausage, allow it to defrost in the refrigerator; then place in 350°F oven until it is warmed throughout.

Raw sausage can be frozen for several months. Wrap in aluminum foil and place in freezer bags. Allow frozen sausage to defrost in the refrigerator overnight and then cook according to the recipe directions.

Stuffed Pork Chops

Costolette di Maiale con Erbe

Preparation Time: 30 minutes   •   Baking Time: 30 minutes

After thirty-five years of marriage, my husband still talks about the wonderful pork chops I made for our first dinner together after our honeymoon in our little brownstone apartment on 103rd Street and Riverside Drive in New York City. It is a meal we enjoy just as much today.

For the Stuffing:
1 tablespoon extra-virgin olive oil
1 tablespoon butter
1 stalk celery, finely chopped
1 small yellow cooking onion, finely chopped
¼ pound pancetta, chopped
1 apple, peeled, cored, and finely chopped
2 tablespoons golden raisins
⅛ teaspoon salt
A pinch of freshly ground black pepper
2 tablespoons chopped Italian flat-leaf parsley
1 cup dry fine bread crumbs

For the Pork Chops:
4 center-cut bone-in loin chops, 1 inch thick, cut a pocket into the chop or you can have your butcher do it for you

¼ cup unbleached all-purpose flour
Salt and freshly ground black pepper
2 large eggs, beaten
1 cup bread crumbs
1 tablespoon extra-virgin olive oil
1 tablespoon butter

For the Sauce:
2 tablespoons extra-virgin olive oil
2 tablespoons butter
½ pound mushrooms (any type), wiped clean with damp paper towel and sliced
Salt and freshly ground black pepper
½ cup white wine
½ cup cream

PROCEDURE

1. Place a large skillet over medium-high heat. When the skillet is warm, add the oil and butter. When the oil is hot and the butter is foamy, add the celery, onion, and pancetta and sauté for 4 minutes. Add the apple, golden raisins, salt, and pepper. Stir and sauté for an additional 2 to 3 minutes. Add the parsley. Remove from the stove, toss with the bread crumbs, place in a bowl, and set aside.

2. Preheat the oven to 350°F. Pat the pork drops dry with paper towels. Season both sides with salt and pepper.

3. Divide the stuffing into 4 equal portions. Stuff the pork chops and sew closed with toothpicks.

4. Place the flour, eggs, and bread crumbs in 3 separate shallow bowls. Season the chops, and dredge in flour; dip in eggs and then in the bread crumbs, making sure to pat the bread crumbs firmly onto the chops so they adhere. If you have time, place the chops in the refrigerator for ½ hour to allow the breading to set. (They will absorb less oil if you refrigerate them before frying.)

5. Place the same large skillet over medium-high heat. When the skillet is warm, add the oil and butter. When the oil is hot and the butter is foamy, add the chops and sauté on both sides until lightly golden. Set the skillet aside and don't wash it yet.

6. Line an ovenproof baking dish with aluminum foil. Place the chops in the pan and bake for 30 minutes. While they are baking, make the sauce.

7. Return the same skillet to stove and heat to medium-high. When the skillet is warm, add the oil and butter. When the oil is hot and the butter foamy, add the mushrooms, season with salt and pepper, and sauté 3 to 4 minutes. Remove mushrooms from the pan and place in a bowl.

8. Deglaze the skillet with white wine, scraping up any browned bits and pieces. Cook until the wine is reduced to about 2 tablespoons. Add the cream and mushrooms and simmer for 5 minutes. Pour over the pork chops. Serve immediately.

Yield: Serves 4 people

NOTES

The sauce can be omitted if you prefer.

Store any leftovers in the refrigerator in a covered container; they will keep for several days. To reheat, place in the microwave or oven. I do not recommend freezing these chops.

Stuffed Pork Tenderloin

Tasca di Maiale Ripiena

Preparation Time: 45 minutes • Roasting Time: 30 to 45 minutes

I love preparing stuffed pork tenderloin in a variety of ways. It is very tender and moist, easy to prepare, and so flavorful. It is very economical—one tenderloin can go a long way. You can't top this pork recipe for taste and presentation. If you want to make a lasting impression on your family, friends, or guests, try serving this at your next dinner party!

2 pork tenderloins, about 1 pound each
Salt and freshly ground black pepper

For the Stuffing:
3 tablespoons extra-virgin olive oil, divided
1 medium yellow cooking onion, chopped
1 clove garlic, chopped (about ½ teaspoon)
2 tender celery ribs, chopped
½ red bell pepper, chopped
½ teaspoon salt
¼ teaspoon freshly ground black pepper

¼ cup golden raisins
8 dried apricots, coarsely chopped
½ cup dry white wine, plus more if needed to moisten stuffing
3 cups dry bread cubes, coarsely chopped
¼ cup chopped Italian flat-leaf parsley
2 large eggs, lightly beaten

For the Assembly:
½ pound sliced provolone cheese
2 yards kitchen twine
½ cup dry white wine
¼ cup chopped red bell pepper, for garnish

PROCEDURE

1. Butterfly the pork tenderloins by horizontally cutting each one almost in half, starting at one edge and cutting up to but not through the other side. Proceed to open it like a book. Pound to a little less than ¼ inch thick. Salt and pepper both sides of the flattened tenderloins. (If you don't have the time or inclination to butterfly your tenderloins, ask your butcher to do it for you.)

2. Place a large skillet over medium-high heat. When the skillet is warm,

add 2 tablespoons of the olive oil. When the oil is hot, add the onion, garlic, celery, and red pepper. Stir and season with the salt and pepper. Cook until softened (about 5 minutes). Add the raisins, apricots, and white wine, stir, and cook for an additional 5 minutes, or until most of the wine is absorbed. Remove from the heat. Transfer the contents of the skillet to a large bowl. Set the skillet aside without washing it. Add the bread crumbs and parsley to the stuffing, and stir. Taste for seasonings and adjust accordingly. Add the beaten eggs and mix lightly until all ingredients are combined. If the stuffing seems too dry, add a little more white wine.

3. Place each flattened tenderloin on a sheet of parchment paper. Place the provolone cheese in one layer over their entire surface. Dividing the stuffing in half, spread it over the cheese. Roll each tenderloin from long side to long side and tie securely with kitchen twine.

4. Preheat the oven to 350°F. Heat the remaining tablespoon of olive oil in the skillet over medium-high heat and sear the rolls on all sides. Line a baking pan with aluminum foil. Place a roasting rack in the pan and put the seared rolls side by side on the rack.

5. Roast for about 30 minutes, or until the internal temperature reaches 140°F. Don't overcook; the meat continues to cook after it is removed from the oven. Allow the meat to rest 10 minutes while you make the sauce.

6. Reduce the drippings in the skillet with the remaining ½ cup dry white wine over high heat, scraping up the browned bits and pieces while stirring. Remove from the heat.

7. Transfer the rolls onto a cutting board and remove the string. Slice the tenderloin on a diagonal into ½-inch-thick slices. Arrange on a platter, drizzle with the sauce, and garnish with the red pepper. Enjoy!

Yield: Serves 8 people

NOTES

Store any leftovers in the refrigerator in covered containers; they will keep for several days. Reheat in the microwave or in a 350°F oven until warm. Leftovers may be frozen and will keep in the freezer for a few months.

Dad's Quick Sautéed Steak with Mushrooms

....

Bistecca Veloce con Funghi del Papà

Preparation Time: 10 minutes • Cooking Time: 15 minutes

My dad had many idiosyncrasies when it came to food. He had only a few favorite meals, and he would stick to the same ones for years with stubborn devotion then suddenly, out of the blue, switch to something entirely different. The first year after we arrived in the States he discovered corn flakes. He fell in love with them and had them every morning without fail. My mother would place a large pasta bowl in front of him and fill it two-thirds full of fresh perked coffee. He would add his flakes and spoonful after spoonful of sugar, while Mom stood by and commented on the amount he could consume. After years of the same familiar ritual, he switched out of the clear blue to Mother's homemade breakfast cookies, 5 of them, broken into his bowl, with more coffee and sugar. He ended this breakfast by eating 2 raw eggs, which was a sight to behold! When he tired of that, he was on to the Italian version of French toast, without syrup or powdered sugar, just a healthy sprinkling of salt. As he got older, he would revisit his old favorites from time to time.

But there was one dish that he remained loyal to throughout his life, and that was his pan-fried steak. I give you this easy recipe, which you will enjoy for its unbeatable flavor and juiciness.

2 Delmonico, porterhouse, rib, or New York strip steaks, seasoned with coarse salt and freshly ground black pepper
1 tablespoon unsalted butter
2 tablespoon extra-virgin olive oil, divided, plus more if necessary for the mushrooms
1 medium yellow cooking onion, sliced

2 cloves garlic, minced (about ½ teaspoon)
½ pound mushrooms of your choice, wiped clean with a damp paper towel, sliced or quartered
Salt and freshly ground black pepper
2 to 3 tablespoons dry red or white wine

PROCEDURE

1. Place a large nonstick heavy-gauge skillet over medium-high heat. (The skillet must be large enough to fit the two steaks comfortably.) When the skillet is warm, add the butter and 1 tablespoon of the oil. When the butter has melted and the oil is hot, add the onions, and stir and sauté for 3 minutes. Add the garlic, and stir and sauté for an additional 2 minutes. Add the mushrooms, sprinkle with salt and pepper, and stir and cook for another 4 minutes, until the mushrooms are cooked throughout. If you need more oil, add as necessary. Remove the mushroom mixture to a bowl and reserve for later.

2. Wipe the bottom of the skillet clean with a paper towel. Place the skillet back on the stove over high heat. Add the remaining tablespoon of oil. When the oil is good and hot (you need to sear the steak, to lock in the juices), add the steaks and swirl around in the oil. Cook on one side for about 2 to 3 minutes, or until browned; then flip them over and cook the other side for an additional 2 minutes or so. Check for doneness by making a tiny slit in the center of the steak with a sharp knife to see what the inside of the steak looks like. Cook to your specifications. Remember, overcooking steak makes it dry and tough.

3. Add the mushroom mixture to the steak, stir, and heat for 45 more seconds. Remove the steaks and mushrooms from the skillet. You can serve the steaks as is, with the mushroom mixture poured over the tops, or cut the steaks into thin slices, fan the slices out, and serve with mushrooms on the side.

4. Set the skillet with pan drippings on high heat. When the pan is hot, add the wine and, with a spatula, scrape up any bits and pieces, cooking until most of the wine has evaporated. Pour this over the steak, or use it to dunk bits of Italian bread in.

Yield: 2 servings

NOTES

Store any leftovers in the refrigerator in covered containers; they will keep for several days. I do not recommend freezing these steaks.

Veal Shanks

Ossobuchi di Vitello

*Preparation Time: 30 minutes, not including
preparation of meat broth, if making from scratch*

Cooking Time: 2 hours

Veal shanks can be cooked in a variety of ways, but they taste the best when they are allowed to cook slowly with vegetables and aromatic ingredients. These shanks are first dredged in flour and then browned. The pan drippings are deglazed with good, dry white wine, and everything is cooked slowly with vegetables and homemade meat broth. At the end of cooking, the veal is succulent and soft and tender, falling away from the bones. Before you plan to make this dish, call your butcher several days in advance to be sure of having the shanks available. You don't want to be disappointed. Ask for the hind shanks; they are meatier.

For the Veal Shanks:
6 veal shanks (see Notes), left whole
    or cut into 1- to 2-inch pieces
Salt and freshly ground black
    pepper
1 cup unbleached all-purpose flour
1 tablespoon butter
1 tablespoon extra-virgin olive oil

For the Vegetables:
3 tablespoons extra-virgin olive oil,
    divided
1 large stalk of celery, finely chopped
2 medium carrots, finely chopped
2 medium onions, chopped
2 cloves garlic, minced
    (about 1 teaspoon)
½ teaspoon salt
¼ teaspoon freshly ground black
    pepper

½ pound fresh shiitake mushrooms,
    stalks removed and discarded,
    surface wiped with a damp paper
    towel and sliced (you may
    substitute fresh porcini or
    portobello mushrooms)

For the Cooking Sauce:
1 cup dry white wine
1 (14 ounce) can whole Italian plum
    tomatoes, seeded (page 3) and
    chopped, with juice passed
    through a strainer or sieve
1¼ cups meat broth
2 bay leaves
2 sprigs fresh thyme (remove leaves
    from stalk and discard stalk)
Rind from ½ lemon, trying to keep it
    in one piece

(cont'd)

For the Gremolata (Optional):
2 tablespoons chopped Italian flat-
  leaf parsley

Grated zest of 1 lemon
1 clove garlic, minced (about
  ½ teaspoon)

PROCEDURE

1. Season the meat with salt and pepper. Dredge in the flour and shake off any excess flour.

2. Place a large heavy skillet over medium-high heat. When the skillet is warm, add the butter and 1 tablespoon of the olive oil. When the butter has melted and stops foaming, add as many pieces of meat as will fit comfortably in the pan. Brown on all sides, about 7 minutes. As the meat cooks, remove it and place on a platter. Continue cooking until all pieces have been browned. This is really the key to the success of this dish. Make sure the meat is browned to a nice golden brown. This not only contributes to a more full, delicious meat flavor, but it adds richness and depth to the sauce.

3. With the heat on medium-high and still using the same skillet (don't bother to wash it), add 2 tablespoons of the olive oil. When the oil is hot, add the celery, carrots, onions, garlic. Season all with salt and pepper. Stir and cook for 5 to 7 minutes. Remove and place on the same platter as the shanks.

4. With the pan still on medium-high heat, add the remaining 1 tablespoon oil. When the oil is hot, add the mushrooms and sauté for 3 to 4 minutes. Remove the mushrooms to the platter with the shanks.

5. With the pan still on medium-high heat, deglaze with the wine. When the wine is reduced by half, add the tomatoes, tomato juice, broth, bay leaves, thyme, and lemon peel along with the browned veal and vegetables in the platter. When the mixture comes to a boil, reduce the heat to simmering and place cover on pan, leaving the lid slightly askew. Stew all the flavorful ingredients slowly for 1½ hours, depending on what size the veal pieces were cut into. (The smaller the pieces, the less cooking time required; the meat is done when it starts to fall away from the bone.) Remove the meat to an ovenproof dish and keep warm in a 250°F oven.

6. Meanwhile, turn the heat under the skillet up to medium-high and cook to reduce the liquids and thicken sauce, about 5 minutes, stirring frequently. Remove the lemon peel and the bay leaves. Put the veal shanks back into the skillet, heat throughout, and place all on a platter.

7. Mix the parsley, lemon zest, and minced garlic to create the gremolata. Sprinkle all over, and serve immediately, nice and hot.

Yield: 6 servings

NOTES

Ask for the hind shanks; they are meatier.

You may choose to make this with lamb shanks. They are uniquely flavorful and an unusual change for family and guests.

Serve this dish as is, with slices of homemade peasant bread. If you want to get a little more elaborate with the presentation, try serving with risotto. Be adventurous, extract the marrow of the bone and eat it; it is a delicacy, and so flavorful!

Store any leftovers in the refrigerator in covered containers; they will keep for up to 4 days. This dish freezes well and will keep in the freezer for up to 4 months. The gremolata can be served as a garnish for a variety of dishes, including baked or broiled fish.

Baked Chicken with Potatoes and Vegetables

....

Pollo con Patate, Pomodori, e Pisellini

Preparation Time: 35 minutes • Cooking Time: 50 to 60 minutes

This is an old standby and worth learning to make with your eyes closed. It provides everything you need to make a nutritious and flavorful meal all in one pan. It can be dressed up for a ball or dressed down for a picnic. Having fresh chicken is key. Find out when your market gets their chicken in and if it has been frozen or partially frozen. Chicken that has not previously been frozen is more flavorful.

1 large frying or roaster chicken, about 3½ to 5 pounds, cut into serving-size pieces (if you don't have the experience or the time to cut it, ask your butcher to do it for you)

Salt and freshly ground black pepper

1 tablespoon butter

2 tablespoons extra-virgin olive oil

4 medium-large baking potatoes, peeled and cut into wedges (place wedges into a medium bowl of cold water to keep them from browning)

1 (16-ounce) package frozen peas

1 large yellow cooking onion, sliced

2 cloves garlic (about 1 teaspoon)

1 (14-ounce) can whole Italian plum tomatoes, seeded (see page 3) and chopped, with juice passed through a strainer or sieve

1 tablespoon Pesto from your freezer (page 25), optional

2 tablespoons chopped Italian flat-leaf parsley

1 teaspoon salt

¼ teaspoon fresh ground black pepper

PROCEDURE

1. Rinse the chicken under cold running water, drain in a colander, and pat dry with paper towels. Season each piece by sprinkling with salt and pepper on both sides. Set aside.

2. Preheat the oven to 350°F. Grease a large baking pan with the butter.

3. Place a large skillet over medium-high heat. When skillet is warm, add the oil. When the oil is hot, add the chicken pieces, being careful not to over-crowd them. As they brown (about 4 to 5 minutes), turn them over. When they have browned on both sides, transfer the pieces to the baking pan. Continue cooking until all the chicken has been browned.

4. Drain and dry the potatoes with paper towels. Place the potatoes, peas, onion, garlic, tomatoes and their juice, pesto, and parsley in the roasting pan on top of the chicken. Season with the salt and pepper. Toss all the ingredients together and bake for 1 hour, stirring every 15 minutes. If you like, place under the broiler for a few minutes to brown. Place all on a platter and serve hot.

Yield: 4 to 6 servings

NOTES

Store leftovers in the refrigerator in a covered container; they will keep for several days. To reheat, place in the microwave or 350°F oven until warm. I do not recommend freezing this dish.

Roast Chicken with Oregano

Pollo Arrostito con Origano

Preparation Time: 10 minutes • Cooking Time: 1¼ hours

This is one of those standbys that keeps coming back to our family table.

1 whole roasting chicken
    (4 to 5 pounds), cut into 8 pieces
1 teaspoon salt
½ teaspoon freshly ground black
    pepper

For the Marinade:
¾ cup apricot or peach preserves

1 medium-large yellow cooking
    onion, chopped (about ¾ cup)
3 cloves garlic, chopped
    (about 1½ teaspoons)
⅓ cup white wine vinegar
1½ tablespoons crushed dried
    oregano

PROCEDURE

1. Preheat the oven to 375°F.

2. Rinse the chicken under cold running water. Drain, and pat dry with paper towels. Place in a baking dish, season, and bake for 30 minutes.

3. While the chicken is baking, prepare the marinade. In a medium bowl, put the preserves, onion, garlic, and vinegar. Rub the oregano between your hands and then add it to the marinade. Stir to combine; then set aside.

4. After 30 minutes, remove the chicken from the oven and drain any liquid into a defatting cup. Discard the fat, but reserve the juice for later.

5. Place the partially cooked pieces of chicken in the marinade, toss to coat all sides, and then replace chicken in the baking dish. Pour any remaining marinade over the chicken.

6. Return the chicken to the oven to cook for another 35 to 45 minutes, checking periodically and turning chicken. If the bottom of the pan starts to dry out, add some of the reserved chicken juice. If you want a nicely browned skin, place the chicken under the broiler for 1 or 2 minutes before serving.

Yield: 6 to 8 servings

NOTES

Store leftovers in the refrigerator in a covered container; they will keep for several days. I do not recommend freezing this dish.

Mama Rosa's Roast Chicken with Honey, Oranges, and Lemon

Pollo al Miele con Arance e Limone

Preparation Time: 10 minutes (does not include making chicken broth from scratch)

Cooking Time: 1 ¾ to 2 hours (to an internal temperature of 180°F;
it usually takes between 20 and 30 minutes per pound to cook roasting chickens properly)

This is one of my happiest experiences; each time I recall it I cannot help but laugh.

One afternoon when my sister Pina and I were visiting my mother in Phoenix, she came to us with empty plastic bags in her hands and said, "Let's go for a walk," which translates into "Let's go for an Italian scavenger hunt." So the three of us set off on an adventure.

After 15 minutes of searching, we discovered a house whose lawn was strewn with pecans. My mother was delighted. I rang the bell and inquired of the kindly lady if she was going to harvest the pecans. She responded that they already had and we should help ourselves. After an hour and a half, we had accumulated enough, even though my mother wanted to continue picking. We approached the owner to thank her for her generosity, but she just gave us more bags and told us she had orange, grapefruit, and lemon trees in the back. Mom was overjoyed. Laden with four bags each of nuts and fruit, we managed to stagger a quarter of a mile down the road before the gentleman of the house found us and offered us a ride in his car. At first we refused, but after considering the alternative, the three of us meekly accepted. What a laugh we had relating the incident to the rest of the family. We feasted on this chicken dish Mom made with some of the oranges and lemons we had gathered.

1 roasting chicken (5 to 6 pounds)
1 teaspoon salt
½ teaspoon freshly ground black pepper
1 large navel orange, cut in half
1 lemon, cut in half

⅓ cup honey
1 medium yellow cooking onion, peeled
1 cup Chicken Broth (page 60) or commercial broth, if necessary, for basting

PROCEDURE

1. Preheat the oven to 400°F. Line a roasting pan with heavy-duty aluminum foil; this will save you a lot of time on cleanup.

2. Rinse the chicken inside and outside with cold running water. Drain in a colander and pat the entire chicken dry, inside and out, with paper towels. Place in the roasting pan. Rub the chicken all over, inside and out, with the salt and pepper. Take one half of the orange and squeeze and rub it in the inside cavity; squeeze and rub the other half on the outside, reserving the orange itself.

3. Seed the lemon and repeat the above procedure.

4. Take some of the honey in the palm of your hand and rub it into both the inside and the outside of the chicken, until all the honey has been used.

5. Cut the onion into quarters, leaving it in one piece at the root end. Cook in the microwave on High for 1½ minutes.

6. Stuff the cavity of the chicken first with one of the reserved orange halves, then one lemon half, followed by the onion, the other half lemon, and ending with the other orange, which will close up the cavity opening.

7. Roast the chicken for 1 hour; then turn the heat down to 325°F and continue to cook for another 45 minutes to 1 hour.

8. While the chicken is cooking, baste it every 15 minutes or so. If you do not have enough natural juices in the bottom of the roasting pan, add some of the chicken broth. If the chicken is browning too quickly, tent a small piece of aluminum foil loosely over the top.

9. Check the chicken for doneness by inserting an instant-read cooking thermometer in the thigh, making sure the probe does not touch the bone. The internal temperature should read 180°F.

10. Serve on a platter with the natural juices. Accompany with rice and vegetables.

Yield: 6 to 8 servings

NOTES

Any leftover chicken should be taken off the bone, placed in a covered container, and refrigerated. It will keep for up to 3 days. Leftovers make wonderful salads, sandwiches, and spreads.

To make broth from the bones, see page 60.

Chicken with Onions and Vinegar

Pollo con Cipolle e Aceto

Preparation Time: 15 minutes   •   Cooking Time: 1 hour

This is a great dish to bring to picnics and tailgating parties. It has a beautiful golden brown color, lovely fragrance, and meat that is moist, tender, and succulent. The sauce that is created by the vinegar, onions, and flour is most flavorful and has a velvety consistency. The reduction of the vinegar combined with sugar, the flavor of the chicken, and onions gives this dish its characteristic taste. It is wonderful whether served hot, warm, or at room temperature.

1 roasting chicken (4½ to 5 pounds), cut into serving pieces—back, ribs, and wing tips removed
Salt and freshly ground black pepper
⅓ cup flour
3 tablespoons extra-virgin olive oil
2 medium to large yellow cooking onions, cut in half lengthwise, and then sliced
½ teaspoon salt
¼ teaspoon freshly ground black pepper
2 sprigs fresh rosemary, needles removed from stems, stems discarded
3 tablespoons sugar
¾ cup wine vinegar

PROCEDURE

1. Rinse the chicken under cold running water. Drain in a colander and pat dry with paper towels. Season each piece by sprinkling both sides with salt and pepper.

2. Place the flour on a platter and dredge the chicken in it until coated all over, shaking off any excess flour.

3. Place a large skillet over medium-high heat. When the skillet is warm, add the oil. When the oil is hot, add as many chicken pieces as will fit comfortably without overcrowding. Brown the chicken on both sides. Remove the chicken pieces as they are browned and place on the platter. Continue until all the chicken has been browned, 15 to 20 minutes, depending on the size skillet you are using.

4. After you have finished frying all the pieces, you will have oil left in the skillet. Turn the heat down to medium and sauté the sliced onion in the same skillet with the oil. Season the onion with salt and pepper, and sauté the onions until tender, stirring occasionally (5 to 6 minutes). With a slotted spoon, remove the onions and place with the chicken. Sprinkle the rosemary needles over the chicken.

5. Drain most of the oil and fat from the skillet. Place the skillet over medium-high heat and put all the chicken and onions back into the skillet. Stir the sugar with the vinegar and pour over the chicken. You will hear a nice sizzling sound. Cook for about 5 minutes, turning the chicken once. When most of the vinegar has been absorbed, turn the heat to low, cover tightly, and cook for an additional 25 to 30 minutes, turning the chicken once.

Yield: 6 to 8 servings

NOTES

Fresh rosemary can be purchased all year long at most grocery stores. Freeze any leftover rosemary for future use by taking the rosemary needles off the stalk, wrapping them tightly with plastic wrap, and placing in a reclosable plastic freezer bag.

If you are making this for a dinner party, you could prepare the chicken earlier in the day, and reheat when you are ready to serve it. Extra chicken will keep in the refrigerator for a few days. I do not recommend freezing leftovers; you lose a lot of that wonderful fresh flavor.

Chicken Salad

Insalata di Pollo

Preparation Time: 25 minutes

This recipe uses the leftover boiled chicken from chicken soup. Many of my cooking class students tell me that when they serve it to guests they get rave reviews.

1 whole boiled chicken
1 small yellow cooking onion, chopped
4 scallions, white part only, chopped
¼ teaspoon finely minced garlic
4 ribs tender celery, chopped
10 Italian chestnuts, cooked, cleaned, and chopped (optional; omit if not in season)
1 roasted red pepper (see page 14), chopped
1½ tablespoons freshly squeezed lemon juice

½ pound mushrooms, cleaned with a damp paper towel and minced
8 ounces cream cheese
½ cup extra virgin olive oil
3 tablespoons wine vinegar
1 tablespoon balsamic vinegar
1 tablespoon finely chopped Italian flat-leaf parsley
1½ teaspoons salt
½ teaspoon freshly ground black pepper

PROCEDURE

1. Bone the chicken and chop it into small pieces. You may do this in a food processor or blender; pulse several times for the right consistency.

2. Place the chopped chicken in a large bowl. Add the onion, scallions, garlic, celery, chestnuts, and roasted pepper. Set aside.

3. Place the lemon juice in a small bowl. Add mushrooms and toss. Let rest for 2 minutes and then it add it to chicken.

4. In a food processor or blender, combine the cream cheese, oil, vinegars, parsley, salt, and pepper until smooth. Add to the chicken.

5. Mix all ingredients together. Taste for seasoning and adjust accordingly.

Yield: 8 servings

NOTES

Store leftovers in a covered container in the refrigerator; they will keep for about a week. I do not recommend freezing this dish.

Stuffed Turkey Breast

Petto di Tacchino Riempito

Preparation Time: 1 hour • Cooking Time: 1¼ hours

This is a very impressive, tasty, aromatic, and economical main course—another small masterpiece. Follow the steps carefully and you will have no problems.

1 whole boneless, skinless turkey breast (3½ to 4 pounds)
Salt and freshly ground black pepper
6 to 8 thin slices baked ham
6 to 8 thin slices provolone
1 recipe Spinach with Garlic and Olive Oil (page 29), drained well

For the Stuffing:
2 tablespoons extra-virgin olive oil
1 medium yellow cooking onion, finely chopped
1 clove garlic, finely chopped (about ½ teaspoon)
1 yellow or red bell pepper, diced
1 stalk tender celery, chopped
¼ teaspoon salt

⅛ teaspoon freshly ground black pepper
6 Marinated Sun-Dried Tomato halves (page 18), finely chopped
4 dried apricots, finely chopped
2 tablespoons chopped Italian flat-leaf parsley
¼ cup pine nuts, toasted (see page 24)
1½ cups bread crumbs
Kitchen twine

For Basting:
½ cup dry white wine
1 cup Chicken Broth—to prepare your own see page 60, or use store-bought broth

PROCEDURE

1. Keep the turkey breast in one piece. Butterfly the thickest portions of both sides of the breast to ⅓- ½-inch thickness and open up like a book. To refresh yourself on the butterflying technique, refer to page 50 on chicken cutlets.

2. Place the turkey breast shinier-side down on wax or parchment paper. Season the surface of the breast with salt and pepper. Place another sheet of wax or parchment paper on the top and pound the breast into a rectangular shape. This will thin and tenderize the meat.

3. Spread the ham slices in one layer over the turkey. Cover the ham with a layer of provolone slices. Add the spinach over the provolone. Let this sit while you prepare the stuffing.

4. Place a large skillet over medium-high heat. When the skillet is warm, add the oil. When the oil is hot, add the onion, garlic, bell pepper, and celery. Stir and season with the salt and pepper. Sauté until the vegetables are tender, about 5 to 6 minutes. Remove from the stove and add the sun-dried tomatoes, apricots, parsley, pine nuts, and bread crumbs. Toss to combine. Spread the stuffing over the spinach layer, leaving a ⅓-inch border all around.

5. Preheat the oven to 425°F.

6. Roll the turkey breast and stuffing up like a jelly roll. Start with the end closest to you and roll away from you to form a long, fat, sausage-shaped roll. Tie with kitchen twine.

7. Put a meat rack in a roasting pan. Place the stuffed turkey breast on rack. Cook at 425°F for 20 minutes. Reduce heat to 350°F and continue cooking. Roast for 60 to 75 minutes total, or until an instant-read thermometer registers 155°F at the center of the roast. Baste with the combined wine and broth every 15 minutes.

8. Remove from oven, allow to rest for 10 minutes, slice into ⅓- to ½-inch rounds, arrange them on a platter, pour the pan juices over them, and serve at once.

Yield: 8 to 10 servings

NOTES

Store any leftovers in the refrigerator in a covered container; they will keep for several days. To reheat, place in microwave or toaster oven until warm. I do not recommend freezing this dish.

*Meats
and Poultry*

Meatless "Cutlets"

"Frogia"

Preparation Time: 10 minutes • Cooking Time: 10 minutes

This dish was inspired by my mother, Rosa. She is the thriftiest, most frugal person I have ever known. I am grateful to have inherited this trait from her. She wastes nothing; to throw food away is a sin—a mortal one, may I add. There would always be leftover egg-and-bread-crumb mixture from the preparation of breaded chicken cutlets. Mom would simply add a little more egg, bread crumbs, and Romano cheese and make these delicious meatless cutlets. This was way before any of us were talking vegetarianism. Now, since some of our children are vegetarians, along with some of their spouses and children, this is a very welcome and often-served dish at our dinner table.

4 large eggs
½ cup freshly grated Romano cheese
1 teaspoon freshly chopped Italian flat-leaf parsley
¼ teaspoon salt
⅛ teaspoon freshly ground black pepper

½ cup plus 1 tablespoon plain dry bread crumbs
1 tablespoon extra-virgin olive oil
1 tablespoon canola oil
4 cups Marinara Sauce (page 5)
Freshly grated mozzarella or Romano cheese (optional)

PROCEDURE

1. In a medium bowl, beat the eggs, cheese, parsley, salt, and pepper. Add the bread crumbs and combine. The mixture will be very sticky. Let it rest 5 minutes and it will become firmer but still somewhat sticky. For this recipe, sticky is good. It will yield a moister cutlet.

2. Place a large skillet over medium heat. When the skillet is warm, add the olive and canola oils. When the oils are hot, drop the bread crumb mixture by heaping tablespoonfuls into the skillet, pressing down gently to flatten the surface somewhat. When golden brown on one side, flip and cook on the other side. These can now be eaten as is. They are fully cooked, or you could proceed to step 3.

3. Heat the sauce in a large skillet and place the cutlets in the sauce to cook

for another 15 minutes. Alternatively, you can bake the cutlets. Put the sauce on the bottom of a baking pan, then layer the frogia on top. Follow with another thin layer of sauce and a sprinkling of cheese. Bake in a preheated 350°F oven for 10 to 15 minutes.

Yield: 8 to 10 cutlets; 4 to 6 servings

NOTES

I often make these for an antipasto tray for dinner parties. Instead of dropping them in the oil in rounded tablespoonfuls, I use a teaspoon, making them small and dainty.

This is our daughter Lisa's favorite thing to make for herself and her friends. Being a vegetarian, she puts her own twist on this recipe by sautéing a variety of vegetables such as zucchini, broccoli, chopped Swiss chard, and shredded carrots, adding them to the bread crumb mixture to make the patties. I must say they are the tastiest veggie burgers I've ever had.

Store leftovers in the refrigerator in covered containers. Reheat in the microwave or eat at room temperature. The cutlets freeze well and will keep in the freezer for up to 2 months.

FISH AND SEAFOOD

With so many miles of Mediterranean coastline, Italians have been able to enjoy a great variety of fresh fish and shellfish of every description, many of which are unfamiliar to us in America. Italians insist on freshness without compromise when purchasing their fish. This should be your creed too; it's better to go home with another product or with frozen fish for your dinner than to try to camouflage smelly, old fish with marinades or sauces. Your goal when purchasing fish is to find flesh that is firm; eyes that are clear, shiny, and unclouded; skin that is glistening; and gills that are rigid, red to bright pink in color, and free of slippery residue. Fish fillets and steaks should have a fresh odor, fine texture, and moist appearance. When buying fish from a reputable dealer, inquire about their delivery schedule—certain fish usually come in at certain times of the week. If possible, ask to smell the fish before you purchase it. If it smells too strong, it has probably been around for some time and has seen better days.

The closer the Italian people live to the coast, the more

fish is a traditional part of their daily diet. It was not so long ago that refrigeration was inaccessible to most Italians; however, with the building of the super-highways called *autostradas,* fish can now be transported from one region to another safely. The Sicilian village in which I was born was far from the coast. Most of the families used sardines and anchovies that were packed in salt or olive oil, or cod that was salted and dried. My mother was very inventive and made a small amount of fish go a long way.

The secrets to cooking fish are the following: buy the freshest fish available to you, cook it the same day, and keep it refrigerated until you are ready to begin cooking. Fish can be cooked quite simply by poaching, steaming, or boiling. You may eat it raw, if you dare. Or it can be baked, broiled, grilled, sautéed, or deep-fried. Use it to make soups or stews.

The recipes included in this book are family treasures, some of which are traditional and some of which I created on vacations with our children. Some are simple and easy to put together in a short period of time, and others, such as the Fish Stew, take a bit more thought, organization, and time. The Baked Stuffed Whole Lobster is in its own category; if you attempt it, picture me at your side, helping you along step-by-step. We can do it!

Fish Stew

Zuppa di Pesce

*Preparation Time: 45 minutes to 1 hour—depending on if the mussels
and clams are farm-raised or fresh; farm-raised requires less cleanup time*

Cooking Time: 40 minutes

This fish stew is utterly delicious and will titillate your taste buds. Looking at this recipe initially, you might get discouraged. *Don't.* It is definitely time consuming, but it is quite simple to prepare. Go one step at a time.

2 pounds mussels
1 pound clams
2 tablespoons salt
2 quarts water
⅓ cup semolina, flour, or cornmeal
1 pound extra-large shrimp
3 tablespoons extra-virgin olive oil, divided
2 medium yellow onions, thinly sliced
4 cloves garlic
A sprinkling of salt and freshly ground black pepper
2 cups Marinara Sauce (page 5)
2 cups dry white wine, divided
¼ teaspoon red pepper flakes, or more to taste

6 fresh basil leaves, chopped
1 quart Fish Broth (page 59), already prepared or use a good brand of canned
1 pound haddock, halibut, or cod, skin removed, rinsed and drained, cut into 1 × 1½–inch pieces
1 pound scallops, rinsed, drained, and any pieces of shiny ligament removed

For Garnish:
2 tablespoons chopped Italian flat-leaf parsley
Zest of 1 lemon

PROCEDURE

1. Soak the mussels and clams in a large bowl of cold water. Add 2 tablespoons salt. Throw away any mussels with broken shells. Add ⅓ cup cornmeal, flour, or semolina to the soaking water and let them soak for 1 hour. The live mussels and clams will feed on the cornmeal and excrete any dirt and sand. Scrub the shells with a stiff brush. Using a knife, scrape away any loose seaweedlike strands (beards) which protrude from the mussels. Rinse the mussels and clams in several changes of cold water until the water is clear.

2. Prepare the shrimp. To remove the shell, start with the large end, get your thumb under the shell, and pull it away. The intestinal vein of the shrimp contains noticeable grit and should be removed. To devein, use a large, pointed knife to cut a shallow slit down the middle of the outside curve of the shrimp. Pull out the dark vein, and discard. (You can also buy farm-raised shrimp that do not have grit in the vein, because they are not fed for several days before they are harvested.) Rinse the shrimp in cold water, drain, and pat dry with a paper towel. Set aside.

3. Place a large skillet over medium-high heat. When the skillet is warm, add the oil. When the oil is hot, add the onions and stir briefly. Sauté for 4 minutes; then add the garlic and sauté for another 2 minutes.

4. Add the 2 cups marinara sauce, 1 cup of the wine, the red pepper flakes, and the basil. Simmer for about 10 minutes. Taste for seasoning, and adjust accordingly. Add the fish broth and the fish chunks and simmer for 7 minutes.

5. Heat another sauce pot over medium-high heat. Add the ½ cup water along with the remaining 1 cup wine. Add the clams, cover, and cook until the clams open. Use tongs and remove the clams immediately as they open and place in a warm oven. Discard any clams that do not open.

6. Place the mussels in the same water as you used for the clams, adding a little more water if necessary. Cover and cook until the mussels open. Remove them immediately as they open and add them to the clams that are in the warming oven. Discard any unopened mussels.

7. Strain any remaining cooking liquid through a coffee filter and add it to the marinara sauce.

8. Place the shrimp and scallops into the marinara pot. Cook with the cover on for 2 minutes. Remove the cover, add the mussels and clams in their shells, stir, add the mussels and clams, and cook for another 2 minutes, or until the shrimp turn opaque and are cooked through.

9. Garnish with the chopped parsley and lemon zest, and serve nice and hot with homemade bread.

Yield: 8 to 10 generous servings

NOTES

Any leftovers should be stored in the refrigerator and eaten the next day. Try pouring over pasta!

Cod from the Christmas Eve Tradition

Baccalà della Vigilia

Preparation Time: 20 minutes (not including soaking time)
Cooking Time: 35 minutes

We lived in a little town called Valguarnera, which is located in central Sicily. Not living on the sea coast, we did not have easy access to all the wonderful seafood caught off the coast. The fish that was readily available to us was salted cod. My mother would soak the cod for several days in water, changing the water several times a day. We looked forward to this fish, which was always cooked on Christmas Eve, when Catholics were not allowed to eat meat. You can still purchase salted cod in many fish markets today, but be sure to order it in advance and soak it several days, changing the water often. This dish may be made with fresh cod if salted cod is not available to you, but as many Italians would say, *Il sapore non e lo stesso*—the flavor just isn't the same. Tradition . . . tradition!

1½ pounds salted cod fillets
⅓ cup flour
4 tablespoons extra-virgin olive oil, divided
3 to 4 potatoes, peeled and cut into large, bite-size pieces
1 stalk tender celery, cut into ¼-inch slices
Tender green leaves from the celery heart
2 medium yellow cooking onions, cut in half lengthwise and sliced
6 plum tomatoes, seeded (see page 3) and chopped, and ½ cup juice from the tomatoes, passed through a strainer or sieve to remove the seeds
8 large green olives, pitted and sliced thin
4 Kalamata or Gaeta olives, pitted and chopped
4 fresh basil leaves, torn into pieces
A sprinkling of salt and freshly ground black pepper
1½ cups Vegetable or Fish Broth (pages 62 and 59) or commercial bouillon or water, divided

PROCEDURE

1. Soak the cod in the refrigerator for 2 to 3 days in cold water, changing the water several times a day; remove any stray bones or loose skin. Drain and wipe dry with a paper towel.

2. Cut the cod fillets into 2-inch pieces and season on both sides with a sprinkling of salt and pepper. Dredge in flour. Place a large skillet over medium-high heat. When the skillet is warm, add 2 tablespoons of the oil. When the oil is hot, add as many pieces of cod as will fit comfortably in the skillet and sauté on both sides until golden. Remove to a platter and continue cooking the rest of the cod in the same manner. Add more of the oil if necessary.

3. Using the same skillet over medium-high heat, add a little more of the oil if necessary and the potatoes, celery, celery leaves, and onions. Sauté for 7 minutes, stirring occasionally. Add the tomatoes, juice, olives, basil, cooked cod, and 1 cup of the broth. Bring to a boil, cover with the lid slightly askew, turn the heat down to a slow boil, and cook until the potatoes are tender, about 15 minutes. If the juice seems to be evaporating, add more broth or water. Taste for seasonings and adjust accordingly. Serve in bowls, piping hot, accompanied by fresh crusty bread.

Yield: 6 servings

NOTES

Store leftovers in the refrigerator in a covered container; leftovers should be eaten the following day. Reheat in the microwave or in 350°F oven until warm. I do not recommend freezing *baccalà*.

Baked Fish, Simplified

Filetti al Forno

Preparation Time: 10 minutes • Cooking Time: 10 to 15 minutes

Easy, healthy, quick, and delicious—who could ask for anything more?

1 tablespoon olive oil or butter, for
    greasing the baking sheet
1½ pounds fillets of flounder,
    haddock, sole, or orange roughy
    (4 pieces or more)
Salt and freshly ground black
    pepper
2 tablespoons butter
2 medium shallots, minced
1 clove garlic minced
    (about ½ teaspoon)

A sprinkling of salt and pepper
2 tablespoons extra-virgin olive oil
2 tablespoons freshly squeezed
    lemon juice
1 teaspoon chopped fresh mint,
    thyme, or Italian flat-leaf parsley,
    or a combination
6 tablespoons dry bread crumbs or
    cracker crumbs made from
    enriched crackers

PROCEDURE

1. Preheat the oven to 400°F. Place an oven rack on the second shelf from the top. Line a baking sheet with aluminum foil and rub 1 tablespoon of butter on the foil.

2. Rinse the fish fillets under cold running water. Drain in a colander and pat dry with paper towels. Season with salt and pepper and place in the prepared baking pan.

3. Place a small skillet over medium-high heat. When the skillet is warm, add the butter. When the butter has melted and stops foaming, add the shallots, garlic, salt, and pepper. Stir and sauté for 3 to 4 minutes, or until the shallots are tender. Place the sautéed shallots and garlic in a medium bowl along with the oil, lemon juice, and herbs. Rub the fillets all over with this marinade.

4. Place fillets on the baking sheet and pour marinade over tops. To ensure even baking of fish, tuck the thin tail-end portions of fillets under. You should now have rectangular pieces of fish of almost even thickness. Sprinkle the tops of the fish with the bread crumbs or cracker crumbs, about 1 tablespoon for each fillet.

5. Bake uncovered for 10 to 15 minutes, depending on how thick your fillets are. When the fish is cooked, it should be opaque and flake easily with a fork. If the fish is still a little shiny and translucent, it needs to cook a little longer. Be careful not to overcook the fish; it will become dry, tough, and rubbery. Serve hot, with a combination of vegetables and rice.

Yield: 4 servings

NOTES

For a more sophisticated version of this dish, make a stuffing using cooked rice, soft cheese, dried craisons and herbs. Incorporate the ingredients and place stuffing on top of the fillets.

Store any leftovers in the refrigerator in a covered container; leftovers should be eaten the next day. Reheat in the microwave or in 350°F oven until warm. I do not recommend freezing this dish.

Elegant Shrimp
with Spinach Stuffing

Gamberi Ripieni con Spinaci

Preparation Time: 45 minutes • *Cooking Time: 10 minutes*

I serve this during the holidays, for special occasions, and at dinner parties. The various steps can be done in the morning and the final dish assembled at the last minute. It is rich in taste and makes a beautiful presentation. People will definitely want seconds, so make extra.

1 pound or extra-large shrimp
¼ teaspoon salt
¼ teaspoon freshly ground black
  pepper

For the Stuffing:
1 medium potato, peeled and cut
  into ⅛-inch dice
⅓ pound mushrooms, wiped with a
  damp paper towel and sliced
4 tablespoons butter, divided
1 medium cooking onion, finely
  chopped
3 cloves garlic, minced
½ pound fresh spinach, cooked
  according to Spinach with Garlic

and Olive Oil recipe (page 29),
  and chopped
1 tablespoon finely chopped Italian
  flat-leaf parsley
1 tablespoon finely chopped fresh
  thyme
Salt and freshly ground black
  pepper to taste
¼ pound Ritz or Townhouse
  crackers, crushed
¼ pound shredded fontina cheese
1 large egg, beaten

For the Garnish:
Thin slices of orange and lemon
or **lemon zest**

PROCEDURE

To Prepare the Shrimp:

1. To shell the shrimp, start with the large end, get your thumb under the shell, and pull it away. The tail fin may remain. Freeze the shells for Fish Broth.

2. The intestinal vein of shrimp contains noticeable grit and should be removed. To devein, use a large, pointed knife to cut a shallow slit down the middle of the outside curve of the shrimp. Pull out the dark vein and discard.

Fish and
Seafood

229

(Farm-raised shrimp are usually free of this.) Rinse the shrimp in cold water and drain.

3. Butterfly the shrimp with a sharp paring knife. Make a cut at the point where the vein was removed. Cut into the shrimp but not all the way through, enough to allow the sides to flatten out. Open each shrimp like a book and flatten. Place on paper towels and pat dry. Season lightly with salt and pepper.

To Prepare the Stuffing:

1. Cook the diced potato in boiling water for 2 minutes; drain and set aside.

2. Sauté the mushrooms in 1 tablespoon of the butter for 3 to 4 minutes. When cold enough to handle, mince and set aside.

3. Melt the rest of the butter in a medium-size skillet over medium heat. Add the onion and cook until tender, about 3 minutes. Add the garlic and cook for an additional 2 minutes. Add the potatoes, mushrooms, spinach, parsley, and thyme and cook for another 1 to 2 minutes. Season with salt and pepper.

4. Stir in the cracker crumbs and shredded cheese and mix with your hands. Taste for seasoning and adjust accordingly.

5. Add the egg and mix well.

To Finish the Dish:

1. Preheat the oven to 400°F and generously butter a baking sheet.

2. Place all the flattened shrimp on a piece of parchment or wax paper. Put 1 heaping tablespoon of stuffing on top of each shrimp. Place the shrimp on the baking sheet and bake for 8 minutes, until the shrimp turn pink and the stuffing is thoroughly heated.

3. Place the shrimp under the broiler for 1 to 2 minutes, until the tops turn golden. Watch closely; you don't want them to burn. Serve hot.

Yield: 20 to 24 filled shrimp,
4 to 6 servings

NOTES

Place leftovers in a covered container in the refrigerator; they will keep for 2 days and may be reheated in the microwave or 350°F oven. Do not overheat or the shrimp will become rubbery. Freezing this dish is not recommended.

Baked Trout

Filetti di Trota Ripieni

Preparation Time: 30 minutes • Cooking Time: 20 minutes

This recipe was created in one of my Intermediate Italian cooking classes. One of the students—Michael, who was always very enthusiastic—would come to class early, ready and raring to go. One night he bounced into class excited; a friend had just come back from a fishing trip and left him a cooler filled with fresh trout. He wanted to know if I had any ideas. We started talking and sharing with the rest of the class and before you knew it, in came the fish and thus came this recipe. This is one of those times that a well-stocked kitchen along with the spirit of improvisation helped to create a recipe that we would use over and over again. I had never prepared trout before; this was the best trout any of us had ever tasted. There is something so special about seizing the moment, going with the flow, and enjoying the pleasures life has to offer.

4 whole trout or 8 trout fillets
1 teaspoon kosher salt
2 tablespoons extra-virgin olive oil
1 small onion, chopped
1 leek, rinsed thoroughly and
   chopped
1 clove garlic, chopped
   (about ½ teaspoon)
2 large celery ribs, chopped
1 small zucchini, chopped
3 dried figs, finely chopped
¼ cup roasted red pepper
   (see page 14), chopped

¼ pound Ritz or Townhouse
   crackers, crushed
2 tablespoons chopped Italian flat-
   leaf parsley
Salt and freshly ground black
   pepper to taste
2 tablespoons butter, melted, plus a
   little extra for greasing the
   baking sheet
Zest of 1 lemon, for garnish

PROCEDURE

1. Rinse the fish under cold running water, drain in a colander, and pat dry with paper towels. Sprinkle with kosher salt and set aside while you make the stuffing.

2. In a medium skillet, heat the olive oil over medium heat. Add the onion, leek, garlic, and celery and sauté for about 4 minutes, stirring, until softened. Then add the zucchini and continue cooking and stirring for another 4 minutes. Remove from the heat.

3. Add the figs, red pepper, crushed crackers, and parsley. Mix lightly until combined. Season with salt and pepper.

4. Preheat the oven to 400°F. Line a baking sheet with foil and lightly grease.

5. If using whole fish, divide the stuffing into fourths and insert it into the cavity of each trout. Lay the fish onto the baking sheet. Drizzle each fish with melted butter and bake for about 20 minutes, or until the flesh comes away from the bone when tested with the point of a sharp knife.

6. If using trout fillets, lay four of the fillets on the baking sheet. Divide the stuffing into fourths and spoon onto each fillet. Cut the remaining fillets in half lengthwise and lay two pieces over each stuffed fillet, pressing slightly on the outer edges so the stuffing shows in the middle. Drizzle with melted butter and bake for about 15 minutes, or until done. The fish should be opaque, and flake off nicely with the tines of a fork.

Yield: 4 to 6 servings

NOTES

Store any leftovers in the refrigerator in a covered container; they will keep for a day or two. Reheat in the microwave or 350°F oven until warm. I do not recommend freezing this dish.

Decadent Baked Lobster

Aragosta Ripiena al Forno

Preparation Time: 1 hour 15 minutes (varies with experience)

Baking Time: 30 to 40 minutes, depending on the size of the lobsters and how many you are baking in the oven at the same time (the meat on the lobster tail should be opaque in color and fork-tender)

This decadent lobster dish should only be attempted if you are experienced in the kitchen, if you have an enthusiastic, high-spirited assistant, or you are a gutsy, adventuresome person who welcomes a good challenge. Because of the expense, I suggest you try it for the first time on a smaller scale—2 or 3 people. My friend Louisa, from Boston, is a lobster connoisseur and this special dish is my improvisation on her recipe. To this day, it does not fail to evoke images of Louisa, knife in hand, giving a lesson on the anatomy of lobster, during our wonderful family vacations at Lake George. When the lobsters arrived at the table donning stuffed bellies and red cloaks, the collaborative exclamations of hungry delight filled the room. Ramekins of butter followed the parceling out of lobster, and the sounds of snapping, slurping, and unbuttoning of waistbands with the occasional "I can't eat anymore" dominated.

8 (1½-pound) fresh live lobsters (order them about 1 week before you need them to make sure your fishmonger will have plenty of time to get them for you)

For the Stuffing:
2 medium-large boiling potatoes, peeled, sliced, and chopped into ⅛-inch dice
1 (1-pound) box Ritz or Townhouse crackers
½ pound (2 sticks) butter, divided
1 medium yellow cooking onion, chopped
2 cloves garlic, minced

Salt and freshly ground black pepper
1 pound fresh scallops, rinsed, drained, and patted dry with paper towels
½ pound mushrooms, wiped clean with a damp paper towel and then sliced ¼ inch thick
Tomalley and roe from the lobsters
½ pound fontina cheese or creamed Havarti, shredded
3 tablespoons chopped Italian flat-leaf parsley
4 fresh basil leaves, chopped

(cont'd)

For the Table (Optional):
2 lemons, cut into wedges   **1 cup melted butter**

PROCEDURE

To Prepare the Lobster for Stuffing:

1. If you feel uncomfortable killing the lobsters yourself, tell your fish-monger when you will be picking them up and ask him to do this for you, along with removing the stomachs and cutting the lobsters. I would advise calling him just before you leave your home so they will be freshly killed, probably 1 hour before you plan to start preparing them. You can have most of the stuffing prepared (through step 5) and only have to sauté the tomalley and the roe. He can show you where the tomalley and roe are if you are not familiar with them.

2. If you are adventuresome and want to do it all yourself, the directions follow. Give yourself plenty of time if this is the first time you are doing this. First, prepare the stuffing through step 5.

To Prepare the Stuffing:

1. Place the diced potatoes in a small saucepan with the cold water. Bring to a boil and boil for 3 to 4 minutes, or until tender, drain well, and place in a large bowl.

2. Pulse the crackers in a food processor or blender until they are fine crumbs; then place them in the bowl with the potatoes.

3. Place a large skillet over medium-high heat. When the skillet is warm, add 2 tablespoons of the butter. When the butter has melted and stops foaming, add the onion and garlic. Season with salt and pepper. Stir and sauté for 4 minutes, until the onions are tender and are staring to turn golden. Remove the onion and garlic with a slotted spoon to the stuffing bowl.

4. Use the same skillet (don't wash it) and put it back over medium-high heat. When the skillet is warm, add 2 additional tablespoons of the butter. When the butter has melted and stops foaming, turn the heat up to high and add the scallops. Season with salt and pepper. Sear on high heat for 2 minutes without turning. Turn and cook for another 2 minutes. Take the skillet off the stove. Remove the scallops with a slotted spoon and place on a cutting board. Chop into large chunks and add to the stuffing bowl along with any pan juices. Do not wash the skillet yet.

5. Place the same skillet over medium-high heat again. When the skillet is warm, add 4 more tablespoons of the butter. When the butter has melted and has stopped foaming, add the mushrooms, season with salt and pepper, and stir and sauté until tender, about 4 minutes. Remove with a slotted spoon to the cutting board and mince. Add the mushrooms and any juice to the stuffing bowl. Set aside to prepare the lobster, as directed below.

To Prepare the Lobsters:

1. Keep the rubber bands on the claws. Holding the lobster with its back on a wooden board, insert a sharp knife at the top of the lobster between the head and the thorax cavity, cutting down the entire length of the lobster to the first joint of the tail, being careful to leave the back shell intact. Pull the body of the lobster gently apart, exposing the inside cavity. If you see a dark intestinal vein that runs close to the center, remove and discard. About 2 inches below the head behind the eyes is a sac (the stomach), which is gray and filled with waste. It can be scooped out by running your finger underneath it, grasping it firmly, and gently tugging. Remove and discard. Sometimes a spoon can be used in the same manner.

2. The greenish-brown material is the tomalley (liver) and is considered a delicacy. Remove it and place it in a small bowl. There may also be the coral (roe) if the lobster is female. This is also considered a delicacy and should be removed and be placed in the bowl with the tomalley. The two will be used to flavor the stuffing.

3. Rinse the lobsters under cold running water, drain in a colander, and pat dry with paper towels.

4. Using kitchen shears or a knife, cut through the remaining joints of the tail, not going into the flesh of the tail.

To Finish the Dish:

1. Prepare the oven by arranging one oven rack on the bottom shelf and the other on the second from the top shelf. Preheat the oven to 375°F. Line two baking sheets with heavy-duty aluminum foil.

2. Return the sauté pan in which you are preparing the stuffing to the stove. Over medium heat, add the remaining butter. Melt the butter and place all the tomalley and roe into the skillet. Sauté for 2 minutes. Transfer to the stuffing bowl. Toss all the ingredients, mixing evenly but lightly. Taste for seasoning and adjust accordingly.

3. Divide the stuffing into eight equal portions and mound it loosely in the body cavity of each lobster. Place the lobsters on the baking sheets, alternating heads and tails to fit them comfortably. You can fit four to a sheet.

4. Bake for a total of 30 to 40 minutes, switching the pans from top to bottom after 15 minutes of cooking. The shells will have turned reddish and the flesh should be opaque, tender, and firm to the touch.

5. Place the lobsters on a large platter or individual serving dishes, and serve hot with lemon wedges—and melted butter, if you dare! I usually accompany the lobster with fresh corn on the cob and a tossed salad—which is soothing after a rich meal. Enjoy, take your time, close your eyes, and just savor all the wonderful flavors and thank God for this wonderful feast!

Yield: 8 servings

NOTES

If there are any leftovers, hide them under lock and key and store them in the refrigerator or they will not be there the following morning. Don't keep them longer than 1 day.

VEGETABLES

Vegetables have always played an important role in Italian cooking and command a place of honor at the Italian table. Italians are able to transform vegetables into the simplest as well as the most complex works of art that are sublime, teasing, and exciting to the palate. Italians eat vegetables primarily because they love them and secondly because these foods are so healthy.

For many families living in Italy years ago, vegetables were the primary staple along with pasta. Meat and poultry were served in very small amounts, on special occasions, and for holidays. In contrast, vegetables have always reigned in Italy, their quality being matchless. The hot sun, fertile land, and perseverance and ingenuity of the people make it so. Throughout most of the countryside, terraced hillsides provide evidence of how the Italians use their natural resources to the utmost efficiency, producing some of the world's tastiest vegetables and fruit.

For the freshest taste and best nutritional value, buy vegetables that are in season. When vegetables are in season and you do not grow your own, buy them fresh from your local farmers' markets and roadside stands. I particularly enjoy those vegetables that are fresh picked and dressed simply with the best olive oil, fresh herbs, and sprinkling of coarse salt and a few grinds of black pepper. If you are allowed to handle the vegetables—feel, fondle gently, and smell for freshness—do it. One of my most memorable visual experiences on a recent trip to Italy was the open-air market. The vegetable stalls were overflowing with fresh fruits and vegetables. A collage of textures and colors—reds, oranges, golds, yellows, purples, and greens—was arranged in harmonious order. There, shoppers were not allowed to touch the fruit and vegetables; that privilege was left to the local vendors. It was impossible for me to resist, however, and I did get myself into trouble a few times; even that was fun.

There are so many ways to cook vegetables. They can be prepared quite simply, in a straightforward and uncomplicated manner by boiling, steaming, or blanching. With just a little more effort they can be sautéed, roasted, grilled, or baked, or you can get a little more elaborate by deep-frying, or stuffing and baking them. Vegetables can be used as an antipasto, as the complement to the second course (*contorno*), or as the featured main course. They can be used to create pasta dishes, to enhance sauces, to stuff breads, as toppings for pizza, and in polenta or risotti.

I use vegetables widely throughout this book, from the antipasti to the pastas, in salads and frittatas, and for stuffing breads, meats, poultry, and fish. Try these recipes and you will soon crave vegetables for the sheer love of them, just like the Italians do.

Green Beans with Balsamic Vinegar and Oregano

Fagiolini con Aceto Balsamico e Origano

Preparation Time: 15 minutes • Cooking Time: 5 to 7 minutes

This makes a wonderful addition to your antipasto tray, or it can be served separately as a vegetable. It does not need to be served hot; it is delicious served at room temperature or right out of the refrigerator. The beans can be cooked the day before and marinated a few hours before serving. The nuts add a nice crunch to the texture of the dish. We often take this on picnics because it keeps very well.

3 to 4 quarts water
1 teaspoon salt
1 teaspoon sugar
1 pound fresh green beans, washed, stem ends removed
¼ cup pine nuts or slivered almonds, toasted (see page 24)

For the Marinade:
2 tablespoons balsamic vinegar
1 tablespoon freshly squeezed lemon juice
½ cup extra-virgin olive oil
3 cloves garlic, chopped (about 1½ teaspoons)

1 tablespoon Pesto from your freezer (page 25), or 6 fresh basil leaves, chopped
6 fresh mint leaves, chopped
1 teaspoon dried oregano
⅛ teaspoon sugar
½ teaspoon salt
¼ teaspoon freshly ground black pepper

For the Garnish (Optional):
Grated rind of 1 lemon
or 1 roasted red bell pepper (see page 14), diced

PROCEDURE

1. Bring the water to a boil in a large nonreactive pot. Add salt, sugar, and the beans and boil for 7 to 10 minutes, depending on the size of the beans. They should be fork-tender when done. Drain in a colander and run under cold water. Drain again. The less water remaining on the beans, the better the marinade can adhere to them.

Vegetables

239

2. Mix the ingredients for the marinade in a bowl. Pour over the cooked beans and allow to marinate for 15 minutes or longer. Just before serving, toss with the toasted nuts and sprinkle with the lemon rind.

3. Alternatively, you may enjoy serving these in bundles, wrapped with strips of roasted pepper or carrots and arranged artistically on a platter.

Yield: 3½ cups; 6 servings

NOTES

You can use this marinade for salads and many different vegetables, such as spinach, asparagus, Swiss chard, and cauliflower.

The string beans taste better as they marinate, although the color will darken as time goes by. They will keep in the refrigerator in covered containers for up to 5 days. I do not recommend freezing them.

About Green Beans

When buying green beans, select fresh ones that have a bright green color and unblemished skin that is firm and smooth to the touch. They should be crispy and firm enough to snap when bent in half. Snap off the ends and wash beans just before using. If the beans are stringy, remove the string by pulling down and off the pod.

Use a large pot to cook the beans; they should have plenty of room to move freely in the water as they are cooking. Boil beans in plenty of salted water until fork-tender, then remove and place in an ice-water bath. When beans are cold, drain very well, pat dry, and store in the refrigerator in a plastic bag. These will come in handy as a ready-to-eat snack, marinated with oil and vinegar and seasonings, and for use in tossed salads, antipasto trays, pasta dishes, and frittatas.

Baby Peas with Sun-Dried Tomatoes and Toasted Pine Nuts

Pisellini con Pomodori Secchi Sott' Olio e Pinoli

Preparation Time: 7 minutes • Cooking Time: 10 minutes

For this recipe, use fresh baby peas when in season; all other times use frozen baby peas (sometimes called early June peas or petite peas). They are young, tender, sweeter in taste, and thinner-skinned.

2 tablespoons extra-virgin olive oil
1 small onion, chopped
4 pounds fresh peas or 1 (16-ounce) package frozen baby peas
¼ teaspoon salt
½ teaspoon sugar
¼ teaspoon freshly ground fresh black pepper

2 tablespoons toasted pine nuts (see page 24)
4 Marinated Sun-Dried Tomato halves (page 18), cut into thin strips

PROCEDURE

1. If using fresh peas, remove the peas from the pods and boil in salted water until tender, 5 to 10 minutes, and proceed with the recipe. Place a medium saucepan over medium-high heat. When the saucepan is warm, add the oil. When the oil is hot, add the chopped onion and stir for 2 to 3 minutes. Add the frozen peas, salt, sugar, and pepper, and stir.

2. Cover, turn the heat to medium, and continue to cook for 8 to 10 minutes, until the peas are tender. Adjust for seasoning. Add the marinated sun-dried tomatoes and pine nuts. Stir, and serve hot or warm.

Yield: 3⅓ cups; 4 servings

NOTES

Store leftovers in a covered container in the refrigerator; they will keep for up to 5 days. To reheat, warm in a saucepan or in the microwave.

Fried Green and Red Peppers

Peperoni in Padella

Preparation Time: 15 minutes • Cooking Time: 15 minutes

4 large green bell peppers
1 large red or yellow bell pepper
3 tablespoons extra-virgin olive oil
½ teaspoon salt
¼ teaspoon freshly ground black
  pepper
2 large onions, sliced

3 cloves garlic, chopped
  (about 1½ teaspoons)

Optional:
½ cup homemade Marinara Sauce
  (page 5)
or 2 tablespoons balsamic vinegar

PROCEDURE

1. Wash and dry the peppers. Slice them in half, and remove the core and seeds. Slice each half into strips the width of your finger.

2. Place a large skillet over medium-high heat. When the skillet is warm, add the oil. When the oil is hot, add the peppers, season with salt and pepper, and sauté 5 to 7 minutes. Add the sliced onion and chopped garlic and sauté for another 5 to 7 minutes, or until tender. Taste for seasoning and adjust accordingly.

3. Serve as is, or add either the balsamic vinegar or the Marinara Sauce and cook for another 1 to 2 minutes.

Yield: 6 servings

NOTES

These peppers are excellent in sausage sandwiches made with homemade Panini (page 177). Or if you have shredded fresh mozzarella cheese, put a layer of cheese over the peppers and place under the broiler for 1 to 2 minutes, until the cheese melts, fill your sandwich, and eat. The peppers are also delicious fried with beaten eggs.

Store leftovers in the refrigerator in a covered container; they will keep for up to 5 days. I do not recommend freezing this dish.

Roasted Fennel

Finocchi Arrostiti

Preparation Time: 15 minutes • Cooking Time: 30 minutes

Fennel is a bulbous vegetable that grows above ground. It has a white color with pale green celery-like stems and bright green frilly leaves coming from the stems. All parts are edible.

2 quarts water
3 bulbs sweet fennel
1 bunch scallions, cleaned and
 chopped
1 clove garlic, minced
 (about ½ teaspoon)
1 tablespoon chopped Italian flat-
 leafed parsley

⅓ cup freshly grated Romano cheese
¼ teaspoon salt
⅛ teaspoon freshly ground black
 pepper
3 tablespoons extra-virgin olive oil

PROCEDURE

1. Preheat the oven to 400°F.

2. Bring the water to a boil in a medium saucepan. Wash the fennel bulbs and cut off a small slice from the root end. Remove the stalks and leaves for future use. Slice the bulbs lengthwise in half and slice each half into quarters. Boil for 8 minutes.

3. Drain fennel and place in a baking dish. Toss remaining ingredients.

4. Bake in the preheated oven until tender, 20 to 30 minutes, stirring at 10-minute intervals. Taste for seasoning and adjust accordingly. Serve hot.

Yield: 4 to 6 servings

NOTES

To add a little more color and flavor, try adding some Marinated Roasted Peppers (page 15) or Marinated Sun-Dried Tomatoes (page 18).

Leftovers will keep in the refrigerator in a covered container for several days. Reheat in microwave oven or skillet. I do not recommend freezing fennel.

Vegetables

Asparagus with Pancetta and Caramelized Nuts

Asparagi con Pancetta e Noci

*Preparation Time: 30 minutes—preparation and cooking time vary
depending on what you have on hand in your pantry*

Cooking Time: about 40 minutes overall cooking time

This dish blends many flavors and textures and is magnificent in its presentation. This recipe has many steps—take one step at a time and it will go smoothly.

**For the Asparagus
(Cooking Time 4 Minutes):**
1½ pounds asparagus, fresh
¼ teaspoon salt
⅛ teaspoon freshly ground black
    pepper
1 tablespoon extra-virgin olive oil
1 clove garlic, finely chopped

**For the Pancetta
(Cooking Time 9 Minutes):**
4 ounces pancetta or bacon, cut into
    ½-inch strips
1 tablespoon extra-virgin olive oil, if
    necessary
1 small onion, chopped
1 clove garlic, chopped

**For the Nuts
(Preparation Time 3 Minutes;
Cooking Time 7 to 10 Minutes):**
1 tablespoon butter

¾ cup walnuts or pecans, coarsely
    chopped
⅔ cup sugar
½ teaspoon grated lemon or orange
    rind
½ teaspoon pure vanilla extract

**For the Marinade
(Preparation Time 3 Minutes):**
3 tablespoons extra-virgin olive oil
1 tablespoon freshly grated Romano
    cheese
1 tablespoon wine vinegar
1 tablespoon balsamic vinegar
1 teaspoon sugar
⅛ teaspoon salt
½ teaspoon freshly ground black
    pepper

Garnish:
1 roasted red or yellow bell pepper
    (see page 14)

PROCEDURE

To Prepare the Asparagus:

1. Soak the asparagus in cold water for 1 minute; then toss lightly in the water to wash away any sand and grit. Remove from the water. If you notice dirt in the bottom of your bowl, repeat the process.

2. Snap off the tough bottom ½ to 1 inch of the stalk. This is easily done by holding the bottom end of the stalk in one hand and snapping the tough end off with the thumb and forefinger of the other hand. If the asparagus spears are very thick in diameter, use a vegetable peeler to peel the lower half of the asparagus.

3. Place the asparagus in a large reclosable plastic freezer bag. Sprinkle with the salt, pepper, olive oil, and garlic. Close the bag, leaving an inch of space for ventilation. Shake the bag to evenly distribute the seasonings.

4. Cook in the microwave on High for 3 to 4 minutes, depending on the size of the asparagus. Check for tenderness and microwave longer if necessary. The asparagus should be a beautiful bright green color and fork-tender.

5. Unzip the bag to stop further cooking; set aside. (Note: Be careful when opening the bag to avoid steam burns.)

To Prepare the Pancetta:

1. Heat a medium-size skillet over medium heat. Add the pancetta or bacon. Cook for about 5 minutes, stirring occasionally, until the pancetta or bacon starts to turn golden but not crispy. Often the pancetta is very lean and does not throw off much fat. In this case, add the olive oil.

3. Add the onion and garlic and stir and cook for another 3 minutes. Stir and cook until the pancetta, onion, and garlic are crispy and golden. Set aside, removing and discarding all but 1 tablespoon of the grease.

To Prepare the Caramelized Nuts:

1. Place a sheet of parchment paper on your work surface and lightly coat it with butter or oil. Set aside.

2. Heat a medium-size nonstick skillet over medium-high heat. Add the nuts and toast for 2 minutes, stirring constantly. Add the sugar and stir continuously until all the sugar has melted, about 6 to 8 minutes. Stir for another minute, until the sugar is golden and syrupy. Do not let it get brown.

3. Remove from the heat, quickly add the citrus rind and the vanilla, and

Vegetables

stir. Turn out onto the prepared greased paper. Be careful not to touch or taste the mixture—you will get quite a burn.

4. Allow the mixture to cool; then crumble into bite-size pieces with your fingers or a kitchen mallet. Use about half the nuts for this recipe if necessary.

To Prepare the Roasted Pepper Garnish:

1. To roast your own peppers, follow the instructions on page 14.

2. Cut the roasted peppers (your own or purchased) into long, thin strips about ¼ inch wide. Set aside.

To Prepare the Marinade and Assemble:

1. Place all the marinade ingredients in a large, shallow bowl, and whisk to combine. Add the asparagus and toss lightly. Let stand for about 10 to 15 minutes. Add the caramelized nuts and cooked pancetta and toss again.

2. Bundle together 3 or 4 asparagus stalks and wrap with a strip of the roasted pepper. Bundle the rest of the asparagus similarly. Place the asparagus bundles on a large circular platter in a spoke pattern. In the center, place any remaining marinade, nuts, and pancetta, making sure to place a small serving spoon with the nuts and pancetta so guests can help themselves.

Yield: 8 servings

NOTES

This recipe can be served as is, without making bundles.

Each simple step of this recipe can be used on its own or in conjunction with other recipes. The asparagus preparation may be used for a quick and tasty vegetable dish. The caramelized nuts can be made and placed in attractive jars and given as gifts. The marinade is wonderful on green, leafy vegetables and salads. Cooking the pancetta with onion and garlic could be the beginning of many pasta dishes. Explore the possibilities!

Store any leftovers in the refrigerator in covered containers; they will keep for up to 3 days. The asparagus will darken as they set, but this does not affect its flavor.

Eggplant Sicilian Style

....

Melanzane Ripiene di Formaggio

Preparation Time: 20 minutes • Cooking Time: 25 minutes

This is a recipe we made when we lived in Italy and still make today. It can be used as a vegetable, in antipasti or as a main course. I've even placed the eggplant halves over a bed of *aglio/oilo* pasta. It is unique to the region of Sicily where I was born and I love its wonderful flavor. This stuffed eggplant is a spectacular vegetarian dish.

4 to 6 baby eggplants (see Notes)
Salt and freshly ground black
    pepper
1 cup Marinara Sauce (page 5)
4 cloves garlic, sliced in very thin
    rounds or slivered

½ (2-ounce) can anchovies
    (flat fillets), finely chopped
8 fresh basil leaves, finely chopped
⅛ pound Romano cheese, cut into
    very thin strips (1 × ⅛ × ⅛–inch)
2 tablespoons extra-virgin olive oil

PROCEDURE

1. Wash and dry the eggplant and cut in half lengthwise through the stem. Do not remove the stem or skin. Place the eggplant, flesh-side down on your work space.

2. With the tip of a knife, cut little pockets (slits) lengthwise on the eggplant, making sure that you stop the slit ⅛ inch before you go through the eggplant. Depending on the size of the eggplant, try to get four pockets in each half of the eggplant. Salt and pepper each pocket lightly.

3. Place the Marinara Sauce, garlic, anchovies, and basil in a small bowl and mix until incorporated. Determine how many pockets you have to stuff and portion out stuffing for each pocket.

4. Stuff the eggplant pockets lightly and then add the slivered cheese.

5. Heat a large nonstick skillet over medium-high heat. When it is warm, add the olive oil. When the oil is hot, add the eggplants, flat-sides down. Cook for 4 minutes; then check to see if the bottoms have turned golden brown. Turn with a wide spatula and brown the upper parts, adding more olive oil as necessary to prevent burning.

6. Place a cover on the pan, turn the heat to low, and continue cooking until tender. The size of the eggplant determines how much longer they have to cook (7 to 20 minutes). They should be fork-tender. Serve hot, warm, or at room temperature.

Yield: 8 servings
as part of an antipasto platter
(½ baby eggplant each)

NOTES

If you can't find baby eggplants, you may substitute medium ones.

Place leftovers in the refrigerator in a covered container; they will keep for up to 5 days. I do not recommend freezing this dish.

My family's approach to food was born of the economic hardship. Each fall was a time for canning and wine-making. Opening the side door to our home in Rochester in September always meant being greeted by the aromas of tomatoes, peaches, pears, cherries, apricots, eggplants, and green peppers. My parents' fruit cellar was wonderful—row after row of gleaming, clear glass containers filled with bright colors. When you turned on the light, they glistened like jewels. The reward of all of our work was the secure feeling I would get seeing that abundance, knowing that we were capable of making wonderful things.

But more than this, the best part of this whole canning and wine-making experience was all of the talking, laughing, and listening that went on during canning. We've cooked and canned in my own kitchen, too, over the years, three generations of Pilatos and Tomasellis working and laughing together.

Sautéed Broccoli

Broccoli Fritti

Preparation Time: 18 minutes • Cooking Time: 7 minutes

The technique of first boiling the vegetables until they are fork-tender, draining and sautéing them in garlic and olive oil is used often in Italy.

1 head broccoli
4 quarts boiling water
1 tablespoon salt
3 tablespoons extra-virgin olive oil
1 tablespoon butter
1 medium onion, chopped
2 shallots, chopped

2 cloves garlic, chopped
½ teaspoon salt
¼ teaspoon freshly ground black
   pepper
2 tablespoons toasted pine nuts
   (see page 24), optional

PROCEDURE

1. Cut the broccoli head from the stems and break into florets. Peel the tough fibrous skin from the stems. Cut the stems into small, bite-size pieces; this will help florets and stems to cook in the same amount of time. Wash the broccoli in cold water and drain in a colander.

2. Heat the water in a large stockpot. When the water comes to a boil, add the salt and broccoli and cook on medium-high heat for about 5 minutes. The broccoli should be fork-tender. Drain immediately and rinse under cold running water. Drain again.

3. Heat a large skillet on medium-high heat until warm. Add the olive oil and butter. When they are hot, add onion, shallots, and garlic; stir and cook for 3 to 4 minutes, until golden; then add the broccoli. Turn the heat to medium and cook for 3 minutes, until the broccoli is hot and flavored throughout. Add the salt and pepper. Taste for seasoning and adjust accordingly.

4. If using the pine nuts, toss with the broccoli just before serving.

Yield: 4 to 6 servings

NOTES

Store any leftovers in the refrigerator in covered containers; they will keep for several days. Reheat in the microwave.

Vegetables

Stuffed Zucchini

Zucchini Ripieni con Riso

Preparation Time: about 45 minutes, including the rice
Cooking Time: 30 minutes

I have gardened with our children on and off for many years and still do so even though they are grown. One summer is still very vivid in my mind. The sun and the rain were perfect for the growing season. We grew enough vegetables to feed a small army, which in a way we were. The children helped in planting the seeds, pulling out weeds, watering the plants, and harvesting the bounty. They were enthralled watching the plants mature, producing glorious fruits and vegetables. This particular summer, the joy of harvesting the zucchini came to an abrupt halt with the advent of what our son Tommy called the Attack of the Killer Zucchini. They grew wildly out of control. As fast as we could pick them, more and larger zucchini grew in their place. I tried many new recipes and improvised as much as I could to camouflage them into soups, sauces, stews, breads, cakes, and even pancakes. The children said, "Not zucchini again!" Our daughter Lisa insisted that we were all turning green and swore that she would never eat another zucchini in her life. However, zucchini were and still are her favorite vegetable.

4 medium zucchini
    (7 to 8 inches long)
Salt and freshly ground black
    pepper

For the Stuffing:
2 tablespoons extra-virgin olive oil
2 mediums carrots, washed, peeled,
    and diced
⅛ teaspoon salt
⅛ teaspoon freshly ground black
    pepper

¾ cup frozen baby peas, defrosted
1 roasted red bell pepper (see page
    14) or equivalent jarred variety,
    diced
3 cups Quick, Delicious, and Simply
    Elegant Rice (page 136) or plain
    cooked rice
⅓ cup freshly grated Romano cheese
1 cup shredded fontina cheese
1 tablespoon chopped Italian flat-
    leaf parsley
4 fresh basil leaves, chopped

PROCEDURE

1. Cut each zucchini in half lengthwise. Using a melon baller, grapefruit spoon, or teaspoon, scoop out the inside pulp, leaving ⅛-inch shell all around. Reserve the pulp. Season the inside of the zucchini with salt and pepper.

2. Coarsely chop the zucchini pulp and set aside.

3. Heat a medium-size skillet over medium heat until warm. Add the oil. When the oil is warm, add the carrots and sauté for 3 to 4 minutes, stirring occasionally. Add the chopped zucchini pulp, salt, and pepper and cook for another 3 to 4 minutes, stirring every now and then.

4. Remove from the stove, transfer to a large bowl, add the peas, red pepper, the cooked rice, cheeses, parsley, and basil. Stir, taste for seasonings, and adjust accordingly.

5. Preheat the oven to 350°F.

6. Pat the zucchini shells dry with paper towels. Stuff each half generously so that you have a nice mound on top.

7. Place the stuffed zucchini in a baking pan and bake for 30 minutes. When done, the zucchini should be fork-tender and hold its boatlike shape. The top of the stuffing mixture should be golden and somewhat crispy.

9. Arrange on a beautiful platter and serve warm.

Yield: 4 to 8 servings

NOTES

Store any leftovers in the refrigerator in a covered container; they will keep for up to 4 days. To reheat, sprinkle 1 tablespoon water and heat in the microwave or toaster oven until warm.

Making extra stuffed zucchini to freeze for another time is easy. Bake them for only 20 minutes, allow to cool completely, and then freeze in a covered container. They will keep in the freezer for up to 2 months. When ready to use, allow to defrost in the refrigerator overnight. Place uncovered in baking pan and cook in a preheated 350°F oven until heated completely throughout, about 20 minutes.

Vegetables

Roasted Potatoes with Cheese and Herbs

....

Patate Arrostite con Formaggio e Erbe

Preparation Time: 25 minutes • Cooking Time: 1 hour

½ cup extra-virgin olive oil, plus
    more for greasing the pan
10 medium Russet or Idaho potatoes,
    peeled and placed in a bowl of
    cold water
2 cloves garlic, minced
    (about 1 teaspoon)

3 sprigs fresh thyme, (leaves only)
2 tablespoons chopped fresh basil,
    mint or parsley
1 tablespoon kosher salt
½ teaspoon freshly ground black
    pepper
½ cup freshly grated Romano cheese

PROCEDURE

1. Preheat the oven to 450°F. Oil a large shallow roasting pan with olive oil, making sure to coat the sides as well as the bottom.

2. Cut the peeled potatoes in half. Turn them cut-side down and cut each half lengthwise into 4 or 5 wedges, and place in a large bowl.

3. Dry the potatoes thoroughly with paper towel and place back in the bowl. Pour the olive oil over the potatoes and add the herbs and seasonings. With your hands, toss all the ingredients together, making sure the potatoes are coated all over with the mixture.

4. Place potatoes in the oven. Stir every 15 minutes, being careful not to break the potatoes. After the potatoes have been roasting for ½ hour, add the cheese, toss again, and turn the heat down to 375°F. Continue to roast for another ½ hour, until the potatoes are tender and golden.

5. Remove from the pan and place on a serving platter; serve hot or warm.

Yield: 8 servings

NOTES

Store leftovers in the refrigerator in a covered container; they will keep for several days.

DESSERTS AND SWEET THINGS

With the exception of fruit and sometimes cheeses, desserts do not play an important part of the everyday diet of most Italians. They are used primarily for special occasions such as holidays, birthdays, baptisms, communions, confirmations, weddings, anniversaries, and formal meals. Italians choose to end their meals on a light note, preferring ripe and supple native fruit that is in season. They believe that fruit cleanses the palate and aids in digestion. Often when there is an abundance of fresh fruit they make a salad (*macedonia di frutta fresca*), which can be enhanced with sweet wines or liquors.

Sometimes Italians choose cheese as a way to end their meal, either accompanied by or followed by fruit, nuts, or wine. Choices include mozzarella (buffalo or cow's milk), mascarpone, Gorgonzola, fresh ricotta, Taleggio, Parmigiano-Reggiano, fontina, provolone, or Asiago fresco. In Sicily, our family had its own trees, the fruit and nuts of which were enjoyed by all. I have fond memories of my dad peeling oranges and slicing fruit. He would amaze us with his skill of slicing the peel or skin in one continuous cutting. He would then slice the fruit into perfectly equal pieces and divide them among us. This was his job, and he always performed it with such grace.

Of course, Italian desserts are not limited to fruit; there are a variety of baked goods, cookies, fried treats, wonderful creams, custards, and gelatos. Many would agree that Sicily's great gift to Italian cooking is her desserts, particularly her pastries. There are few people who have not heard of the crisp and flaky, luscious cannoli, the decadent cassata cake, the many varieties of biscotti, and fried puffs (fritelli). I offer you my family's special cannoli recipe, which is unequaled, and my version of the Sicilian cassata, and the ricotta sfingi, all of which use the ricotta recipe from the "Stepping-Stone Recipes" chapter. Try making our traditional cookies and the special fried treats from the holiday tradition and from the St. Joseph's Day table. Many are very basic and simple to make, require only a few steps, and use inexpensive ingredients. Some are more complex, calling for organization, planning, and time.

As in many countries around the world, baking in Italian families was thought of as a rite of passage, handed down from mother to daughter or from grandmother to grandchild. This was so in my mother's family, as well as in my own, with one main difference—I have included my sons in this initiation. Change is good.

Most of us don't have dessert often, and when we do, we should indulge ourselves, guilt free, and enjoy every last morsel!

Fresh Fruit Salad

....

Macedonia di Frutta Fresca

This is a wonderful way to end a meal, especially in the summer or fall, when the fruit is in season and is firm, juicy, sweet, and succulent.

The recipe has no exact amounts and no specific ingredients. Choose fruit that is in season in the amounts you require. The fruits should complement one another in flavor, color, and texture.

Peel the fruit if you wish and cut it into bite-size pieces. Before peeling oranges and lemons, you may want to remove the zest and reserve it for the garnish or freeze it for another use. Place the cut fruits into a bowl and dress with a little sugar to suit your taste. When fruit is locally grown it often does not need any extra sugar. Add a little fresh lemon or orange juice to help retain the vibrant color of the fruit. To dress this salad and make it more upscale, you can add a small amount of aged balsamic vinegar, marsala, sweet white wine, brandy (plain or flavored), or fruit or nut-flavored liqueurs.

Make the salad several hours before serving, allowing the flavors to blend and mellow. Preserve it by placing plastic wrap directly on top of the fruit. This prevents air from getting to the top layer and delays the oxidation process. Store it in the refrigerator.

Serve chilled in attractive goblets or bowls with garnishes of citrus zest or mint (allow about ¾ cup per serving). If you are feeling particularly festive, go for a dollop of whipped cream.

Tips for Making Cookies, Cakes, and Pastry

Regardless of where one grew up, the memory of freshly baked cookies and desserts conjures up images of the carefree days of childhood. We all remember the time when licking chocolate off our fingers and devouring batches of cookies came without any guilt or whispers about fat content. Those days may be long gone, but my passion for cookies and desserts remains intact.

As I have passed entire afternoons chatting with family and friends over flour and dough, I know that people of all ages can derive pleasure from baking together. The best advice I can give you is be organized and use the finest, freshest ingredients available.

Get yourself organized for cookie-making. There are a number of things you can do beforehand to make the actual preparation easier.

1. Read the recipe thoroughly before you begin.
2. Remove the butter from the refrigerator so it can begin to soften or come to room temperature.
3. Toast and chop the nuts.
4. Zest or grate the citrus rind.
5. Melt the chocolate before preparing the dough.
6. Use unsalted butter for freshest unsurpassed flavor. Substitute some vegetable shortening to yield puffier, fuller cookies.
7. Assemble the ingredients in the order you will need them.
8. Prepare the cookie sheets, and cake and pie pans according to recipe directions.

After you mix your dough, following the directions, check baking times and make sure to check doneness a minute or so before the recipe suggests.

When measuring the ingredients, always use appropriate measuring cups and spoons. For dry ingredients, use standardized dry measuring cups and measuring spoons. Fill to overflowing and then level the top off with a straight-edged utensil. Use dry measure to measure flour, sugar, baking powder, peanut butter, chocolate chips, cream cheese, sour cream, nuts, chopped fresh fruit and vegetables, preserves, and jams. When measuring flour, lightly spoon it into a measuring cup; then level it off. Do not tap or bang the measuring cup—this will pack the flour, giving you more flour than you intended. To measure liquid ingredients, use a standardized glass or plastic measuring cup with a pouring spout. Place the cup on flat surface that is at eye level and fill to the desired mark.

Cream your sugar and butter mixture well before adding the eggs. Once you have added the flour mixture to your egg, creamed sugar, and butter mixture, mix only until all the flour has been incorporated. Over-mixing, -kneading, and -handling develops the glutens in the flour and can produce tough cookies, cakes, and pastry.

Most unbaked cookie dough can be refrigerated for up to 1 week and frozen for up to 6 months when properly wrapped. Wrap, airtight, in heavy-duty plastic freezer bags or aluminum foil. When you are ready to make cookies, remove the dough from the freezer and let it stand at room temperature for 30 minutes before forming. Bake according to the directions.

When forming cookies, try to make them approximately the same size and shape; this will promote even baking and browning. Shiny, heavy-gauge aluminum baking sheets are good conductors of heat and will produce the most evenly baked cookies. Nonstick coated cookie sheets are also acceptable. Dark sheets absorb more heat and cause cookies to overbrown. Place parchment paper on cookie sheets. Usually one sheet will cover two cookie sheets. The parchment can be used several times before discarding. Parchment sheets may be purchased in kitchen stores and many supermarkets in the bakery department.

Halfway through the baking, rotate the cookie sheet from the bottom to top of the oven to ensure even browning and add a second sheet to the bottom; this allows you to bake two sheets at a time. Allow the cookie sheets to cool between batches. Remove the cookies to a rack to cool, making sure they are completely cool before storing.

Store cookies in airtight containers in a cool, dark place but not in the refrigerator. Never store crisp and soft cookies together; the crisp ones will absorb moisture from the soft ones and loose their crispness. If freezing cookies that call for frosting, don't put the frosting on until the cookies have been defrosted and have reached room temperature. It takes most cookies 10 to 15 minutes to defrost.

Mariella's Biscotti

Biscotti alla Mariella

Preparation Time: 20 minutes • Baking Time: 50 minutes

My sister Mariella and I spent some time together perfecting this biscotti recipe. She is the best baker of the family, probably because her husband has the sweetest tooth! We make these cookies throughout the year but always around the holidays, having them ready to serve to friends. They are a crisp biscotti, wonderful to dunk in a cup of coffee or tea, a glass of milk, or Vin Santo. Children love making these and giving them as gifts to teachers and special friends. Try them in place of the traditional all-American chocolate chip cookie—much less fat and sugar!

⅓ cup unsalted butter
1 cup sugar
2 large eggs
2 tablespoons milk
1 teaspoon vanilla extract
Zest of 1 orange, grated
2 cups unbleached all-purpose flour

⅛ teaspoon salt
1 teaspoon baking soda
1 cup almonds, lightly toasted
   (see page 24) and coarsely
   chopped
Egg wash (1 egg and 1 teaspoon
   water, beaten together)

PROCEDURE

1. Arrange one oven rack on the bottom shelf and the other on the second from the top shelf. Preheat the oven to 300°F.

2. In a large mixing bowl, cream the butter and sugar with an electric mixer on medium speed for 1 minute until combined. Add the eggs, milk, vanilla, and orange zest and beat until incorporated.

3. Mix the flour, salt, and baking soda together in a separate, medium bowl. Add this mixture to the egg and butter mixture ¼ at a time, mixing at low speed. Fold in the chopped almonds by hand.

4. Line a cookie sheet with parchment paper. Divide the dough in half and form two logs about 2 inches wide and 9 inches long. The dough will be thick and sticky. To aid in forming the logs, dust your hands with flour often. Place the logs on the cookie sheet about 4 inches apart brush the top of each log with egg wash.

5. Bake for 30 to 35 minutes, until golden but not brown. The logs will spread out considerably. Cool for 10 minutes and cut with a serrated knife into ½-inch diagonal slices. The biscotti can be eaten now, at this softer stage, or toasted. If toasting, arrange cut-sides down on a plain unlined cookie sheet and continue to bake for about another 10 to 15 minutes, until toasted, drying the inside of the cookies. Cool the biscotti on a wire rack.

Yield: 34 slices

NOTES

Thoroughly cooked, twice-baked biscotti can be stored in an airtight container for several months. If you choose not to toast them, they should be eaten within a couple of days or frozen in reclosable plastic freezer bags. Biscotti freeze well and will keep in the freezer for up to 6 months.

Since this is such a wonderful base recipe for biscotti, I suggest these variations:

- Use toasted skinned hazelnuts, pine nuts, pecans, or walnuts, instead of the almonds.
- Add ⅓ cup unsweetened cocoa powder, to make chocolate biscotti.
- Add about ½ cup chopped dried apricots.
- Add about 1 cup golden raisins or currants, soaked in hot water for 10 minutes and drained.
- Add ½ to 1 cup miniature semisweet chocolate chips.
- Add 1 teaspoon cinnamon or ⅛ teaspoon nutmeg.
- Add ½ teaspoon almond extract or 1 teaspoon orange extract.
- Add ½ teaspoon ground ginger.
- Dip the baked biscotti in melted chocolate to coat all or part of the cookie.
- Drizzle the tops of the baked biscotti with melted chocolate or sugar glaze.
- Use lemon rind in place of the orange rind.

The possibilities are endless, and I am certain you will come up with some I haven't thought of.

Lemon Ricotta Drop Cookies

Biscotti di Ricotta con Limone

Preparation Time: 25 minutes (not including preparation of the ricotta)
Frosting Time: 15 minutes • Baking Time: 15 minutes per cookie sheet

This is one of the easiest types of drop cookies to make. The cookies are light and moist, not overly sweet, with a thin coating of frosting. There is no rolling, cutting, refrigerating, or filling. Prepare the dough in your mixer or by hand, and simply drop it by teaspoonfuls onto the cookie sheet. The dough is a little sticky, so be sure to dust your index finger with flour before pushing the dough off the teaspoon.

¾ cup butter
2 cups sugar
3 large eggs, beaten
2 cups Homemade Fresh Ricotta
  (page 8), passed through a sieve
  or food mill
Rinds of 2 lemons, grated
1 teaspoon lemon extract
5 cups unbleached all-purpose flour
  (a little more if necessary)

1 teaspoon baking soda
1 tablespoon baking powder
1 teaspoon salt
1 recipe Frosting (page 264),
  changing the flavoring to lemon
  by substituting 1¼ teaspoons
  lemon extract for the orange
  extract

PROCEDURE

1. Prepare the oven by arranging one oven rack on the bottom shelf and the other on the second from the top shelf. Preheat the oven to 350°F. Line 3 cookie sheets with parchment paper.

2. In a large bowl, using an electric mixer, cream the butter and sugar. Add the eggs, ricotta, lemon rind, and lemon extract on medium speed until well blended, about 1 minute. Sift the flour, baking soda, baking powder, and salt.

3. With the mixer on the lowest speed, add the flour mixture to liquid ingredients ½ cup at a time and mix until the last bit of flour has just blended. Do not overmix. The dough will be a little sticky.

4. Drop the dough from a teaspoon onto prepared cookie sheets, spacing

the cookies about 1½ inches apart. Place a little flour in a bowl and dust your index finger each time you form a cookie. Try to make them uniform in size.

5. Bake each sheet of cookies for about 15 minutes total. Bake the first sheet for 8 minutes on the bottom rack and then 7 to 8 minutes on the upper rack, until the cookies are just golden on the bottoms. Do not allow them to brown. When you transfer the sheet to the top, place a second cookie sheet on the bottom, continuing to bake each sheet for 8 minutes on the bottom rack and 7 to 8 minutes on the upper rack. Remove the cookies from the oven as they start to turn golden. Cool for 2 minutes on the cookie sheet; then remove to wire racks to cool completely before frosting. (You can reuse the parchment paper several times.)

6. Frost the cooled cookies with Frosting (page 264), substituting 1¼ teaspoons lemon extract for the orange extract.

Yield: Approximately 70 cookies

NOTES

These cookies keep for several days if stored in a single layer in an airtight container. They freeze very well and will keep in the freezer for several months when stored in reclosable plastic freezer bags. If you are going to freeze the cookies, I recommend you do not apply frosting to them before freezing, but rather after the cookies have defrosted.

This is such a versatile cookie batter you can use it as a Stepping-Stone recipe, substituting whatever flavorings and extracts you prefer and adding ingredients such as nuts, currants that have been soaked in warm liquid, mini chocolate chips, golden raisins, sprinkles, and so on.

Sesame Seed Cookies

....

Biscotti di Gigiolena

Preparation Time: 40 minutes • Baking Time: 15 minutes per cookie sheet

Italians love their sesame seed cookies. They are sturdy and healthy cookies, unusual in appearance, not very sweet—a nice blend of flavors and textures. They're perfect for dunking in coffee, milk, and tea, and they make a wonderful snack for children and adults alike. This recipe is an improvisation based on my sister-in-law Jane's recipe.

4 cups unbleached all-purpose flour	Zest of 1 orange, grated
4 teaspoons baking powder	1 teaspoon vanilla extract
⅛ teaspoon salt	Egg wash (2 large eggs beaten with
1 cup unsalted butter, softened or	2 tablespoons water)
vegetable shortening, softened	1 pound unhulled sesame seeds (see
1⅔ cups sugar	Notes)
4 large eggs	

PROCEDURE

1. Prepare the oven by arranging one oven rack on the bottom shelf and the other on the second from the top. Preheat the oven to 375°F. Line 3 cookie sheets with parchment paper.

2. Sift the flour, baking powder, and salt together into a medium bowl. Set aside. Cream softened butter with the sugar in another medium bowl with an electric mixer or by hand. Add the eggs, one at a time, beating until each is incorporated. Add the orange zest and vanilla.

3. Add the flour mixture, ½ cup at a time, to the butter-and-egg mixture, blending the dry and wet ingredients with an electric mixer, a fork, or your hands. This should take about 1 minute. Do not overmix. If the dough is too sticky, add a little more flour. The dough may be refrigerated at this point until you are ready to finish the cookies.

4. Prepare the egg wash in a shallow bowl. Place the sesame seeds on a platter.

5. Roll the dough into coils about 12 inches long and ¾ inch in diameter.

Cut the coils into 3-inch diagonal lengths. Dip each 3-inch piece into the egg wash; then roll it in the sesame seeds. Place the cookies 1 inch apart on a parchment-lined cookie sheet.

6. Bake each sheet of cookies for a total of 15 minutes. Bake the first sheet for 8 minutes on the bottom rack; then switch to the upper rack and continue for 7 to 8 minutes. As you move the first cookie sheet to the upper rack, place another sheet of cookies on the bottom rack. The cookies are done when they are just golden on top and bottom. Do not allow them to become brown. Remove the cookies with the parchment paper to a work surface to cool or use a wire rack.

Yield: 6½ dozen

NOTES

Unhulled sesame seeds can be purchased at natural foods stores or Italian markets.

Store cookies in an airtight container for several weeks or freeze for up to 4 months. This cookie recipe is an old standby I like to have in the freezer for when unexpected guests drop by. Besides, if they are in the freezer, I have to think twice before going down to get them for myself. The cookies defrost in about 10 minutes—just about the same time it takes to make the coffee. You can place the defrosted cookies in a preheated 350°F oven for 5 minutes to rejuvenate them.

Millie's Orange Drop Cookies

Biscotti all'Arancia

Preparation Time: 25 minutes • Frosting Time: 15 minutes
Baking Time: 15 minutes per cookie sheet

I have included this moist, not overly sweet, and very flavorful cookie in memory of my husband's sister Millie. It's an excellent cookie to keep on hand: it is moist, has a wonderful texture and a delicate orange flavor, and stores extremely well.

For the Cookie Dough:
½ cup unsalted butter, vegetable shortening, or a combination of the two, softened
½ cup sugar
3 cups unbleached all-purpose flour
5 teaspoons baking powder
⅛ teaspoon salt
½ cup milk

2 large eggs
1 tablespoon grated orange rind
1 teaspoon orange extract

For the Frosting:
1½ cups confectioners' sugar
4 to 5 tablespoons half-and-half or evaporated milk
1 teaspoon orange extract

PROCEDURE

To Make the Cookies:

1. Prepare the oven by arranging one oven rack on the bottom shelf and the other on the second from the top shelf. Preheat the oven to 350°F. Line 3 cookie sheets with parchment paper.

2. In a medium bowl, cream the butter and sugar with an electric mixer. In another bowl, sift the flour with the baking powder and salt; set aside.

3. Pour the milk into a glass measuring cup and heat in the microwave to warm (30 seconds on High). Add the eggs and orange rind and extract to the measuring cup and mix with a fork. Add the milk mixture to the creamed butter-and-sugar mixture and beat with the electric mixture for 1 minute.

4. With the mixer on low speed, add the flour mixture about a ½ cup at a time until the mixture has been used.

5. Drop the dough by rounded teaspoons onto the parchment-lined cookie sheets, leaving 1 inch around each cookie.

6. Bake the first sheet for 8 minutes on the bottom rack; then transfer it to the upper rack and continue baking for another 7 minutes. When you transfer the first sheet to the top, place a second sheet on the bottom, continuing to bake each sheet for 8 minutes on the bottom rack and 7 to 8 minutes on the upper rack. Remove the cookies from the oven as they start to turn golden. Cool for 2 minutes on the cookie sheet; then remove and place on wire racks to cool completely before frosting. (You can reuse the parchment paper several times for other batches.)

To Frost:

1. When completely cool, the cookies can be frosted. Take the parchment paper you used to bake the cookies and place it on the work surface.

2. Combine the confectioners' sugar, half-and-half or evaporated milk, and orange extract in a bowl. Stir until all the sugar is dissolved.

3. Use your index finger like a paintbrush to frost each cookie all over, even on the bottom; then place the cookie on the parchment paper to dry. Frosting the cookies all over makes a nice seal and keeps them moist.

Yield: 5 dozen cookies

NOTES

Try using grated lemon rind instead of grated orange rind in the dough for a variation on this recipe.

These cookies may be stored in an airtight container for up to 1 week. To freeze cookies, place them in a heavy-duty freezer bag; they will keep for up to 3 months. If you are planning to freeze the cookies, don't frost them now. Frost them once they are completely thawed.

Chocolate Spice Cookies

Biscotti Speziati al Cioccolato

Preparation Time: 40 minutes • Baking Time: 10 minutes per cookie sheet
Frosting Time: 15 minutes

I recently made a trip to Arizona, where my family gathered four generations to celebrate my mother Rosa's ninety-third birthday. What joy and renewal of life! This cookie recipe is one of her favorites and she still makes it from memory, insisting that the only way to make it is by starting with 5 pounds of flour. It would be a sin (*un peccato*) to make less. After all, you have to get the ingredients out anyway, use the same amount of utensils, and it's not that much more work.

For the Cookie Dough:
⅓ cup cocoa powder
1⅓ cups milk
1⅓ cups sugar
⅔ cup vegetable shortening
⅓ cup oil
2 large eggs, beaten lightly with a
    fork
¾ cup currants
¾ cup chopped pecans
2 teaspoons cinnamon
⅓ teaspoon ground cloves

5½ cups unbleached all-purpose
    flour
2 tablespoons baking powder
2 teaspoons baking soda
⅛ teaspoon salt

For the Frosting:
4 cups confectioners' sugar
1½ teaspoon vanilla extract
6 tablespoons milk, or more if
    necessary to make a spreading
    consistency

PROCEDURE

To Make the Cookies:

1. Prepare the oven by arranging one oven rack on the bottom shelf and the other on the second from the top shelf. Preheat the oven to 375°F. Line 3 large cookie sheets with parchment paper.

2. In a saucepan, heat the cocoa and milk to lukewarm over medium-low heat, stirring until dissolved. Add the sugar, shortening, oil, beaten eggs, currants, and nuts and keep over medium-low heat until the shortening has dissolved. Cool to room temperature and add the cloves and cinnamon.

3. Meanwhile, in a large bowl, mix the dry ingredients thoroughly. Make a deep well in the center, pour the liquid ingredients into the well, and, using your hands or a fork, start in the center of the well and incorporate the flour slowly with the liquid, going around until all the flour has been incorporated and the nuts and currants are evenly distributed. Don't overwork the dough or the cookies will be tough. If the dough is too sticky, add a *little* more flour.

4. Take small pieces of dough (a little smaller than a walnut) and roll gently in between the palms of your hands to form a ball and press the nuts and currants inside the dough. (The currants will burn if they are sticking out.)

5. Place the balls of dough 4 rows across and 6 rows down on a prepared cookie sheet. Bake on the lower oven rack for 5 minutes; move to the upper rack and bake for about another 5 minutes. Cookies are done when you press lightly on top of the cookie and it does not leave a depression. Do not overcook. The bottom of the cookies should be *just* golden. When you transfer the first sheet to the top, add a second sheet to the bottom shelf, continuing to bake each sheet for 5 minutes on the bottom shelf and 5 minutes on the top.

6. Cool for 2 minutes; then remove the cookies from the cookie sheet and place on the counter to continue to cool.

To Frost:

1. When the cookies are fully cooled, they can be frosted. Combine the frosting ingredients.

2. To frost the cookies, hold a cookie with the fingers of one hand and dip it into the frosting. Use the index finger of the other hand like a paintbrush to coat the cookie top and bottom with frosting. Place on wax paper to dry.

Yield: 6 dozen

NOTES

These cookies will stay fresh when stored in an airtight container for up to 1 week. Stored in heavy-duty freezer bags they freeze very well and keep for up to 3 months. When making large batches to freeze I usually do not frost them until after they have thoroughly defrosted. They take about 15 minutes to defrost at room temperature.

Sicilian Creams

Pasticiotti

Preparation Time: 20 minutes, plus 15 minutes to prepare the cream filling

Baking Time: 18 to 20 minutes per cookie sheet

For the Cookie Dough:
4 cups unbleached all-purpose flour
1½ tablespoons baking powder
¾ teaspoon salt
½ cup (1 stick) cold unsalted butter,
    cut into small pieces
1 cup sugar
2 large eggs
¾ cup lukewarm milk (heated in
    microwave for 30 seconds)
zest of 1 lemon, grated
2 teaspoons lemon extract

For the Syrup:
⅓ cup rum or fruit- or nut-flavored
    liqueur
⅓ cup hot water

For the Decoration:
¼ cup powdered sugar
or ½ cup semisweet chocolate chips

For the Filling:
½ recipe Mama Rosa's Lemon
    Custard Cream (page 74)
or ½ recipe Chocolate Custard
    Cream (page 278)

PROCEDURE

1. Sift the flour, baking powder, and salt into a large mixing bowl. With an electric mixer or pastry cutter, cut in the pieces of butter until they resemble fine crumbs. Add the sugar and mix well.

2. Lightly beat the eggs in a small bowl. Stir in the milk, lemon zest, and lemon extract.

3. Form a well in the dry ingredients, pour the wet ingredients into the well, and stir to form a soft, pliable dough. If dough is too dry, add a tiny bit of milk. If dough is too sticky, add a little bit more flour.

4. Lightly flour your work surface and turn the dough onto it. Knead a few times to form a nice cohesive dough. Form into a 1-inch-thick disk, cover with plastic wrap, and place in the refrigerator to rest for 30 minutes or so.

5. Meanwhile, prepare the oven by arranging one oven rack on the bottom shelf and the other on the second from the top. Preheat the oven to 350°F. Line 2 cookie sheets with parchment paper.

6. Roll the dough to a ¾-inch thickness. Cut circles with a 2-inch round cookie cutter. Dip the cutter into flour if the dough starts to stick to it.

7. Place the cookies on a prepared cookie sheet, leaving a 1-inch space between them. Bake for a total of 18 to 20 minutes, 10 minutes on the bottom rack and then 8 to 10 minutes on the upper rack. As you move the first cookie sheet to the upper rack, place the next sheet on the bottom rack, cooking the second sheet the same as you did the first. The cookies are done when they are a blondish-golden color on the top and bottom. Do not allow them to become brown. Remove from the oven and place on a wire rack to cool.

8. While cookies are cooling, mix the rum or liqueur with the water.

9. When the cookies completely cool, slice them in half horizontally with a serrated knife, making a top and a bottom half. Brush the insides of the cookies with the syrup and fill with the cream, allowing a generous portion for each cookie.

10. To decorate the tops, dust with confectioners' sugar, or go one step further, and melt ½ cup chocolate chips and pipe melted chocolate through a fine-tipped pastry bag into a myriad of designs. Start simple and get more adventurous as you become more secure with the process.

11. Refrigerate the cookies until you are ready to serve. Before serving, let the cookies stand at room temperature for about 30 minutes.

Yield: 20 to 30 cookies

NOTES

These cookies can also be baked and placed in an airtight container a day or two in advance before soaking and filling. After the cookies are filled, they taste best when eaten the same day or the following day. Store in the refrigerator.

Ricotta Puffs

Sfingi di Ricotta

Preparation Time: 10 minutes (not including preparation of the ricotta)
Cooking Time: 15 to 20 minutes

Sfingi are deep-fried doughnutlike puffs that are made throughout Italy—especially in Sicily. They remain an important part of the St. Joseph's table tradition (see page 37) and are made as a devotion to him. There are a variety of recipes for sfingi throughout Italy. My mother makes a version that uses yeast, flour, and a large amount of eggs; I, however, use a batter that includes my wonderful homemade ricotta. Sometimes I take the Cream Puffs recipe dough (page 272) and make another variety of sfingi from that base recipe. Sfingi made with the Cream Puffs dough are very light, airy, and fluffy and can be filled with whipping cream or Ricotta Cloud Cream (page 280). The ricotta sfingi are more substantial and doughnutlike than the yeast-based batter or the one using the Cream Puffs dough. I like eating all three types because each evokes its own cherished memory.

1½ cups unbleached all-purpose
   flour
2 teaspoons baking powder
2 tablespoons sugar
⅛ teaspoon salt
4 large eggs
1 teaspoon vanilla extract
1 pound Homemade Fresh Ricotta
   (page 8)

1 quart canola oil, or more
   depending on the size of the
   deep-fryer or saucepan

For the Glaze:
1 cup honey
2 tablespoons water

PROCEDURE

1. Sift the flour, baking powder, sugar, and salt into a medium bowl. Set aside. In another bowl, beat the eggs and vanilla with a fork or an electric mixer for 30 seconds. Add the ricotta and continue to beat on medium until well blended, about 2 minutes.

2. Add the flour mixture to the ricotta ¼ cup at a time and continue to beat only until all the flour is incorporated into the batter. Do not overbeat. The batter should be very thick.

3. Place several sheets of paper towels on a cookie sheet. Heat the oil in a deep-fryer or deep-sided, heavy pan set over medium-high heat until it reaches 360° to 375°F. Gently drop batter by rounded teaspoonfuls into the oil, no more than 4 to 5 sfingi at a time, and fry until puffed to a golden brown. Each puff doubles in size as it cooks and needs plenty of room to dance around. By watching the first batch, you can gauge how many puffs you can effectively fry at one time in your fryer. As each puff is done, remove it with a slotted spoon or spider and place on the paper towels to drain. Continue until all the batter is used.

4. Heat the honey with the water in the microwave for 1 minute on High. Stir and heat again for 30 seconds. Pour the heated honey into a shallow bowl and roll each sfingi in it to coat the puff. Place the honey-coated puffs on a platter for serving, drizzling any extra honey over them.

Yield: 2½ dozen

NOTES

Sfingi taste best when eaten within an hour of cooking.

Store any leftovers in an airtight container in the refrigerator; they will keep until the next day. Reheat in a 350°F oven to rejuvenate them.

For very special occasions, these sfingi can be filled with Mama Rosa's Lemon Custard Cream (page 74), Ricotta Cloud Cream (page 280), or whipped cream. If you fill them, omit the honey coating and simply sprinkle powdered sugar over them before serving.

To make the sfingi using the Cream Puffs dough, prepare the dough on page 272 and drop it by rounded teaspoonfuls into the hot oil. Allow for expansion—they do a lot of bopping around. Keep them moving around with a slotted spoon so they get golden brown on all sides.

Desserts and Sweet Things

Cream Puffs

....

Bigné di San Giuseppe

Preparation Time: 15 minutes (not including preparation of the cream)
Baking Time: 25 to 30 minutes per baking sheet

These puffs are one of the easiest desserts to make and one of the most impressive to serve. I serve them for holidays, special occasions, St. Joseph's Day, and any other day when I feel like a quick dessert. They are wonderful to showcase the Ricotta Cloud Cream, Chocolate Custard Cream, and Mama Rosa's Lemon Custard Cream.

1 cup water
½ cup unsalted butter
1 cup unbleached all-purpose flour
⅛ teaspoon salt
4 large eggs, at room temperature

1 recipe Mama Rosa's Lemon Custard Cream (page 74), Chocolate Custard Cream (page 278), or Ricotta Cloud Cream (page 280)
Confectioners' sugar

PROCEDURE

1. Prepare the oven by arranging one oven rack on the bottom shelf and the other on the second from the top. Preheat the oven to 400°F. Line two 11 × 17–inch baking sheets with parchment paper.

2. Place the water and butter in a medium-size, heavy-gauge saucepan. Heat over medium-high. When the mixture comes to a boil and butter has melted, reduce the heat to medium and add the flour and salt all at once. Stir quickly until the mixture leaves the sides of the pan, forms a ball, and looks dry, about 1 minute. Remove from the heat and cool for 5 minutes.

3. Add the eggs, one at a time, beating each one in completely with a wooden spoon or an electric mixer until it has been incorporated into the mixture. When all the eggs have been added, the mixture should be velvety smooth in consistency.

4. Drop dough by rounded teaspoonfuls onto the parchment-lined baking sheets, about 1½ inches apart. This could be done using a pastry bag with a ½-inch tip. Smooth any peaks or points (which would brown prematurely).

5. Bake for 25 to 30 minutes total, 15 minutes on the bottom rack and 15 minutes on the upper rack, until the puffs are dry and golden in color. If they are undercooked, they will turn soggy and deflate when cooled. Carefully remove from the parchment paper and place on a wire rack to cool.

6. When the puffs are cool, cut in half and fill. The inside of the puff is all air, so be generous with the filling. If you have a pastry bag, you can fill the puffs whole. Place the point of the tube into the bottom of the puff and squeeze until the puff is full.

7. Arrange on a beautiful platter and dust with confectioners' sugar or drizzle with chocolate sauce (see below).

Yield: 24 small to medium puffs

NOTES

You can make the puffs the morning of the day you plan to serve them and store them in a paper bag. Fill the puffs 1 or 2 hours before serving. You can freeze unfilled puffs for up to 2 months.

If using frozen puffs, defrost; then 1 hour before serving, place the thawed puffs in a preheated 350°F oven for 5 minutes to rejuvenate them. Cool and fill.

The pastry dough from this recipe can be used to make a version of the St. Joseph's sfingi (Ricotta Puffs, page 270)—just follow the cooking instructions.

Melting and Drizzling Chocolate for Decorating

Place ½ cup chocolate chips in small reclosable plastic freezer bag. Close the bag, leaving a small ¼-inch opening for venting. Microwave on High for 45 seconds, or until the chocolate is melted. Fold top of the bag over slightly, pushing chocolate down into one of the two corners. With scissors, snip a *tiny* piece off that corner. Holding the top of the bag tightly, drizzle chocolate through the opening, squeezing gently but firmly on the bag as you decorate.

If you do not have a microwave, melt the chocolate on the stove in a double boiler over low heat. Place the melted chocolate in a plastic bag and follow the above directions.

Cannoli

....

Cannoli

*Preparation and Cooking Time: 2 to 2½ hours
(not including preparation of the ricotta)*

Cannoli are one of the best known pastries in the world. Most people have heard of these special crispy tubular-shaped treats that are filled with ricotta cream that is light, fluffy, soft, and voluptuous in texture, not overly sweet, with a hint of chocolate chips and cinnamon and sometimes candied orange peel. The shells are light-colored, delicate, and flaky. They are pleasant-tasting and not greasy. The cream filling is like a cloud, weightless and absolutely decadent.

You will need a pasta machine and eight metal cannoli tubes or forms for making the shells; these tubes are available in kitchenware stores and Italian specialty shops. Don't let the multiple steps scare you. Recruit help, take the steps one at a time, and prepare as much as possible in advance. After my family makes cannoli, we love to sit around the table and just admire them, anticipating what they are going to taste like and how many each of us gets to eat!

2¼ cups unbleached all-purpose
    flour
¼ cup sugar
A pinch of salt
¼ cup vegetable shortening or
    unsalted butter, or a combination
    of both
1 large egg, beaten
½ teaspoon vanilla extract
⅓ cup dry white wine or more—
    whatever it takes to form a ball
1½ quarts canola or vegetable oil, for
    deep-frying

For the Filling:
1 pound Fresh Ricotta (page 8)
1 cup or less confectioners' sugar
1 teaspoon vanilla extract
1 cup *already* whipped cream
⅓ cup mini semisweet chocolate
    chips
⅛ teaspoon ground cinnamon
½ cup ground almonds or pistachios
    (optional)

For Decorating:
Confectioners' sugar

PROCEDURE

Making the Pastry Dough:

1. In medium bowl, combine the flour, sugar, and salt. Cut in the shortening with a pastry blender or fork until the pieces are the size of small peas.

2. Make a well in the flour mixture. Pour the beaten egg, vanilla, and wine into the well. Using your hands or a fork, start in the center of the well and incorporate the flour slowly with the liquid, going around until all the flour has been incorporated. Knead the dough on a floured surface for a couple of minutes until the dough is smooth and does not stick to the work surface or your hands. Cover the dough with plastic wrap and place in the refrigerator for 30 to 60 minutes. (Alternatively, the dough for the shells may be done in the food processor. Place dry ingredients in the bowl and, with the motor on, add the wet ingredients through the feed tube until incorporated, *almost* forming a ball. Use the pulse mode so you do not overprocess.)

Shaping the Shells:

1. Roll the dough out very thin, to between $\frac{1}{16}$ and $\frac{1}{32}$ inch. This can be done with a rolling pin or, better yet, with a pasta machine. First, cut the dough into six pieces and cover loosely with plastic wrap so it does not dry out. Dust each piece with flour, flatten it slightly, and run it through the pasta machine with the rollers set at the widest opening. Dust the piece again, fold it in thirds, and pass it through the rollers again. Do this a couple of times until you see that the dough is smooth and elastic. Continue to do this with the other five pieces.

2. To roll the dough to the proper fineness, take one piece at a time and dust it lightly with flour and now begin decreasing the width of the rollers so the dough becomes thinner with each roll. The third or the second to the last setting is what we are looking for. Lightly dust your whole work surface with flour, set each ribbon of dough on the lightly floured surface, and, using a 3½-inch round cookie cutter, cut out circles, stacking them 8 to a stack and keeping them covered so they don't dry out. The scraps can be saved and rerolled at the end to make more cannoli. Total yield is about 45 to 50.

3. Start to heat the oil in a deep-fryer or heavy saucepan to 350° to 375°F. While the oil is heating, place each cannoli form around a circle of dough horizontally, gently pulling the dough at both the north and south ends so you get a slight oval shape. Roll one end of dough *loosely* over the tube. To seal, wet the far edge of the other side of dough (a very small portion) with water and gently roll up so the edge overlaps slightly. Press firmly to create a good seal. The dough should fit loosely around the tube. As the shells cook, they puff up and enlarge, making it difficult to remove the tube from the shells if they are wound too tight. You will be frying them three or four at a time and then removing the tubes and shaping more shells.

Frying the Shells:

1. Place a cookie sheet lined with paper towels near the frying pan or deep-fryer. When the oil has reached 350°F, you are ready to begin frying the cannoli shells. Place one shell at a time into the hot oil by holding the metal end of the tube with your finger and gently lowering the tube into the oil. You can fry three or four at a time depending on the size of the pan. Be careful not to crowd them, turning as necessary. They will puff up and turn golden quickly— in about 1 to 2 minutes. Remove them with tongs or a slotted spoon, holding them over the oil momentarily to allow excess oil to drip back into the pan. Place them on the prepared cookie sheet. This will help absorb any extra oil.

2. Let them cool briefly; then with a kitchen towel hold on to one end of the tube and with the other hand hold the cannoli pastry shell and gently twist and pull it off the tube. Do not wash the tubes before shaping more shells. Keep repeating the process until you have used up all the circles of dough. Set the fried shells aside.

Making the Ricotta Cream Filling:

1. Pass ricotta through a food mill or ricer. Place the ricotta, sugar, and vanilla in the bowl of a food processor or electric mixer and process until the texture is smooth and blended. Do not overmix. Using a spatula or your hands, fold in the already whipped cream and mini chocolate chips, and the cinnamon. Cover with plastic wrap and place in the refrigerator until ready to use.

To Assemble:

1. Half an hour before you plan to serve the cannoli, take the filling out of the refrigerator and scoop into a pastry bag fitted with a plain ½-inch tip or ½-inch star tip.

2. Pipe the filling into each of the shells. Fill one half and then fill the other half, making sure that the shells are completely filled.

3. Arrange on a beautiful platter or dish. Finish by sprinkling or dusting confectioners' sugar over the tops. Serve immediately. You cannot imagine how delicious these freshly made cannoli taste.

Yield: 46 medium cannoli

NOTES

The shells can be made in advance and stored in an airtight container in a cool, dry place for several weeks. Or they can be frozen in heavy-duty freezer bags; they will keep for up to 4 months. This recipe always makes enough shells for several servings. It pays to do the whole recipe.

The shells should not be filled until you are ready to serve them; they will get soggy if they are filled too soon. You can have the shells ready and the ricotta cream filling made and waiting in the refrigerator. It takes only a short time to pipe or spoon the filling into the shells.

Eat the cannoli with your hands as they do in Italy. The pastry is impossible to cut with a knife; the shell will crumble and you will have a mess on your hands.

Try These Variations
- Dab each end with toasted coconut.
- Drizzle melted chocolate over the top (see page 273).
- Add ground pistachios or almonds to both ends of the filling cream.
- Add small pieces of candied citrus to the filling.
- Fill the shells with Mama Rosa's Lemon Custard Cream (page 74) or Chocolate Custard Cream (page 278) instead of the ricotta cream.

Chocolate Custard Cream

Crema di Cioccolato

Preparation Time: 10 minutes • Cooking Time: 10 minutes

If you love chocolate mousse but find that it is too rich and has more calories than you would like to consume, try this recipe. It uses cocoa powder rather than chocolate, and it does not use whipping cream. The flavor and texture are exquisite. I use this as a filling for cream puffs, cakes, crêpes, and pies. Pour it into champagne glasses and serve it as a light dessert at the end of a heavy meal. If you are sick in bed with a cold or flu, have someone you love make it for you. It is one of my favorite comfort foods.

1 cup sugar
4 cups milk (whole or 2%), divided
⅓ cup cocoa powder
½ cup cold water
½ cup cornstarch

5 large egg yolks, lightly beaten
1 teaspoon orange extract
¾ teaspoon almond extract or
    3 tablespoons orange liqueur,
    or 3 tablespoons nut liqueur

PROCEDURE

1. Combine the sugar and 3 cups of the milk in a heavy, medium-size saucepan. Place over medium heat and stir to dissolve the sugar. In a small bowl, combine the cocoa and water to form a thick syrup. Add to the milk-and-sugar mixture in the saucepan and stir.

2. In another bowl, combine the cornstarch with the remaining cup of milk. Stir until the cornstarch is completely dissolved. Add the beaten egg yolks and stir. Make sure this is nice and smooth, with no lumps (check it with your fingers); then add this mixture to the saucepan.

3. Continue to cook on medium, stirring continuously in a spiral, starting from the center of the pan, going to the edge and back to the center, being sure to stir the entire bottom surface of the pan.

4. Be alert; the sauce will start to thicken quickly. The cream will start to get steamy and then you will notice, just before the boiling point, that it starts to get lumpy. Don't panic. Stir very quickly until the mixture comes to a boil; then turn the heat off, keeping the pot on the burner. Stir briskly for 1 minute. This will make the cream velvety.

5. Take the pan off the stove. Add the orange and almond extracts or liqueur and stir to blend. Pour the cream into a bowl. Place a sheet of clear plastic wrap directly on the surface of the custard to prevent a skin from forming, making sure the entire surface is covered. Serve hot, at room temperature, or cold. If using the cream as a cake filling, cover the top with plastic wrap and allow to cool at room temperature for 1 hour.

Yield: 4½ cups;
more than enough to fill
24 small to medium cream puffs

NOTES

For a more intense chocolate flavor, try stirring 4 ounces of melted chocolate into the hot mixture. For a cream that is a little richer and fluffier, try folding in 1 cup of whipped cream when the pudding is completely cooled. This cream is perfect to serve with ladyfingers.

Store leftover cream in the refrigerator in a covered container; the cream will keep for 2 or 3 days. If you have stored it for several days, whip it by hand or with an electric mixer before serving to restore the creaminess. I do not recommend freezing this cream.

Ricotta Cloud Cream

....

Nuvola di Ricotta

Preparation Time: 10 minutes (not including preparation of the ricotta)

This very easy, decadent, light and airy dessert cream resembles a mousse in appearance and texture. It is the perfect ending to a main-course meal as well as a light supper.

1 recipe Homemade Fresh Ricotta
   (page 8)
1½ cups confectioners' sugar
1 teaspoon vanilla extract
½ teaspoon ground cinnamon
   (optional; it will darken the

cream somewhat so if you want it
   to be perfectly white, omit it)
1½ cups whipping cream, whipped
⅔ cup semisweet miniature
   chocolate chips

PROCEDURE

1. Place the ricotta, sugar, and vanilla in the bowl of a food processor or electric mixer and process until the texture is smooth and blended. Do not overmix. Using a spatula or your hands, fold in the whipped cream and mini chocolate chips.

2. Place in a medium bowl and cover with plastic wrap or in dessert cups or champagne glasses and refrigerate until ready to serve.

Yield: 5½ to 6 cups

NOTES

This cream can also be used to stuff Cream Puffs (page 272), fill the Ricotta Puffs (page 270), Graziella's Decadent Cake (page 284), or pies.

Store any leftovers in the refrigerator in a covered container; it will keep for several days. Whip with a mixer or by hand to restore the creaminess before serving. I do not recommend freezing this cream.

About Sponge Cakes

This is an exceptional all-purpose cake that is used often in my household. Very light in texture, pale lemon in color, and rich in flavor, it stands well on its own, unadorned. Sponge cakes are cakes that are leavened solely by the beaten eggs, their texture depending entirely on how they are mixed. That is why these cakes have to go into the oven as soon as they are mixed. Often, cake flour, a soft wheat flour with fewer glutens, is used for sponge cakes, yielding cakes with high volume, fine texture, and a delicate tenderness.

Sift the flour several times before adding it to the egg mixture. Sifting the flour aids in producing its light and airy character. Be forewarned when reading a recipe that there is a big difference between 1½ cups sifted flour and 1½ cups flour, sifted. In the first case, you sift the flour first, then measure, giving you less flour. In the second case, you measure the flour first, then sift, which yields more flour. Very often in baking the addition of only a couple of tablespoons of flour can adversely affect the quality of the final product.

When adding the flour, add ¼ cup at a time, sprinkling it over the surface and folding it in carefully with a rubber spatula. Be careful not to deflate the batter. When whipping the egg whites, use a balloon whisk attached to your mixer, if you have one. This helps incorporate more air, yielding a higher, lighter cake. Be careful not to overbeat the whites; they should be stiff, but moist and glossy.

The egg yolk mixture gets beaten with the sugar for about 6 to 8 minutes. Don't cut this time short. Let your eye be the judge. The color and consistency of the batter goes from the orange yolk color to a very pale lemon color with a thickened consistency.

This cake is done when it springs back when lightly touched in the center with your fingertips. You can also test it with a long, thin skewer. Insert the skewer in the center section; if it comes out dry and clean, the cake is done. If not, give it another 5 minutes and check again.

A sponge cake has the perfect networking for soaking up rum, liqueurs, and syrups. It is able to soak up a considerable amount of liquid and still hold its form quite well. Use this characteristic to your advantage, if you would like, making the cake richer and even more flavorful. Make sure that the liquid you choose complements the original flavor of the base cake.

Don't grease the sides of the tube pan when making this cake. The ungreased sides of the tube pan allow traction for the delicate batter to climb the sides of the pan as it bakes and cools.

Basic Eight-Egg Sponge Cake

Pan di Spagna

Preparation Time: 25 minutes • Baking Time: 50 minutes

8 large eggs, at room temperature,
    separated
¼ teaspoon cream of tartar
1¼ cups sugar, divided

Grated rind from 1 lemon
3 tablespoons fresh lemon juice
3 tablespoons water
1½ cups sifted cake flour

PROCEDURE

1. Remove the top rack from the oven. Set aside. Place the other rack in the bottom position. Preheat oven to 350°F.

2. Prepare a tube pan by greasing *only* the bottom of the pan. Cut out a circular pattern from wax or parchment paper by placing the tube pan on paper, tracing the bottom of the pan with a pencil, and cutting out the circle with scissors. Fold the circle into quarters and cut the center hole to match the diameter of the tube. Place the circle of paper in the bottom of the tube pan.

3. Place the egg whites into a 4-quart mixing bowl and the yolks into a 3-quart mixing bowl.

4. Beat the egg whites with an electric mixer until frothy (about 1 to 2 minutes); then add the cream of tartar and ¼ cup of the sugar slowly and continue to beat until the whites form stiff peaks. (Do not overbeat or the egg whites will get dry.) Set aside.

5. Using the electric mixer again, beat the yolks for 1 minute. Add 1 cup sugar slowly and continue to beat until the yolks are a pale lemon color, about 6 to 8 minutes. Add the lemon rind. Pour the lemon juice and water in a slow stream and beat for 1 minute more.

6. Add the flour a couple of tablespoons at a time into the yolk mixture, mixing gently until all the flour is incorporated. Do not overmix.

7. Stir about 1 cup of the beaten egg whites into the batter. (This will help loosen the thick batter.) Fold in the remaining egg whites. I like using my hands to do the folding; I can feel how the batter is being incorporated. Try it my way and see what you think, or use a rubber spatula.

8. Pour the batter immediately into the prepared tube pan and bake for

15 minutes at 350°F; then reduce the temperature to 325°F and bake for another 40 to 50 minutes. The cake is done when the top is a golden color and springs back when lightly pressed with your fingertips. You can also test it with a long, thin skewer. Insert it in the center section; if it comes out dry and clean, the cake is done. If not, give it another 5 minutes and check again.

9. Remove the cake from the oven, turn it upside down, and let cool for 1 hour in the pan. If your tube pan does not stand on its side supports, invert it over a large funnel or bottle.

10. When the cake is cool, run a knife gently around the sides of the pan to loosen the cake. Remove the outer rim from the pan and with knife loosen the center pole from the cake. Remove the cake from the form and place it on a platter.

Yield: 1 plain 10-inch cake
(about 12 servings; as you add fillings,
you will be able to serve more people)

NOTES

You may serve the cake as is, or slice it into three or four layers, soak it with rum, and fill with fruit, custard creams, or frosting. Once the cake is filled, wrap with plastic wrap and place it in the refrigerator, where it will keep for several days.

To cut the cake into even layers, first measure the height of the cake and divide by how many layers you will need. With your ruler, go around cake and insert toothpicks every 2 inches where the layers will be cut so that the cake looks like it has spokes all around the edge. To split the layers, slice along the toothpick lines with a serrated knife.

This cake freezes very well either whole or sliced into layers, allowing you to use as many layers as necessary. Wrap the cake with aluminum foil or plastic wrap and then place it in a reclosable plastic freezer bag. It will keep very well frozen for up to 6 weeks.

Graziella's Decadent Cake

Cassata di Graziella

Preparation Time: see individual recipes   •   Assembly Time: 15 minutes

I devised this version of cassata, a truly decadent cake, by combining various recipes in this book. Don't let the number of steps scare you. Organization and preparing in advance is the key to the ease and success of this cake. Everything but adding the whipped cream frosting can be done a day in advance. In fact, preparing it a day ahead allows the rum syrup to soak through and flavor the cake.

I make this cake for very special occasions and holidays. When my mom comes to visit, we make this together. It is wonderful to have the companionship and an extra pair of hands. This is definitely a work of art and a treat for all your senses.

This rich cake is smooth, velvety, and light in texture and appearance, with an unsurpassed taste. My students say that this cake is to die for. Serve small pieces, but don't be surprised if everyone asks for seconds!

1 recipe Eight-Egg Basic Sponge
   Cake (page 282), cut horizontally
   into four layers
1 recipe Rum Syrup (page 286)
2 cups Mama Rosa's Lemon Custard
   Cream (page 74)

2 cups Chocolate Custard Cream
   (page 278)
1 recipe Ricotta Cloud Cream (page
   271)
1 recipe Whipped Cream Frosting
   (page 287)

PROCEDURE

1. You will need a tube pan, four long thin wooden skewers to keep the cake standing tall and straight during assembly, a metal frosting spatula, wax paper, and a beautiful serving dish that will fit in your refrigerator. This helps you organize yourself, making it easier to follow along.

2. Place a sheet of wax paper on your work surface. Put the individual layers of cake separately on top of the wax paper. Brush or drizzle Rum Syrup equally over all layers until you have used up all the syrup.

3. With both hands and your fingertips, gently get underneath the bottom layer and place it on a serving platter that will fit in your refrigerator. Cover the top of this layer evenly with Mama Rosa's Lemon Custard Cream.

4. Place the second layer of cake on top of the first layer and spread with 1½ cups Ricotta Cloud Cream.

5. Place the third layer of cake over the Ricotta Cloud Cream (making sure that the cake is straight) and spread it with Chocolate Custard Cream.

6. Place the fourth layer of cake over the Chocolate Custard Cream and spread this layer with the remaining Ricotta Cloud Cream.

7. Insert four long wooden skewers straight down through all the layers and fillings to prevent the cake from shifting.

8. Cover the cake with plastic wrap and place in the refrigerator until you are ready to put the layer of Whipped Cream Frosting on the top and sides, which should be done a couple of hours before serving. Remove the wooden skewers before frosting.

Yield: 18 to 20 servings

NOTES

The cake will keep in the refrigerator for up to 5 days. It can be frozen and will be tasty, but never as good as when it is fresh. It will keep in the freezer for up to 1 month. Defrost it in the refrigerator before serving.

Rum Syrup

Sciroppo al Rum

Preparation Time: 5 minutes • Cooking Time: 30 minutes

1 cup water   **¾ cup light rum**
½ cup sugar

PROCEDURE

1. Place the water and sugar in a heavy saucepan over medium heat. Stir to dissolve the sugar. When the mixture comes to a boil, reduce the heat to low and simmer for 30 minutes.

2. Remove from the heat, add the rum, stir briefly, and allow to cool.

Yield: 1 cup

NOTES

This syrup can be made a couple of days in advance and stored in the refrigerator in a tightly fitting container. It can be used to soak sponge or chiffon cake and ladyfingers.

Whipped Cream Frosting

Copertura di Panna Montata

Preparation Time: 5 minutes • Cooking Time: 30 minutes

This whipped cream includes the addition of cornstarch to help hold its shape and allow you to use it in a pastry bag with tips for piped decorating.

⅓ cup confectioners' sugar
1 teaspoon cornstarch
2 cups heavy whipping cream,
    divided

1 teaspoon vanilla extract

PROCEDURE

1. Place the sugar, cornstarch, and ½ cup of the cream in a small saucepan over low heat. Stir until the sugar and cornstarch are dissolved. Turn the heat to medium and bring to a boil, stirring constantly. Turn the heat to low and simmer for 2 minutes, until the liquid has thickened.

2. Remove from the heat and cool to room temperature. Add the vanilla.

3. Place the remaining 1½ cups whipping cream in a bowl that has been chilled in the refrigerator. Beat with an electric mixer until soft peaks start to form. Add the cornstarch mixture into whipped cream, beating continuously until soft peaks form and hold their shape. If you would like to color the whipping cream, do so now. Place it in the refrigerator until ready to use.

Yield: 4 cups

NOTES

You may wish to use different flavorings in place of the vanilla, such as 1 teaspoon almond, lemon, or orange extract or 3 tablespoons (at most) of a liqueur.

I do not recommend freezing this cream. Instead, store it in the refrigerator in a covered container for up to 2 days.

DIRECTORY OF
PARTICIPATING ARTISTS

Photos are numbered in the order they appear in the book.

Clay

James Aarons (2, 8, 12, 19)
Natoma Ceramic Designs
P.O. Box 78093
San Francisco, CA 94107
(415) 495-0440

Richard Aerni (cover)
2975 County Road 40
Bloomfield, NY 14469
(716) 657-6045 (phone)
(716) 657-6023 (fax)

Dr. Kenneth Beittel (2, 10)
2014 Pine Cliff Road
State College, PA 16801
(814) 234-4428

David Calvin Heaps (2)
P.O. Box 184
Lloyd, FL 32337-0814
(850) 997-9606 (fax)

Melissa Carpenter (20)
355 Ridge Avenue
State College, PA 16803
(814) 237-6705; claytime@vicon.net

Jack Charney (9)
369 Montezuma Avenue, H 150
Santa Fe, NM 87501
(505) 983-8081

David Dontigny (17)
7991 East Back Mountain
Reedsville, PA 17084
(717) 667-3792
dldontigny@lcworkshop.com

Maishe Dickman and Tina Menchetti
   (14, 16)
519 George Street
New Haven, CT 06511
(203) 776-3957

Linda Fox (1)
290 Cedar Avenue
Highland Park, IL 60035
(847) 475-9697

Louise Harter (3)
7 Carrington Road
Bethany, CT 06524
(203) 393-9273

Clay

Mary Hosterman (12)
264 South Main Street
Pleasant Gap, PA 16823
(814) 359-2475

Daniel Levy (4, 10, 11)
155 W. 29th Street, 3N
New York, NY 10001
(212) 268-0878 (phone and fax)

Lois MacDonald (7)
17 Herber Avenue
Delmar, NY 12054
(518) 439-6839 (phone)
(518) 439-6145 (fax)

Grace Pilato (15)
524 South Allen Street
State College, PA 16801
(814) 238-5828

Hunt Protro (18)
P.O. Box 61
Rohrersville, MD 21779
(301) 432-2941

Ian Stainton (15)
P.O. Box 105A R.R. 1
Spring Mills, PA 16875
(814) 364-9974

Ikuzi Teraki and Jeanne Bisson
Romulus Craft (2, 13, 19)
8495 VT Route 110
Washington, VT 05675
(802) 685-3869

Metal

Kim Lucci Elbually (2, 3, 20)
Artistic Concepts
P.O. Box 1194
Lewistown, PA 17044-1194

Deb Jemmott (cover, 9, 14)
Enhancements
269 Solar View Drive
San Marcos, CA 92069
(760) 471-7963
twinoaks@logos.calvary.net

Joy Raskin (19)
P.O. Box 1422
Concord, NH 03301
(603) 224-4395 (phone)
(603) 228-6284 (fax); pichnjr@aol.com

Fiber

Doris Manahan Rohrbaugh (5, 12)
454 Woolverton Way
Alexandria, PA 16611
(814) 669-9170

Wood

Edward S. Wohl (6)
6154 Brotherhood Lane
Ridgeway, WI 53582-9555
(608) 924-9411 (phone)
(608) 924-3115 (fax)

Glass

Jan and John Gilmore (21)
Gilmore Glass
P.O. Box 961, Routes 22 and 44
Millerton, NY 12546
(518) 789-6700; gilmor@taconic.net

Leanne and R. Guy Corrie (11)
Union Street Glass
833 South 19th Street
Richmond, CA 94804
(510) 620-1100

Directory of Participating Artists

ACKNOWLEDGMENTS

I send a big heartfelt thank you for the kindness of all those who shared my dream, and whose enthusiasm helped bring this book to life. This work would have proved impossible were it not for their simple and pure generosity. I am very grateful to my husband, Guy, the most enthusiastic admirer of my food, for his discriminating palate, his honest critique, and for his proofreading; and to my children, Lisa Pilato, Thomas and Tracy Pilato, Mark and Alyssum Pilato, Michael and Keiko Pilato, and Natalia and Emory Pipersburgh, for their unending love and faith in me. A special thank-you goes to Lisa for her loyalty and hard work in helping with many aspects of the manuscript. I will always remember her many invaluable long-distance telephone conversations that cheered me on and left me with good advice.

I am indebted to my mother, Rosa, to my siblings, Pina, Angela, Augie, and Maria, and to their spouses, who have contributed recipes and have helped in the building of wonderful traditions and memories that will sustain me for a lifetime.

I will always cherish the encouragement and advice of the hundreds of cooking class students who have shared my kitchen with me over the years. Together we have searched for harmony and balance.

Charles DuBois and Angela Rogers shared my dream when this book was in its beginning stages. They gave much of their time and considerable talents in helping to get this book off the ground.

The friendship, support, and vitality of Deborah Cameron and Gretl Collins was lifeblood to me. They spent endless hours, days, nights, and weekends typing, plugging recipes into the computer, editing, and always being there when I needed encouragement. They are true friends.

Special thanks go to the following individuals: to Federica Verra, my dear

Italian friend, for her help in translating English food titles into Italian; to James Porterfield for his guidance and expertise in how to go about getting published; to James Collins, my photographer, for his artistry and his critical and sensitive eye; to American Craft Council Library and to Jo Ann Brown from the American Craft Enterprises for their help in locating some of the artists whose works were included; to all the national artists, as well as to the owners of the Artisan Connection and Art Alliance Gallery Shop, for their submission of work to be photographed. (I am only sorry that space and design considerations prevented me from including all of the excellent works that were sent to me); to Gretl Collins, Gina Bellissimo, John Mentzell, Sara Olsen, Steve and Lynn Jablonsky, and Susan Hammerstedt for helping in the preparation of the food used in the photographs; to Jana King, publisher of *State College* magazine, for publishing my monthly food column; to all who had a hand in typing, namely, Denise Olivett, Diane McDermott, Catherine Griffiths, Monika Matthews, John Sherer, Elizabeth Goreham, Donna Conway, Gina Bellissimo, Cheryl Coles, Maria Smilios, Glen and Nancy Gamble, and Trish Hummer, for their stalwart support; to the staffs of the Penn State University Agronomy Department, Extension Service, Nutrition Department and Dairy Facility for their valuable advice on the science of cooking; and finally to Peter Bordi, Marg Sente, Fran Osseo-Asare, Carol Anne Colombo, Martha Bellanti, Ron Hand, Ann Schement, John Bellanti, Laura Brown, Tom Rhodes, Joey Martain, Connie Tomaselli, Angela Maltese, and to all my dear friends in our State College family for the many ways they supported and encouraged me.

My extensive list of thanks would not be complete without mention of my amazing editor, Marian Lizzi of St. Martin's Press. From the very beginning she gave me enthusiastic support, kind words of advice, insights, and wise guidance. At times when I'd get discouraged, her cheerful belief in the worth of this book sustained me. All authors should be so fortunate.

INDEX